1,001
IDEAS
to *Create*
RETAIL
EXCITEMENT

EDGAR A. FALK

PRENTICE HALL

Library of Congress Cataloging-in-Publication Data

Falk, Edgar A.
    1,001 ideas to create retail excitement / by Edgar A. Falk.
      p. cm.
    Includes index.
    ISBN 0-13-292393-9
    1. Retail trade.   2. Sales promotion.   3. Marketing.   I. Title.
II. Title: One thousand one ideas to create retail excitement.
III. Title: One thousand and one ideas to create retail excitement.
HF5429.F242   1994   94-1050
658.8′2—dc20   CIP

Printed in the United States of America

10 9

ISBN 0-13-292393-9

PRENTICE HALL
Paramus, NJ 07652

On the World Wide Web at http://www.phdirect.com

This book is dedicated to Jilly and Oliver

ACKNOWLEDGMENTS

A book on retailing cannot be written without acknowledging the millions of men and women who have dedicated their lives to the profession. We come in contact with them day-in and day-out and learn so much from these daily visits to their stores and shops. Much of what we have written has been inspired by what we have observed over the past twenty-five years as we have traveled and shopped throughout the United States. While we are based in New York City, the so-called "retail hub of America," we have met some of the sharpest and most knowledgeable retailers in some of the smallest cities and towns in the country. We thank them for the knowledge they imparted to us.

We also want to thank the many trade associations, government agencies and retail resources for their time and input. We want to particularly thank Margaret Padin-Bialo of the New York regional office of the Bureau of the Census, and Herbert Austin of the New York district office of the Small Business Administration for their cooperation. To Mike Snell, our agent, thanks for representing us.

Finally we want to thank Karen Hansen and the staff at Prentice Hall Career & Personal Development, for their support.

CONTENTS

CHAPTER 3 Deciding Which Promotional Programs to Conduct

CHAPTER 4 Looking Good from Your Front Window to the Back of the Store

How This Book Will Help You Meet The Marketing Challenges of the '90s

"It's not the size of the dog in the fight . . . but the size of the fight in the dog."

It is a corny saying and as old as the hills but it pretty well sums up the current picture in retail.

While it is probably the most challenging and competitive form of business in America today, retail is also the one business where success is not necessarily determined by size. The smaller retailer has just as good a chance for success as the giants of the industry so long as he, or she, takes a very professional and sophisticated approach to running the business.

The days of just opening the doors and waiting for the customers to come are long gone. To be a successful retailer today, you must become a well-rounded expert in all phases of the business. You must know what you are doing at all times, and leave nothing to chance.

- You must know who your audience is.
- You must know what your audience wants.
- You must know how to reach that audience.
- You must know how to broaden the base of that audience.
- You must know how to get that audience to shop more often.

- You must know how to get that audience to spend more money each time it shops.

You must know how to create excitement at retail!

This book is aimed at helping you meet these challenges whether you operate one store or four, own or manage a franchise location, or run a branch store for a national chain.

It shows you how to become more aggressive, competitive, and promotion-minded in marketing your store.

It shows you how to make your store a more exciting and interesting place at which to shop—a place where people will *want* to visit, and will go out of their way to visit.

It shows you how to attract new customers, and keep old ones coming back.

1,001 Ideas to Create Retail Excitement is a book of ideas.

It provides you with an extensive menu of ideas and suggestions from which you can develop a high-profile marketing program.

- Ideas on how to develop information, and statistical data about your customers and potential customers so that you will have a better handle on who they are and how to reach them.
- Ideas for seasonal and holiday promotions.
- Ideas for sales and special events.
- Ideas for building repeat business and incremental sales.
- Ideas for using sports to promote your store.
- Ideas for cross-promoting with other stores.
- Ideas for developing community involvement programs.
- Ideas for getting publicity in local media.

How many of these ideas a retailer will use will vary from store to store.

It will depend upon your objectives, your budget, your staff, your merchandise, your pricing and your customers.

Only you—being on the scene—are in the position to develop the necessary data, evaluate the situation, and make the final decision on how to market your store.

And only you can decide which of the many ideas will help you fulfill your objectives, and have the greatest amount of impact upon your customers and potential customers.

Retail marketing is an idea-driven industry, and there is no such thing as "too many ideas" in the business.

That's why *1,001 Ideas to Create Retail Excitement* will be equally valuable to larger retailers, franchisees, and local managers of national chains as it is to smaller retailers.

The unique ideas found within these pages regarding the approaches toward cross-promoting, building repeat business and incremental sales, getting publicity in local media, and community involvement programs will help any size store become more competitive in its community.

Edgar A. Falk

CHAPTER 1

Paying Attention to Your Product Line, Pricing, Service and Sales Force

The name of the game in retail is to attract new customers and get old ones to keep coming back. If you cannot accomplish this, your business is going to go down the tube. While there are many external factors that play a role in determining the success or failure of a retailer, all too often the retailer must share in the blame. Too many just don't do their homework, analyze the situation and the trends, or create the environment and excitement customers want when they go shopping.

To be a successful retailer, you must pay close attention to your product line, your pricing, your sales force, the services you provide to your customers and how you provide them, and the convenience of your location and shopping hours.

These key factors will determine your success as a retailer, and how you market your store and products to your customers and those whom you want to become customers.

SELECTING THE RIGHT PRODUCT LINE

You must offer your customers a good selection of quality products for which they perceive they are paying a fair price. Your product line should be, if at all possible, distinctive from that of your key competitors unless you plan to go head-to-head against them. If you sell clothing you should also stock a wider variety of sizes in all styles. *Most important, you want to position yourself as the store providing something different, and beyond what your competitors have to offer.*

SETTING A SOUND PRICING POLICY

Pricing is not as simple as it may appear.

You want your customers to perceive that they are paying a fair price for the products they purchase, but "fair price" may have a different meaning to different people. The convenience of your location and hours, the quality of your products, and the services received can be strong influencing factors on how your customers determine a "fair price." If these factors are all positive influencers, a "fair price" will be perceived to be higher than if they are negative influencers.

You must also decide upon a general pricing policy for the store. Are you going to hold the line and keep firm prices on your merchandise? Are you going to consistently place merchandise on the shelves at full price with the intention of quickly marking it down? Are you going to establish a policy of "everyday low prices"? Or are you going to follow a policy so many customers are used to: sales, sales, sales?

Each has advantages and disadvantages and *only you can make the decision.*

A very upscale store can often hold the line on its regular pricing, conducting just one or two sales a year. The argument is that the image of the store will suffer if it becomes too promotion-oriented. However, upscale customers like bargains, too.

Some retailing experts are critical of stores that initially display merchandise at full price so that they can quickly mark it down. Their argument is that consumers become aware of the tactic and will delay their purchases. The feeling is that it also kills the credibility of the store's pricing policy.

Under the everyday low pricing concept, products are introduced at a lower than usual price which is sustained for a period of time. Markdowns and sales, for the most part, are very limited. Once you have effectively established awareness for this pricing policy among your customers and in the community, you can usually spend less money on promotions. A negative can be that people may perceive your merchandise to be of lower quality (even though it isn't). Also, many people like sales and even though your prices may be lower, their perception may be that they are not getting a bargain because they do not see that the prices are being marked down.

The "sales . . . markdowns . . . sales" policy of the 1980's remains very popular among consumers. They are still conditioned toward expecting sale-after-sale-after-sale, and large numbers automatically delay making any purchases until a sale comes along. This has become so habit-forming that large numbers of retailers are still operating under this policy.

OFFERING CONVENIENCE

Every retailer should reflect upon the meaning of the description of a convenience store. It is usually a store which is convenient for its customers both in its location and in its hours. As a result, convenience stores can often command premium prices for their products.

That's not to say that every store should be located around the corner from the majority of its customers, and should be open till midnight. Rather, the convenience of location and business hours should be realistically established in order to fulfill the needs of your present and potential customers. For example, if you are operating a dry cleaning store and your customers leave for work at 8 AM and return at 6 PM, you are not offering convenient service to them if your hours are 9–5. Nor are you offering convenient shopping hours if you are located in the downtown shopping area and close your doors at 5:30, just thirty minutes after people get out of work. And, if demographics show that the types of consumers most likely to be attracted to your business live on the north side of the city, you may not be getting too much business from them if you are located on the south side.

Other convenience factors include your store's location in relationship to public transportation, traffic flow, highways and highway exits, and public parking.

What you must do is determine what factors impact on the convenience needs of your present and potential customers. This is discussed in greater depth in Chapter Two.

PROVIDING SERVICE THAT MEETS CUSTOMER NEEDS

Customers consider service to be a very important part of the retail experience. Good customer service will keep them coming back, while bad service experiences can mean the end of a relationship with the store. In addition, a store's reputation for providing good service can, through word-of-mouth advertising, attract a lot of new business.

Most important, good service can mean greater profits. Customers are usually willing to pay more for that extra service.

What are the tenets of good customer service?

- The awareness of everyone on the store's staff that only a satisfied customer will become a regular customer. Conversely, a regular customer can quickly become an ex-customer if his or her level of expectation and satisfaction is no longer met.
- The acknowledgment that customer service is *everyone's* responsibility. There cannot be a single weak link in the chain.
- The anticipation of the customer's needs, and fulfilling those needs.
- The solution of potential problems before they have a chance to develop into serious problems.
- Good two-way communications with the customers. Listening to what they have to say, and implementing their suggestions.
- The recognition that the customer is always right and that you need the customer more than the customer needs you.

A good customer service program can include a multitude of elements:

- Free or low-cost gift wrapping.
- Free or low-cost packaging and delivery.
- A clearly defined and promoted exchange and refund policy.
- Free or low-cost installation of products which require that service.
- Contacting a customer who has made a large purchase to inquire about his or her satisfaction.
- If you sell clothing, a policy of sewing on buttons anytime they come off. (All the customer has to do is bring the item to the store.)
- Keeping a supply of matching extra buttons on hand in case a customer loses one.
- Having a buffing machine at the store so that customers can shine their shoes free-of-charge anytime they come in.
- A free shoe shine anytime a customer purchases a new pair of shoes.
- Taking telephone orders from credit card customers, and a telephone reservation system so that customers can call in to have a product put on hold for them.

- An answering machine so that customers who call after the store has closed can leave a message. Have someone check the machine every two hours so that calls can be promptly returned.
- Offering hot coffee and tea on cold days, iced tea or lemonade on hot days.
- Carrying customers' packages to their cars.
- Offering a baby-sitting service to mothers while they shop at the store.
- Conducting customer seminars so that they may become more familiar with your products, especially if they are of a technical nature.
- Encouraging customers who purchase technical products to call anytime they have a question.

EMPLOYING THE VERY BEST SALES STAFF

You can have the right pricing, the right products, offering the right convenience that appeals to everyone, and a good service policy on paper — *and still fall flat on your face if you do not have the right sales help.*

Customers not only have to feel comfortable when dealing with your sales staff but also must have confidence that they are knowledgeable about the products they are selling. In today's highly competitive marketplace, the salesperson can be the difference between a steady customer and one who never returns after that first purchase.

That's why there are several important factors: who you hire; how you train the person; how you motivate him or her; how you get the salesperson to be more responsible to customer needs.

Who You Hire

Hiring is not an easy job. Even the most successful executives will readily admit that they have made many mistakes in hiring the wrong people. But hiring mistakes can be minimized if you carefully analyze your needs and look for people who will fulfill those needs. For most retailers, those needs are very similar. They need people

- Who like to sell and take pride in closing the sale.
- Who are dependable and whom you can count on to show up for work every day.

- Who are intelligent, quick learners who have the curiosity to expand their knowledge.
- Who project a pleasant and positive image which mirrors that of the store.
- Who like people and relate well to them.
- Who are neither impressed with their importance nor overwhelmed by the importance of VIP customers.
- Who are helpful to customers as well as to their fellow employees and management.
- Who are ambitious and hope some day to have your job — or their own store.

There are, of course, other factors to take into consideration. These include appearance, speech, "chemistry," past employment history, and references. In addition to former employers, ask the candidate to supply names of former customers whom you might call for a reference.

After Hiring

Once you hire a salesperson, gradually break in him or her by assigning the new employee to a senior staff member or by taking charge yourself. Emphasis during the first two weeks should be on familiarizing the new salesperson with the merchandise and the store's standard operating procedures. Have the new employee positioned close enough to the trainer so that he or she can overhear the conversations between salesperson and customer. It should give the new employee a feeling as to how things are done at the store. Likewise the trainer should be close enough to overhear the conversation when the new salesperson is talking to a customer. At the end of the day, the trainer can then offer any suggestions which he or she might have. At the end of the two-week period, you should sit down with the new salesperson and offer a general critique along with any suggestions you might have for improving his or her performance. Periodically sit down for a "one-on-one" with all staff members to review their performance (even if it is excellent) and to ask them for ideas on how the store might improve its services to customers.

Sales Training

An ongoing product training program should be a "must" for every retailer. *It is the only way your staff will acquire the thorough product knowledge required to do a superior job on the sales floor.* At least one hour every other week should be spent on sales training if you have a limited, or uncomplicated line of products. A broad or more complicated line requires at least one training hour every week. Ask the manufacturer (or its distributer) to provide the training, or video tapes, lesson plans and handbooks so that you can conduct it. A technique often used is to assign a different salesperson to conduct each class. In order to be effective, the salesperson will have to become an "expert" in the products he or she covers. As a result, whenever a fellow salesperson has a question about those products, the "expert" on the sales floor can be consulted. Using this technique, each member of your staff is not only trained in every product line, but also becomes an "expert" in at least one of them. This is an excellent technique to motivate your sales force to learn and to encourage teamwork.

Another good technique to use to reinforce on-the-job training for the sales staff and provide product information is to place special "talking points" point-of-purchase materials at the product. This P-O-P material usually lists the most important features of the product. The salesperson can use this as a cue card for reference purposes while talking to a customer. Customers will also find them informative and helpful when they are browsing without a salesperson.

Whenever a new product or product line comes in, immediately schedule a sales training session. This is especially important if it is a nationally well-advertised, highly technical product like a computer or a home entertainment system. Chances are that customers will have seen the manufacturer's advertisements and will have many questions about the product.

Keeping the Sales Staff Motivated

To motivate your sales staff, you must realize that what works for one person may not work for the next. Some people will be motivated by a pat on the back; others have to be talked to; a large number of people respond to money as a motivating factor; still others are turned on by gifts and other nonmonetary rewards. You have to decide what is going to work for your staff.

If you offer rewards to motivate your staff, you have several options: each salesperson can be rewarded on an individual basis; can be teamed with a partner; or placed on a larger team. The latter two methods may be more effective because of peer pressure. This is a very structured system of rewards. It might involve points awarded per sale, per dollar total, or per specific product sold. It might be an ongoing program, or cover just a specific period of time. If it is the latter, it might be conducted for a one-month period each quarter. You have a lot of flexibility in structuring such a program. You might also consider a weekly program. Give a "night out on the town" to the salesperson who brings in the most dollars that week, a bond to the salesperson who records the greatest number of sales, etc. When a salesperson goes that extra mile to help a customer (drove five miles in a blizzard to deliver a birthday gift, etc.), don't hesitate to reward him, or her. If any of your manufacturers are offering retail salesperson incentive programs, consider participating. They provide another way of rewarding your people for doing a good job. Offer product to your staff at a very good discount. If you sell clothing, it is important that your sales people wear what they are trying to sell. To encourage them to dress in what is being sold, you may want to offer them product at cost.

You should also invite customers to nominate a "Salesperson Of The Month," and a "Salesperson Of The Year." The winners could be selected by a special in-store ballot available to all customers.

A "mystery shopper program" will also keep your sales force on its toes, and motivated. Have family and friends — none of them identified as such, or as mystery shoppers — report back to you on their shopping experiences. Give them questions you want asked of the sales help, as well as the correct answers, and have them report back to you on the results. Reward the sales staff members who answered correctly, telling them the mystery shopper had visited. By never identifying these mystery shoppers, you will be motivating your sales staff to be ready anytime for a visit.

Your product line, your pricing, the convenience and service you offer, and your sales force are the anchors for the rest of your marketing program. You just cannot afford to neglect them!

CHAPTER 2

Gathering the Data to Help You Make Your Marketing Decisions

It is impossible to make sound marketing and promotional decisions unless you have comprehensive information about your present customers and your potential customer base. You must know who your audience is, what it wants, how to reach it, and how to expand it.

You need general statistical information about the people who live in your area and whose patronage you seek. You also need very specific information about their buying preferences and shopping habits.

All too often, smaller retailers overlook this important requirement. They feel that the development of demographics and other research data is too time consuming and expensive.

It is just the opposite.

Much general data about the people who live within your shopping area is available free of charge from government sources. It is also possible to obtain free assistance for structuring and conducting the original research so important for your store's success. Other data can be obtained at relatively low cost, or even through shared costs among similar-sized non-competitive retailers.

HOW TO OBTAIN EXISTING GENERAL DEMOGRAPHIC DATA

Existing general demographic data is readily available from both Federal government and private sources in just about every community in the United States at little or no cost to retailers.

U. S. Bureau of the Census

The primary source for all types of this demographic data is the U. S. Bureau of the Census. (It is part of the Department of Commerce.)

Of greatest interest to a retailer will be the data accumulated and available on what is called "Census Tracts" and "Block Numbering Areas." Each metropolitan area is subdivided into "Census Tracts" of approximately eight square blocks within which live anywhere from 2,500 to 8,000 people, with 4000 the average number. In addition, approximately 200 other counties, not within metropolitan areas, are also subdivided into "Census Tracts." "Block Numbering Areas" are subdivisions in other counties for which "Census Tracts" have not been established. Your first step is to identify the areas where your customers live and from which you want to draw new customers. It will then be easy, from Census maps, to identify the tracts and block number areas.

The data you will be able to find in the Census reports for each will include:

- A breakdown by age and sex of all people living within each tract or block number area. Ages are given, by sex, in five-year increments from under five years to 24, and then in ten-year increments from 25-84.
- Persons per household and persons per family.
- Household and family incomes, and median household incomes.
- Aggregate retirement income by households.
- Occupations.
- Time leaving home to go to work.
- Travel time to work in minutes.
- Means of transportation to work.

- Marital status of residents: never married, now married, separated, widowed or divorced.
- Value of single family houses on less than 10 acres with no businesses on the premises.
- Owner costs as a percentage of household income.
- Median rents.
- Persons by languages spoken.
- Race.
- Educational attainment.

This information taken from the recent Census, provides you with much of the basic information you need about your target audience. It is available in both print and CD-ROM format and can be purchased from the Census Bureau at prices which range from $10 to $150. *It is also available for use free of charge* at any of the Federal Depository libraries. There is usually one in each Congressional district. In addition, there is a network of state and local data centers at which this information is also available for use at no cost. See the Resources section at the end of this chapter for further information about how to find these locations.

"The Lifestyle Zip Code Analyst"

Compiled and provided by National Demographics & Lifestyles, and published by Standard Rate & Data, it identifies the lifestyles of residents from the top metropolitan statistical areas as well as from all counties with populations of at least 35,000 people. The information is broken down by ZIP code so that it is easy to pinpoint your target areas.

The general demographic information provided for each ZIP code includes:

- Adult population and number of households.
- Household type: Single (by sex), or married.
- Age of householder (in six age segments from 18-65 plus).
- Household income.
- Whether they own or rent (by percentage).
- Children living at home (analysis by ages).

Fifty-six lifestyles are covered, identifying the percentage of people within each ZIP code who are interested in each:

- "The Good Life," twelve lifestyles ranging from cultural events, fashion clothing, gourmet cooking/fine foods and home furnishings/ decorating to wines, foreign travel, and real estate investments.
- "High Tech," ranging from photography, home video games, personal home computers and electronics to stereo/records/tapes and VCR recordings.
- "Sports & Leisure," including bicycling, boating/sailing, bowling, golf, skiing, tennis and running/jogging.
- Outdoor activities ranging from camping, hiking, fishing, hunting and shooting, to motorcycling, recreational vehicles and wildlife/ environment.
- Indoor activities including automotive work, reading, coin/stamp collecting, gardening, household pets, needlework/knitting.

This information can be very valuable to you if you carry products which appeal to any of these lifestyles. By determining within which local ZIP codes the heaviest concentrations of these people live, you can more effectively plan and target your advertising, direct mail and other marketing programs.

The current price of this book is $375. You may want to get together with several other non-competitive local retailers and split its cost. The book may also be available at your local public or business library.

Local Media

The advertising departments of local newspapers, radio and television stations, cable systems, city magazines and companies selling outdoor and transit advertising are also good sources for data.

The research and data provided by each will probably emphasize the superiority of its product over competitive media. However, the general demographics used as the base for each study will probably provide you with good basic statistics. Of help to you would be any research or data local media has developed on purchases made at your type of store, for your type of product lines, or any local data on seasonal purchasing patterns. To obtain this material, contact the local media advertising departments and ask each for its media kit. Salesmen from each will probably want to call upon you to try to persuade you to advertise. While advertising should be considered when developing your total marketing effort (see Chapter 15), don't feel pressured by the salesman's visit. Explain that you are in the preliminary phases of putting together your plan and are presently evaluating media data. Be sure to also ask for whatever research data on buying patterns the salesman has available.

State, City, and Regional Governments

States, cities and regional development and planning commissions often have extensive statistical data about their areas. Contact these agencies to see what they have available. Local government finance administrations might also have data which they have developed based on tax collections.

Banks, Real Estate Developers, Chambers of Commerce

Banks, real estate developers, chambers of commerce and other business groups may also be sources for statistical data. Contact your bank, for example, to see what information and studies it may have available. Real estate developers may also have statistical data which they use when selling or renting space. However, in order to obtain information from them, you will probably have to show some interest in their services. Local chambers of commerce and other business groups may be able to supply research they have conducted, or at least collected from various sources. Of course, if you are located in a shopping mall, ask its management for any customer research it has done.

Public Libraries

An important potential source of information is your local public and/or business library. Many are depositories for all types of statistical data. Contact the local research librarian who can quickly tell you if the type of local statistical information you need is available.

Small Business Administration Business Information Centers

The Small Business Administration currently operates special Business Information Centers in Atlanta, Houston, Los Angeles, St. Louis and Seattle. If you are located near one of the offices, you should make use of its services, one of which is free access to various market research data bases.

HOW TO OBTAIN LOCALLY GENERATED ORIGINAL RESEARCH FREE OF CHARGE

While basic demographic information is readily available at little or no cost, original research which is going to bring you and your customer closer together must be developed and conducted locally.

It may be possible for you to get original research done at little or no cost.

Assistance from College Marketing Classes

There are several forms of assistance you might be able to get from local universities, especially schools of business. Attempt to arrange for a marketing professor to assign a group of graduate students to conduct research for you as a term project. You may find that the professor will only cooperate if you let the students develop a marketing plan based on their research findings. This, of course, will be a bonus to you. While there will usually be no charge for this type of project, you might give the students an honorarium of $500. Or, you might donate $500 to the university. Check also to see if any local universities have internship programs. If they do, see if you can get one or more interns to help you develop and conduct your research project. Again, sometimes a modest honorarium is given to cover transportation and meals.

While students will do the work involved in term projects, and internships, there is usually some supervision by the faculty which will vary from school to school.

U.S. Small Business Administration

The Small Business Administration, in addition to its other services, has two programs in particular which can help smaller retailers in the research and marketing areas.

Small Business Institute Program   More than five hundred schools of business participate in this Small Business Administration program. Retailers can receive management counseling and other assistance from qualified graduate and undergraduate business students working under expert faculty guidance. Each individual program is tailored to the needs of the specific small business. You might contact your local Institute to see if you can arrange for it to conduct a research project for you. It could also develop marketing, advertising and promotional plans for your store.

Small Business Development Centers   Located throughout the United States, these campus-based centers bring together the resources of the university, the private sector and government. They specialize in providing direct one-to-one counseling on small business problems. They can help you, for example, develop your research program and guide you through its different stages. Unlike the Institute program, the Development Centers do not do the work for you but instead provide you with their expertise in the areas in which you may need assistance.

See the Resources section at the end of this chapter to find out how to contact the Small Business Administration.

ALTERNATIVES TO OBTAINING FREE LOCAL RESEARCH

If you cannot get this research from local colleges, the Small Business Administration programs, or other sources, there are two alternatives:

• Hire a firm to do some or all of your research.

• Use consultants to help you develop and conduct your own research.

Hiring a Firm or Someone to Do Research for You

There are firms that specialize in research in most major U.S. cities; they can be found in the Yellow Pages under the heading "Market Research And Analysis." Some advertising agencies also have research capabilities.

It is always best to deal with a firm that comes highly recommended. For such recommendations ask other businesses, local business associations as well as local advertising agencies that farm out their research projects. Another source for a recommendation would be the advertising departments of local media. As already indicated in this chapter, many have had studies done for them.

In order to keep your research expenses down, consider teaming up with other local, non-competitive retailers to commission a joint research project. This would probably be most effective if your project partners were located in your area, sold merchandise in the same price range, and were interested in reaching out to consumers in the same residential sections as you. You may also want to hire a free-lance research person to do the project, such as a local marketing professor, someone working in research who is looking to moonlight, or even a retired researcher. Another possibility is to hire one or more highly recommended advanced graduate students.

Conducting Your Own Local Research

While it will take planning, time, and staff, it is possible to conduct some of your own research. However, it is recommended that even if you choose this option, you should use a free lancer or some other person experienced in the field to develop the questionnaires and structure the projects. Ideally, you might be able to accomplish this—at no cost to you—with the help of your local Small Business Development Center (see page 15). Some simple, basic questionnaires are included at the end of this chapter.

Consumer interviews and the collection of other data can be conducted by employees, or you can hire students or other individuals on a part-time or "per interview" basis. If your interviewers are not experienced, they should be provided with very specific information on all aspects of their work, including scripts to use during telephone interviews.

WHAT INFORMATION YOUR LOCAL RESEARCH SHOULD DEVELOP

There are two different *prime* audiences on which your local research should focus: People who already shop at your store, and people you would like to attract to the store.

Much of the information you seek from both audiences is similar in nature. From your present customers you will get data based on their experiences at your store. From your potential customers you will get information on their perception of your store, what might be keeping them away, and what it might take to attract them.

People Who Are Already Customers

Statistical data on the entire community is readily available from Census reports and other research discussed earlier in this chapter. What is important is to develop very specific data about your present customers, including their shopping patterns, attitudes toward your store, staff, and merchandise. The data you develop should provide you with a better understanding of your customers, enable you to improve your services to them, and result in increased sales.

Specific information you want to develop:

- General demographics about your customers—age, income, marital/family status, occupation, where they live (ZIP code, section, Census tract), education, language spoken.
- Information about their lifestyle interests.
- Frequency of visits to store.
- Average purchase per visit.
- Days, times of the day they shop at your store.
- Why do they shop at your store? What are they seeking from you?
- What it is that they like most about your store.
- Evaluation of the quality, styling, and availability of your merchandise.
- Seasons and holidays which have the most influence on their buying patterns.
- Attitude toward promotions, sales, special events.
- Do they already have specific items in mind to purchase when they enter the store?
- Items they buy on impulse.
- Their reactions to your salespeople: Are they helpful? Do they quickly resolve problems? Are they knowledgeable about products?
- What, if anything, do they dislike about your store.

- Other stores in the immediate area at which they shop.
- Newspapers they read, radio stations to which they listen, television channels they watch.
- From which media they receive information about the products/styles you sell.
- The influence advertising has on their shopping.

People You Would Like to Attract as Customers

You should also survey people who are not currently customers in order to determine how you might be able to expand your base. If you have general demographics on your present customers, you might use it to identify the city's Census tract areas in which people with similar demographics can be found. You could then concentrate some research in those areas to see how you might attract more customers from among your prime target audience.

Using the Census tract study, you might also identify areas where a more upscale audience than your present customers live, and do some research to find out what it will take to attract this group to become customers.

The information you want to develop from potential customers includes:

- If they purchase the type of products you sell.
- Where they currently shop for your type of products.
- What they look for when shopping for the products your store carries. Convenience? Pricing? Quality? Service?
- If they have ever heard of your store.
- Their impression of it.
- If they have ever been in it.
- Why they haven't shopped at it.
- What would induce them to shop at your store.
- Other stores in your area at which they currently shop.
- Seasons and holidays which most influence their buying behavior.
- The role promotions, sales, and special events play in attracting them to a store.

- Items they purchase on impulse.
- Shopping times and other patterns.
- Amount of purchases per visit/per month.
- Newspapers they read, radio stations to which they listen and television channels they watch.
- From which media they receive their information about the products/styles you sell.
- The influence advertising has on their shopping.
- Profile by age, income, education, occupation, lifestyles, section where they live. While you may be targeting the Census tract areas in which your present customers live, the individuals you survey may not have the same demographics. It is important to know their demographics since it might open an entire new audience for your store.

Customers You Have Lost

There is also a third audience about which you should be concerned: customers who no longer shop at your store. If you find that you are losing a significant number of customers, you should survey them (if you have a mailing list) in order to determine the problems. The key question to which you want an answer, of course, is why the customer has stopped shopping at your store.

Your survey of former customers should focus on:

- Pricing.
- Quality of products.
- Selection (variety, availability).
- Service.
- Convenience (location, days and hours of operation).
- Competition.

UNDERSTANDING RESEARCH FORMATS

There are many formats which can be used to solicit research data. Some *must* be conducted by professionals; others by individuals under the direction of a professional; still others by virtually anyone.

Here are some examples:

Questionnaires

Questionnaires are generally used to develop the major information concerning customer likes and dislikes, buying patterns, and personal demographics. They can be mailed to survey subjects, given to them in the store to take home to fill out and mail back, or can be used by interviewers during face-to-face sessions with subjects.

Face-to-face interviewing should be done by trained professionals since the interviewer's tone of voice, facial expressions, and attitude can influence answers. Also, some interview subjects may be reluctant to give true answers in face-to-face situations, or may slant their answers toward what they think the interviewer wants to hear.

The key to obtaining valid information is in the structuring of the survey. How questions are written will determine the objectivity of the responses. Questions concerning general demographic data are easy to write. However, questions requesting other information must be carefully written to avoid any form of suggestion or bias. That's why it is important for someone with experience in the research field to prepare the questionnaire. "Mini-questionnaires" can be used to develop information about customer service and other single-subject items. They are easy to prepare—you can probably prepare this type yourself—and can be filled out by customers while they are still in the store. Several examples of "mini-questionnaires" can be found at the end of this chapter.

Focus Groups

Focus groups use group discussions to elicit information you seek. There might be ten to twelve people in the group, with a trained moderator leading the discussion. Focus groups *must* be organized and led by professionals. They are usually conducted in a room with a concealed observation window from where you can view the entire discussion.

Panels

A panel consisting of customers might be set up to serve as a form of "advisory board" for your store. Every month or so, the members would be sent questionnaires aimed at developing whatever information you might seek, as well as trying to determine both problems and opportunities which might exist. For serving on the panel and responding to all the questionnaires during the year, the panelist is usually given a gift in the $25 range. Panelists remain anonymous, identifying themselves by number on the outside of the envelope so that it can be logged in for credit toward the gift. It is important to use a professional to select the panel and write the questionnaires.

Telephone Interviews

It is also possible to conduct interviews over the telephone. Since it is usually difficult to keep people on the telephone for a long period of time, normally less information can be gathered through this method than through written or in-person surveying. Since it is possible to work from a script, telephone surveys are easy to conduct even by inexperienced interviewers. One telephone type of interview is to call customers who have made a recent purchase. The announced purpose of the call is to check up and see if the customer is happy with the product. However, during the course of the conversation the interviewer, following a script, asks a few other questions to elicit information without the customer's awareness that he or she is being surveyed. Sample scripts can be found at the end of this chapter.

Studying Purchasing Patterns

A lot can be learned by studying the purchasing patterns of your customers. An easy way of doing this is through the development of a "Frequent Buyers Program." (See Chapter Ten.) Another technique is to have customers register for a mailing list so that they can be informed of special sales and discounts. Give each customer a membership card with an identification number, and have your cash register programmed so that it can compile sales data. Ask for the customer's membership card each time he or she makes a purchase and punch in the number along with the purchase information. Thus, you will be able to keep a running record of purchases, days and hours shopped, and other information from which you can develop all types of patterns and trends.

"Counting Heads"

From time to time, it is a good idea to station someone outside the store to take a count of passers-by. You want to know the number of people by sex, estimated age (from under 21 to over 60), whether they looked at your windows and whether they entered the store after looking at them, whether they appeared to be casually walking or headed to a specific location. You must take these counts at times when you have different windows—for example, when you have a window with movement in it, when you have specials, bright colors, etc. One purpose is to determine if any one type of window has more impact than another. A tally sheet for such a survey can be found at the end of this chapter.

License Plates

If there are many public parking spaces in the area, you may want to have someone periodically jot down license plate numbers. Very often you can tell from the plates the area where the car owner lives. In some states it is possible to purchase the names and addresses of car owners by submitting license plate numbers. This information will give you data about where area customers live. It will also enable you to get names for a mailing list if you do any direct mail. This project can be done by an employee or part-time worker; furthermore, you might get several non-competing retailers to split the cost with you.

Day-to-Day Analysis of Sales

Every retailer should keep a day-to-day analysis pattern of business. Included should be: sales broken down into one or two hour increments; number of customers entering the store during these same increments; sale or promotion taking place; weather; competitor activity (sales or promotions); other events taking place (local college football game, special on television, etc.).

GET TO KNOW YOUR COMPETITORS!

Of major importance in your fact-finding efforts should be as complete an analysis as possible of your competitors' marketing operations. This should be conducted on an ongoing basis. The information you collect should include:

- The type, quality, and selection of merchandise they sell, as well as pricing policies.
- Store hours, and amenities they offer customers (free deliveries, free alterations, return policy, telephone ordering, frequent buyer's programs, etc.).
- Marketing program, including advertising, special promotions and events, sales, etc.

The techniques to use in studying your competitors include:

- Frequent shopping at their stores.
- If possible, have one of your staff, or a relative become friendly with a sales person at each store. By earning their confidence, they might learn about special upcoming sales and other information which might be helpful to your store. To accomplish this, some of your "shoppers" might have to purchase products from these competitors.
- Get on their mailing lists, and in any special sales programs or clubs. Naturally, you will have to be discreet as to whose name is on the list. Perhaps you could use one of your relatives who has a different family name.
- Monitor the media to determine their advertising programs and estimated expenditures. Determine the patterns of the programs (days they usually advertise), as well as their creative approach.
- Try also to determine the pattern they might be following in scheduling promotions and sales.

YOUR RESEARCH MAY TELL YOU OTHER THINGS, TOO

It is important to use research to also gather data which will help you in your long-range planning, and to make important strategic decisions.

What areas should you look at?

- Are there any significant special markets, or new customer segments to which you should devote attention?
- Are you pursuing the right direction by trying to appeal to the entire market, rather than just segments of that market?
- Are you closely monitoring your target audience in order to track any possible changes taking place which could significantly affect your business?

SAMPLE QUESTIONNAIRES, TELEPHONE SCRIPTS AND TALLY SHEETS

To assist you in your research activities, the pages that follow present a series of sample questionnaires, telephone scripts and tally sheets.

Each questionnaire and telephone script contains a description of its purpose and the audience to whom it is directed.

SAMPLE MINI-QUESTIONNAIRE TO DETERMINE WHICH MEDIA CUSTOMERS READ, LISTEN TO OR WATCH

Here is an example of a mini-questionnaire which you might use to determine which media your customers read, listen to, and watch. It will assist you in determining where you might place your advertising. This questionnaire can be distributed in-store, or via a special or regular mailing.

HOW CAN WE BEST REACH YOU?

We are interested in determining how we can best reach you with our specials and other information about our store. Won't you please take a few minutes to answer this questionnaire and drop it in the box near the cash register. Thank you!

What is the radio station to which you most frequently listen?

_____

At what times do you usually listen? _____

What newspapers do you read (daily and weekly)? _____

What sections of the daily newspaper do you read? _____

What newspapers do you read on Sunday? _____

What sections of the Sunday newspaper do you read? _____

What sections of the weekly newspaper(s) do you read? _____

What television channels do you most frequently watch? _____

Do you watch the local television news programs? _____

If you do, at what times, and on what channels? _____

Do you watch cable television? _____

What cable systems do you watch (other than your regular television channels)? _____

Please list on a scale of 1-6 which advertising you see, hear or watch has the most influence on your buying decisions. 1 would be the medium with the most impact, 6 with the least.

        Radio _____
        Television _____
        Daily Newspapers _____
        Weekly Newspapers _____

Cable Television _____

Received In The Mail _____

Do you usually read, listen to, or watch our advertising? _____

Where?　Radio _____　　Weekly Newspapers _____

Television _____　　Cable Television _____

Received In Mail _____　　Daily Newspapers _____

NOTE: This question regarding your store's advertising should be asked even if you do not advertise, or do not use all of the media listed. It tests validity of answers, also possible confusion with competition's advertising.

SAMPLE MINI-QUESTIONNAIRE TO DETERMINE CUSTOMER SATISFACTION

On page 27 is a sample mini-questionnaire aimed at determining customer satisfaction. The customer can be asked to fill it out and leave it in a "ballot box" at the counter. Or it can be given to the customer when he or she makes a purchase, requesting return in the stamped, addressed envelope you provide. To encourage responses, you might hold a drawing for prizes among all customers who return their questionnaires. All they would have to do is list their name and address on the outer envelope. Because this is a customer service questionnaire, we also recommend that customers be given the option of providing their name and address on the questionnaire. If they do, and express unhappiness with your service or products, we recommend that contact be made with the customer.

HOW HAS OUR SERVICE TO YOU BEEN?

We are interested in learning if we are living up to your expectations during your visits to our store. We would appreciate a few minutes of your time to let us know how we are doing.

How do you rate our sales help overall?

Excellent ⎯⎯⎯⎯⎯⎯⎯⎯⎯⎯
Good ⎯⎯⎯⎯⎯⎯⎯⎯⎯⎯⎯
Fair ⎯⎯⎯⎯⎯⎯⎯⎯⎯⎯⎯
Poor ⎯⎯⎯⎯⎯⎯⎯⎯⎯⎯

Do you find that they are knowledgeable about our products?

Yes ⎯⎯⎯⎯⎯⎯⎯⎯⎯⎯
No ⎯⎯⎯⎯⎯⎯⎯⎯⎯⎯⎯
Sometimes ⎯⎯⎯⎯⎯⎯⎯⎯

Do you find exactly what you are looking for when you shop at our store?
Yes ⎯⎯⎯⎯⎯⎯⎯   No ⎯⎯⎯⎯⎯⎯⎯

What attracts you to shop at our store?
(Check as many as applicable)

Convenience ⎯⎯⎯⎯⎯⎯⎯⎯
Pricing ⎯⎯⎯⎯⎯⎯⎯⎯⎯⎯
Selection ⎯⎯⎯⎯⎯⎯⎯⎯⎯
Quality ⎯⎯⎯⎯⎯⎯⎯⎯⎯⎯
Service ⎯⎯⎯⎯⎯⎯⎯⎯⎯⎯

Now, please rate those factors you have checked above on a scale of 1 to 5, with 1 being the most important, and 5 the least important.

Convenience ⎯⎯⎯⎯⎯⎯⎯⎯
Pricing ⎯⎯⎯⎯⎯⎯⎯⎯⎯⎯
Selection ⎯⎯⎯⎯⎯⎯⎯⎯⎯
Quality ⎯⎯⎯⎯⎯⎯⎯⎯⎯⎯
Service ⎯⎯⎯⎯⎯⎯⎯⎯⎯⎯

How do you rate our prices?

Above Average ⎯⎯⎯⎯⎯⎯⎯
Below Average ⎯⎯⎯⎯⎯⎯⎯
Average ⎯⎯⎯⎯⎯⎯⎯⎯⎯

How do you rate the quality of our merchandise?

Above Average ⎯⎯⎯⎯⎯⎯⎯
Below Average ⎯⎯⎯⎯⎯⎯⎯
Average ⎯⎯⎯⎯⎯⎯⎯⎯⎯

How do you rate the selection of merchandise we have on hand?

Excellent _____

Good _____

Fair _____

Poor _____

Do you make it a habit to shop during our sales?

Yes _____

No _____

Sometimes _____

Do you make it a habit to shop during our special promotions or events?

Yes _____

No _____

Sometimes _____

Do you have problems finding your size(s)?

Yes _____

No _____

Sometimes _____

We would appreciate receiving any additional comments you have about our store, its merchandise, and our sales help. _____
_____
_____
_____

Optional: If you would like to provide your name and address, please do so.

Name _____   City _____

Address _____   ZIP Code _____

SAMPLE MINI-QUESTIONNAIRE ON CUSTOMER DEMOGRAPHICS

The sample mini-questionnaire on page 29 is designed to develop demographic data on customers.

CONFIDENTIALLY, PLEASE TELL US A LITTLE ABOUT YOURSELF

This is a confidential questionnaire which we developed in order to find out more about our customers so that we may better serve your needs. *DO NOT WRITE YOUR NAME OR OTHERWISE IDENTIFY YOURSELF.* Thank you for your cooperation.

Sex: Male _____ Female _____

Are you: Married? _____ Single? _____
        Separated? _____ Divorced? _____
        Widowed? _____

Education: High-schoolgraduate _____ College graduate _____
        Post-graduate work _____ Technical school _____

Languages spoken other than English _____

Your age:
        Under 18 _____ 18-24 _____
        25-34 _____ 35-44 _____
        45-54 _____ 55-64 _____
        65-74 _____ 75-84 _____

Hobbies/Special Interests _____
_____

Annual household income:
        Under $10,000 _____ $10,000–$29,999 _____
        $30,000–$49,999 _____ $50,000–$74,999 _____
        Over $75,000 _____

Occupation _____

If you work, what are your hours? _____

Total number of family members who are customers _____

How often do you shop at the store?
        Once A Week _____ More Than Once A Week _____
        Every Two Weeks _____ Every Three Weeks _____
        Once A Month _____ Once A Quarter _____

Approximate number of times a year _____

Approximate number of years a customer _____

Usual shopping day(s) at store:
        Monday _____ Tuesday _____ Wednesday _____
        Thursday _____ Friday _____ Saturday _____
        Sunday _____

Usual shopping hours (If you checked more than one day, please indicate the hours usually shopped at the store for each of the days) _____

How do you reach the store?

          Walk _____   Drive _____

          Bus _____   Train _____

If you take public transportation to the store, identify the bus route or train line _____

Thank you for your cooperation!

SAMPLE QUESTIONNAIRE TO SEND TO A FORMER CUSTOMER

If a good customer stops shopping at your store, it is important to determine the reason. If you have his or her name and address on file, you should make contact. One way is through a questionnaire similar to the one on page 31.

WE MISS YOU!

We notice that you haven't visited with us for some time, and we wonder if you have found some serious problems with our service, merchandise, or some other aspect of our store.

We would appreciate a few minutes of your time to fill this out and return to me in the attached stamped addressed envelope.

While it is not necessary to identify yourself in this questionnaire, I would like to discuss with you any problems you might have had with us. Please call me at 668-6667 anytime at your convenience.

John D. Owner

Do you still have a need for the type of merchandise our store carries?
Yes _____ No _____
(If you checked "yes," please complete the rest of the questionnaire.)

How did you find our prices?
        Above Average _____
        Below Average _____
        Average _____

How did you find the quality of our merchandise?
        Above Average _____
        Below Average _____
        Average _____

How did you rate the variety of merchandise offered?
        Above Average _____
        Below Average _____
        Average _____

Was the merchandise you wanted usually available when you shopped at our store? Yes _____ No _____

How would you rate our sales people?
        Excellent _____
        Good _____
        Fair _____
        Poor _____

Were you satisfied with the service you received at the store?
Yes _____ No _____

Please check off as many of the reasons as necessary to describe why you stopped shopping with us.

Pricing _____

Quality of Products _____

Selection of Products _____

Sizes Needed _____

Sales Help _____

Service _____

Location _____

Store Hours _____

If there are any other reasons, please list them _____

_____

_____

If you have any other comments about our store, we would like to hear them

_____

_____

_____

_____

_____

Thank you for filling out this questionnaire.

As a former customer, your opinion is highly valued and we hope to learn from it how we may have failed to serve your shopping needs, and what we can do to correct these problems.

SAMPLE TELEPHONE SCRIPT TO DETERMINE CUSTOMER SATISFACTION

This is a sample of a telephone script which might be used not only to determine customer satisfaction with a recent purchase but also to elicit other information. While telephone interviews can be formally structured, with the interviewer asking questions and offering a multiple choice of answers, this survey uses open-ended questions. The interviewer must take extensive notes during the conversation since the subjects will be expressing their views in their own words.

Hello. Is this Mrs. Arlene James?

This is Harvey Smith of "The Downtown Boutique." I was just calling to see if you were happy with the blazer and skirt you purchased March 15?

- Are you completely satisfied with its fit?
- How long have you been shopping with us, Mrs. James?
- Do you find that you are getting all of the assistance you need when you come into the store?
- Do you find that our sales help are knowledgeable and can answer all your questions?

We're interested in your comments because we consider customer satisfaction to be our number one goal.

May I ask you a few more questions?

- Can you usually find what you want when you are shopping?
- Do you feel that we have a broad enough selection for you to choose from?
- And do you have any problems finding your size?
- What about our pricing? How do you find it?
- Are you satisfied with the quality of our merchandise?
- One last question. From your point of view, what can we do to improve our services for you?

Thank you very much for your time. And if you have any problems with the blazer and skirt, or anything else you ever purchase from us, please be sure to bring it back.

Thanks again Mrs. James.

SAMPLE TELEPHONE SCRIPT TO A FORMER CUSTOMER

You may also interview a former customer by telephone. It may be advantageous to do a telephone interview instead of mailing a questionnaire since, in addition to getting your information in the customer's own words, during the course of your conversation you may be able to persuade him or her to come back as a customer.

Hello. Is this Ms. Mary Jones?

This is John D. Owner, from John D's Shoe Store. We have noticed that you have not been in to see us for some time, and we were wondering if you were having any problems with our store.

(Note: You may get the answers to all of your questions as she responds. If not, follow the script and ask the questions for which she may not have given you information.)

We value the opinions of our customers and we'd like to ask you a few questions to see how we may have failed to serve your shopping needs.

- Has our pricing been a problem?
- Were you satisfied with the quality of our products?
- Do you feel we have enough of a variety of merchandise?
- Did we always have your shoe size in stock?
- How did you find our salespeople? Were they helpful, and knowledgeable?
- Was there any one reason why you stopped shopping with us?

  (If the answer is no, ask the next question)
- What then were the reasons?

We appreciate your time, and we'll do everything we can to correct the problems you discussed with me. I hope, perhaps, at some future date, you will shop with us once again.

(Note: If answers to your questions are not clear, follow up in a conversational tone and try to get a firmer answer to each question).

SINGLE DAY BUSINESS ANALYSIS

Date _____ Day Of The Week _____

Time	No. Of Customers	No. Of Products Sold	Gross Sales
9 AM			
10 AM			
11 AM			
Noon			
1 PM			
2 PM			
3 PM			
4 PM			
5 PM			

6 PM _____

7 PM _____

8 PM _____

9 PM _____

10 PM _____

TOTALS

Promotion/Sale _____

Weather _____

Competitor Promotions _____
_____

Other Competitive Events _____
_____

HOURLY TALLY SHEET FOR PASSER-BY HEAD COUNT

Day _____   Date _____

Hour _____   Weather _____

	MALES	FEMALES
Under 21		
21–29		
30–39		
40–49		
50–59		
Over 60		

Looked At Windows

Entered Store After Looking

Casually Walking

Fixed Destination

TOTALS

	MALES	FEMALES
Under 21		
21–29		
30–39		
40–49		
50–59		
Over 60		
Looked		
Entered		
Casual		
Fixed		

RESOURCES

The following are the contact points from which to obtain information for services mentioned in this chapter:

U. S. Bureau of the Census

- First check the U. S. Government listings in your telephone directory. If there is a regional office in your area, it will be listed and you will probably be able to do your research there.
- If one isn't listed, contact your nearest regional office (see list below) for the location of the Federal Depository Library, or state or local data centers.

  The Census Regional Offices:

Atlanta, GA	Detroit, MI
Boston, MA	Kansas City, KS
Charlotte, NC	Los Angeles, CA
Chicago, IL	New York, NY
Dallas, TX	Philadelphia, PA
Denver, CO	Seattle, WA

- If you need further help to locate any of the offices, contact Customer Services at 1-301-763-4100.
- To order any reports, documents, or CD-ROM's and to get information about any products available from the Census Bureau, contact Customer Service, Bureau of the Census, Washington, D. C. 20233 (301-763-4100).

The Lifestyle Zip Code Analyst

Customer Service, SRDS, 2000 Clearwater Drive, Oak Brook, IL 60521.

The Small Business Administration

- First look in your telephone directory under U. S. Government listings. Your local office can give you full information on all of the SBA's programs and services. While we only discussed marketing and research assistance in this chapter, the Small Business Administration offers a complete menu of services in all areas of business.

• If you cannot find a listing, then call the Small Business Answer Desk at 1-800-8-ASK-SBA (1-800-827-5722).

Market Research Firms

Look in your local Yellow Pages under "Market Research and Analysis" to find market research firms. If you cannot find any, or would like to find other sources, you might consult the following:

• The Marketing Research Association publishes a directory listing approximately 1000 firms. It is titled, *"Blue Book: Research Services Directory."* It may be found at public, business, or university libraries, or can be purchased from the Association for $100. The address: Marketing Research Association, 2189 Silas Dean Highway, Suite 5, Rocky Hill, CT 06067 (203-257-4008).

• The Council of American Survey Research Organizations (CASRO) can supply at no cost a list of any of its member firms located within your area. The address: CASRO, 3 Upper Devon Belle Terre, Port Jefferson, NY 11777 (516-928-6954).

• The New York Chapter of the American Marketing Association publishes two directories. One is of organizations which conduct focus groups and costs $50. The second directory, known as "The GreenBook," (its actual name is *International Directory Of Marketing Research Companies & Services*) has extensive listings of firms from all over the United States and costs $90. It might be available at local public, business and university libraries. The address to order a copy is American Marketing Association/NY, 310 Madison Avenue, Suite 1211, New York, N. Y. 10017. (212-687-3280).

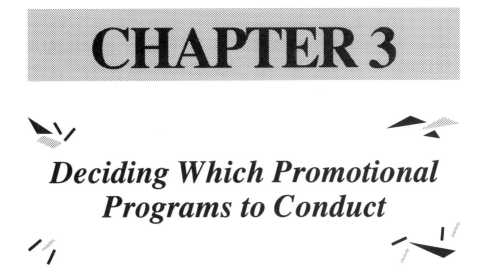

CHAPTER 3

Deciding Which Promotional Programs to Conduct

While there may be over 1000 promotional ideas within the pages of this book, by no means is each one of them suitable for every retail establishment. Rather they comprise a universe of ideas from which retailers can select those which may be appropriate for their stores. Entire categories may be eliminated by some retailers because they may not be appropriate for the store, its product lines, or its customers. Or they might be just too expensive for the store's budget. On the other hand, some retailers may find workable suggestions in all categories.

Only you are in the position to decide which promotions to try at your store. And you should make those selections only after a careful analysis of customer attitudes and costs.

MATCHING THE PROMOTION TO THE CUSTOMERS

Before you even begin work on the financial feasibility of a promotion, you must be convinced that it will be attractive to your customers and to your potential customers as well. This is where your role as "matchmaker" comes in.

Chapter Two, "Gathering The Data To Help You Make Your Marketing Decisions," discussed the data readily available in your community, as well as other information which can be developed locally. This information will help you profile your actual and potential customers. Once you have profiled them, you will have a better idea of the promotions to which they will react positively.

In addition, while a promotional idea is still in its embryonic stage, your sales staff should test customer reaction to it. You should also poll other customers by telephone, as well as some of your targeted potential customers.

Information to Get From Regular Customers

- Try to determine if a regular customer will visit the store during the promotion solely because of it.
- Will a regular customer postpone a visit to the store until the promotion starts? Or will he or she avoid the store during promotions?
- Will a promotion encourage the customer to spend more money than he or she usually does?
- Will added crowds at the store during the promotion upset the regular customer?
- What promotions do your regular customers prefer? Special events, seasonal themes, sales, contests?
- Try to determine, by themes, which promotions your regular customers prefer (sports, exhibits, entertainers, psychics, etc.).
- Would a regular customer prefer lower everyday prices to promotions?
- Do promotions have any effect on how the regular customer feels about the store?
- What do regular customers think of the proposed promotion outlined to them? Would they look forward to it?

Information to Get From Potential Customers

- What do they think of promotions?
- Will they visit a store for the first time because of a promotion?
- Will they visit it even though they may not be looking to purchase a product?

- What promotions would attract them to a store? Special events, seasonal themes, sales, contests?
- What themes would attract them? Sports, nostalgia, psychics, exhibits, holidays, entertainment?
- If they visit a store because of a specific promotion, would they visit it a second time after the promotion is over?
- Would they prefer to patronize a store which offers everyday low pricing rather than periodic promotions?
- What do they think of the proposed promotion outlined to them? Would they look forward to attending?

Another question which might be added to both surveys relates to a list of four or five promotions you have under consideration. Ask each person to rank them in order of their interest.

The information you develop from your customer profiles and surveys will provide you with data to help you decide upon the feasibility of conducting specific promotions. You should use this information to answer the first four of the following **five promotional criteria questions.** The fifth question concerns the financial viability of the proposed promotion. The totality of these five answers will enable you to make your final determination as to whether a particular promotion will help fulfill the marketing and sales objectives of the store.

ANSWERING THE FIVE PROMOTIONAL CRITERIA QUESTIONS

1. *Will this promotion attract new and/or repeat customers, and/or incremental business?*
   The obvious answer must be yes. A promotion should only be conducted if it will attract customers and business. The type of promotion you select, your pricing during the promotion, and those to whom you market each promotion will determine your success in attracting new customers and building incremental sales. It must be a promotion which appeals to your target audience.

2. *Will the new customers it attracts be the customers you want to attract—people who will come back to the store after the promotion is over?*

This is where you have to be careful in selecting a promotion. An up-scale men's clothing store with a sports memorabilia display will attract many sports fans but probably very few will become regular customers. Similarly, if you have a celebrity signing autographs, people may buy the product necessary to get the autograph but never come back a second time. A good rule of thumb is not to hold events which will draw large crowds unless you feature products in the popular price range. An upscale store should carefully target its promotion toward the people it wants to attract as customers. It should be a promotion which will appeal only to a narrower audience, and with all promotional efforts aimed directly at that very group. It doesn't have to attract large numbers of people to the store; in fact, you would be better off drawing a smaller number of quality prospects to whom your salespeople could give more personal attention, and work toward converting into regular customers.

3. *Will the promotion enhance the overall image of the store, or will it possibly detract from it?*
This is the easiest question to answer since you have total control over it. You know what image your store has, or at least what you want it to have. Measure the proposed promotion against it and see if it will detract from your image. If you are known as a conservative store, don't conduct an "off-the-wall" promotion with psychedelic lighting which is going to draw a teen-age crowd. By the same token, if you draw a young upbeat clientele, don't schedule a promotion which is going to attract a senior citizen crowd. Your customers undoubtedly like the image of your store because that's why they shop there. So by tailoring promotions for them, based on their likes, you will be enhancing the overall image of the store.

4. *Will it hurt existing business by attracting so many new customers that you will not have time to tend properly to the needs of your loyal regular customers?*
This is a possibility if your store becomes so packed with people that shopping becomes difficult and your regular customers will not get the usual service. You must try to select promotions that can fit comfortably in the store, and will not draw masses of people who cannot be properly handled.

Another way to approach the problem is that when you schedule promotions that you expect will draw large crowds, hold a preview day or night for your regular customers. This way, they will feel important, have first crack at all merchandise and get the VIP treatment. It will also enable your sales force to spend more time during the promotion cultivating potential new customers.

5. *What is the bottom line? Will it be cost efficient? And how cost efficient will it be when compared to other promotions you could run?* You will need to develop quite a bit of data to answer this important fifth question. If you have been compiling sales statistics over the years, you may already have this information. If you haven't, you should be collecting sales data on a regular basis since it is so important to your promotional planning process. Chapter Two has information on how to do this, including an easy-to-follow form.

The data you must develop includes:

Cost of Promotion/Percentage of Annual Promotion Budget

One of the first things you have to do is price out very carefully the exact cost of the promotion. You must factor in all of the basic costs from planning to execution. This will include:

- Entertainers/personalities (magician, clown, etc.)
- Platform rental, if necessary
- Public address system
- Decorations, costumes, etc.
- Advertising and promotion (Only factor in the costs of advertising and promotional materials purchased exclusively for this promotion.)
- Prizes, if it is a contest
- Props or other material
- Extra security
- Additional staff salaries (Temps, or overtime)
- Refreshments, gifts for customers (Both optional)
- Contingency allowance
- Contribution to charity (If it is a tie-in with a nonprofit organization)

Once you have added up all these expenses, figure out what percentage of your annual promotion budget will be used for this event. Also figure out your profitability of the other promotions you have recently held.

Store's Sales History During Promotion Period

You should have been keeping good records of your sales by week or month. If so, you will be able to get an idea of what your average sales figures have been over the past few years during specific periods. Note whether or not you were conducting promotions during this period in past years. You should also determine the percentage of your annual sales which usually occur during this month. You can then measure it against the national average for your particular type of store. See Chart One on pages 47-48. Does your past performance measure up to this national average? If it does not, this could be an indicator that you must promote your store and product line more vigorously this month.

Square Footage Needed vs. Square Footage Available

You must carefully calculate the amount of square footage needed for this event, including space for customer-spectators. Then calculate the amount of non-display space available. You will then find how much additional space may be needed.

At this point, you must decide whether it will be worth committing the additional space to the promotion. What is the potential income lost by eliminating the display space during the promotion period? If you do not already have this information, start tracking sales from the display area involved over a period of days similar to those during which the promotion will run. Will the additional business generated by the promotion more than make up for the loss? Would any loss be minimized by shifting the products from the eliminated display area to another area in the store? Could you have them temporarily replace less profitable products on display?

Experience Factor

What has been your experience regarding similar promotions or any promotions held during this period of time? Approximately how many additional customers were attracted to the store, and how many of them became permanent customers?

Staffing Requirements

You must factor in the staffing requirements for the promotion or event. This includes both planning time and the time and staff needed for the event itself. If additional people are needed, or staff members are paid overtime, costs must be calculated and added into your budget.

Targeted Goals for the Promotion

You must set some practical profit and customer goals for your promotion.

- Is your main objective to use the promotion to introduce new customers to the store?
- Is it to increase gross sales, or net profits? If so, by how much? And are these reasonable figures?
- Is the objective just to focus attention on the store, or enhance its image, without caring about sales figures and income?

You must put some dollars-and-cents estimates against these questions. For example, you must place a monetary value on a new customer. Based on experience, how much additional revenue will a new customer generate in a year? You must also estimate how much additional revenue will be generated by the promotion. You should be able to use figures from past promotions to get these numbers.

Other Income

Will any manufacturers contribute promotional dollars for the event? If so, how much? Will an increased buy-in of products entitle you to a lower wholesale price?

MAKING THE FINAL DECISION

It is now up to you to make that final decision.

- You should be totally convinced that the promotion you select will appeal to your audience.

- You should be convinced that it will accomplish its goal: to attract new customers; increase sales; create long range excitement; or enhance the image of the store.

- You should also be convinced that there will not be any financial surprises, that you will not be way over budget, and that income from the promotion will be within the parameters of your estimate.

Chart One

PERCENT OF RETAIL SALES DONE EACH MONTH DURING 1992

(By Type Of Store)

Type of Store	Jan	Feb	Mar	Apr	May	June
Auto And Home Supply Stores	7.1	7.1	7.9	8.3	8.5	8.9
Automotive Dealers	7.2	7.5	8.5	8.7	8.7	9.2
Book Stores	9.6	6.5	6.5	6.5	6.8	7.1
Building Materials & Supply Stores	6.5	6.6	7.7	8.5	9.1	9.5
Department Stores	5.8	6.4	7.3	7.6	8.1	7.5
Drug & Proprietary Stores	8.1	8.0	8.2	8.4	8.3	8.1
Eating Places	7.7	7.8	8.3	8.1	8.7	8.3
Family Clothing Stores	5.1	5.7	6.6	7.4	7.3	7.6
Floor Covering Stores	7.1	7.1	8.1	8.3	8.0	9.0
Furniture & Home Furnishings Stores	7.3	7.5	7.9	7.9	8.1	8.3
Gasoline Service Stations	7.6	7.3	7.8	7.9	8.6	8.8
Grocery Stores	8.1	7.7	8.0	8.2	8.6	8.3
Hardware Stores	6.6	6.4	7.6	8.5	9.7	9.2
Household Appliance Stores	7.2	6.9	7.5	7.6	7.7	8.7
Jewelry Stores	5.3	6.9	6.1	6.4	7.9	7.3
Liquor Stores	7.0	7.2	7.3	7.6	8.5	8.4
Meat & Fish Markets	6.6	6.5	7.1	7.6	7.8	8.6
Men's & Boys Clothing/ Furnishings Stores	6.8	6.4	7.2	8.1	8.5	8.3
Radio, TV & Computer Stores	7.8	7.3	7.7	7.3	7.4	7.7
Retail Bakeries	8.5	8.5	8.7	8.3	9.0	8.3
Shoe Stores	6.5	6.8	7.8	9.1	8.6	8.2
Sporting Goods Stores And Bicycle Shops	6.2	7.0	7.7	8.4	8.5	8.5
Variety Stores	6.9	7.4	7.4	8.4	8.1	7.3
Women's Clothing Specialty Stores	5.9	6.2	7.4	8.2	8.6	7.7
Women's Ready-To-Wear Stores	5.8	6.2	7.5	8.3	8.7	7.7

Source. U.S. Department of Commerce
Estimated Monthly Retail Sales By Kind Of Business
January 1 - December 31, 1992

Type of Store	July	Aug	Sept	Oct	Nov	Dec
Auto And Home Supply Stores	9.1	8.7	8.7	9.1	8.3	8.3
Automotive Dealers	9.1	8.5	8.6	8.7	7.7	7.8
Book Stores	7.2	10.6	10.1	7.6	7.7	13.8
Building Materials & Supply Stores	9.3	9.0	9.1	9.1	7.9	7.6
Department Stores	7.4	8.3	7.5	8.5	10.2	15.3
Drug & Proprietary Stores	8.1	8.1	7.8	8.3	7.9	10.4
Eating Places	8.5	8.8	8.2	8.7	8.2	8.6
Family Clothing Stores	8.0	9.1	8.0	8.9	10.1	16.0
Floor Covering Stores	8.9	9.0	8.6	8.6	8.5	8.7
Furniture & Home Furnishings Stores	8.5	8.5	8.3	8.6	8.9	10.1
Gasoline Service Stations	9.0	8.9	8.5	8.8	8.3	8.4
Grocery Stores	8.8	8.5	8.2	8.5	8.2	9.0
Hardware Stores	9.0	8.6	8.3	8.8	8.2	9.1
Household Appliance Stores	9.1	8.6	8.1	8.7	9.0	10.8
Jewelry Stores	7.0	7.3	6.9	7.5	9.1	22.5
Liquor Stores	8.8	8.6	8.2	8.6	8.5	11.3
Meat & Fish Markets	9.5	9.1	8.6	8.6	8.6	11.5
Men's & Boys Clothing/ Furnishings Stores	6.9	7.5	7.4	8.5	9.2	15.4
Radio, TV & Computer Stores	7.9	7.8	7.9	8.3	9.1	13.9
Retail Bakeries	8.2	8.3	8.0	8.6	7.4	8.3
Shoe Stores	7.9	9.9	8.5	8.2	8.0	10.7
Sporting Goods Stores And Bicycle Shops	8.6	8.7	7.7	7.3	7.7	13.8
Variety Stores	7.5	7.5	6.8	8.3	9.0	15.4
Women's Clothing Specialty Stores	7.6	8.4	8.0	8.7	9.3	14.0
Women's Ready-To-Wear Stores	7.6	8.4	8.1	8.7	9.3	13.8

CHAPTER 4

Looking Good from Your Front Windows to the Back of the Store

The first impression a person is going to get of your store is from its windows, front door and outside signage. Many a decision on whether to enter the store or keep on walking will be based upon this first impression. Unlike the familiar saying, "Don't judge a book by its cover," people *do* judge a store by its "cover." Furthermore, if potential customers do get by the "cover" and enter the store, they must feel comfortable inside or chances are they will walk right out.

So it is very important that both the inside and outside of your store are kept as attractive as possible. Both should reflect the personality and image which will appeal to your target audience. Think of the store as you would of an impulse item. You want the passer-by to be stopped in his or her tracks by your windows and signage, and be drawn right into the store. Then, once the customer opens the door, you want him or her to be further drawn to your merchandise.

MAKING YOUR SIDEWALK HEAD AND SHOULDERS ABOVE THE OTHERS

The image of your store begins with your sidewalk. You want it to be head and shoulders above all the other sidewalks on the same street. If someone surveys the entire block from across the street, you want your entire "package"—sidewalk, store, and signage—to stand out from all of the others.

- If zoning laws permit, think of ways to improve the pavement in front of the store. Perhaps a red-brick sidewalk will give you the distinctive look you want. Or perhaps a red brick path or "mat" at the entranceway.

- If you have trees in front of the store, plant flowers in the tree bases. In addition, flower plantings in other appropriate places around the front of the store will create an attractive atmosphere, as will hedges and other plants.

- If you have a wide sidewalk, and zoning laws permit it, consider installing one or two benches near the curb, but facing your windows. It is a nice amenity for the community, and anyone sitting on the benches will be looking right at your windows.

- Keep the sidewalk clean; have it swept several times a day. A dirty sidewalk is a turn-off.

- On snowy days, shovel the sidewalk to keep it clear of snow. You may have to do it several times an hour, but your customers will appreciate it.

USING EFFECTIVE OUTSIDE SIGNAGE, AWNINGS AND CANOPIES

A great deal of thought should go into your decision on how to display the store's name, as well as whether or not you will have a canopy or awning over your windows and/or doors.

Assisting you in developing your outside look should be a designer who should look at the exterior as a package, advising you on color, types and sizes of signs, type of canopy or awning to use, and type of window.

In reaching your conclusions, you must take several factors into consideration:

- Local zoning regulations. There may be restrictions regarding the type and/or size of signage you can use, especially if you are located in a historic district.

- The surrounding stores. Some uniformity in store signs on the same street is usually a good idea. Otherwise you can end up with a maze of signs, each trying to overwhelm the other. To achieve this uniformity, it may be necessary for you to compromise on the signage that you really want. This is one particular area in which your designer can be of great assistance.

- Your location. If your entrance is right on the corner, your signage will probably be different than if you are in the middle of the block. For a corner entrance, you might want an overhanging vertical sign attached to the corner of the building so that it is visible on both streets. If your store is visible on a highway, well-traveled road, or commuter rail line, you will probably want a lighted sign in order to attract attention to the store's name.

- Today a growing number of stores use canvas canopies or awnings which also serve as the identifying signage for the store. While they can be very attractive and eliminate the need for a sign, canvas does get dirty and must be cleaned on a regular basis. So, before installing a canvas sign, you must commit yourself to a regular cleaning schedule.

- Many of the canvas canopy signs do not have an overhead covering. As a result, they will not protect passers-by from inclement weather like an awning. When people take cover under an awning, you have a captive audience for your windows. You never know how many customers you will pick up that way. The added exposure you receive can be very meaningful, especially if you are located right by a bus stop or some other heavily traveled area.

SETTING THE SCENE IN YOUR WINDOWS

One place where you should not cut any corners is with your windows. They might be the most important part of the store because of the influence they have in setting the scene for what the customer will find inside. When properly used, they are probably your least expensive and most effective form of advertising. *They bring customers into the store!*

Your initial step should be to decide on an overall philosophy of how you will use your windows, what you want them to say, and how you want them to deliver your message. There are many options available, and what you do and how you do it will depend largely upon your type of store and your marketing strategy.

A Minimum of Product vs. a Packed Window

Just how much product you put in a window will depend upon what you are trying to accomplish. Retailers who display a minimal amount of product are usually trying to project a very upscale image. By delivering a limited message through their windows, they appear to be saying that they have an exclusive grouping of products for a select audience. Other stores will pack their windows with as much product as possible. Shoe stores do this to show the variety of styles; hardware stores show the variety of products they carry; drug stores display their many specials. Still other stores try to present a cross-section of products they carry so that window shoppers get a sense of what is available inside.

Yes or No on Price Tags

Should you place price tags on products in the window? Stores which usually display prices do it so that shoppers will know the price range of their products, and also be aware of specials and sale items. There are various reasons for not featuring price tags in the window. Some retailers feel the absence of price tags lures shoppers into the store, creating an opportunity to close a sale, while a visible price tag might turn shoppers off and keep them from entering the store. Others feel that they avoid getting involved in open price wars with competitors. Still other retailers look at it as a way to project an upscale image. People with limited budgets will feel they cannot afford to shop at the store while wealthier people will gain an image of the store as upscale, with quality pricing and a rich clientele.

Should Movement Be Incorporated In Your Windows?

Movement adds excitement to your windows and attracts attention. It stops people on the street and draws them toward the window.

Some retailers feel that the use of turntables and other animated devices will focus attention on only that part of the window, while remaining products will be ignored. For the same reason, others feel that you will accomplish your objectives if the key products you are promoting are the ones featured in the moving display. The star products get the star treatment, and the others fill the support role.

There are also different theories as to the effectiveness of "electronic message boards." Again, some retailers feel that message boards detract from what is displayed in the window, while others feel that they actually attract people to the window. This latter group's argument is that people stop to read the message and in doing so are exposed to the store window. Messages can also be used to direct the reader to products in the window. For example, a message might read, "See that pair of boat shoes to the left of the sign? They carry the longest guarantee . . . ."

A third form of movement is the use of live performers in the window. In the chapter on Special Events (Chapter Six), you will find examples of how performers can appear in the window for the specific purpose of attracting a crowd and leading it into the store. Naturally, when you have live performers in the window, you will have little product exposure since people will be concentrating on the performance and not looking at what is on display.

Finding Someone To Decorate Your Windows

Once you have decided on the direction your window project will follow, your next step should be to find a decorator. If the budget permits, you should hire a professional window dresser. How do you find one? Spend some time looking at store windows throughout the area. When you see a window you like, ask the owner for the name of the dresser. Or you can compile a list of three to four and interview each one. See if they agree with your objectives for your windows. Determine their creativity by having them show a portfolio of windows each has decorated. Find out their work procedures. Do they provide you with a sketch of each window? Do they lean toward using expensive props? Are they willing to repaint and reuse old props? How quickly do they work? How long will it take from concept through final execution? And, most important, is the chemistry there? Will you be able to work with one another?

If you cannot afford to use a professional window dresser, you may be able to find help locally free-of-charge, or at a relatively low cost. Contact any local schools of design and see if they have intern programs for their students. You may be able to get free assistance, perhaps even students working under the direction of their teacher. If the school does not have a formal internship program, ask the dean or a professor to recommend a very talented student. Your costs will probably be minimal.

Free-lance help may also be found locally that can save you money. You might find a full-time window trimmer who works for a large department store who is looking to moonlight. You may also find a talented decorator or designer who has the flair for doing windows.

Many retailers and their employees have become skilled window trimmers. While it takes time from their regular duties, it does save the store money. If you will be doing your windows in-house, contact your suppliers to see if there is any assistance they might offer. It might include handbooks or video tapes on decorating techniques, or they may even have a consultant who could visit your store and run an informal seminar.

Making the Windows Work for You

With major decisions made on the look your windows will take and who will be your trimmer, it is time to put those windows to work for you. They have to help you sell your products, motivate window-shoppers to come into the store, and leave an impression of the store on the minds of passersby.

Here are some tips on how to accomplish this:

- Use your windows to tell what's going on inside the store. Always feature your sales, special events, and thematic promotions in them. For example, if you are running a "Back To School" promotion, decorate the windows with school logos, books, blackboards and school desks, as well as your featured products. Also use banners to reinforce the message.

- Be ingenious on how you display your products. Sometimes use props instead of mannequins and fixtures. Display waterproof boots by having them stand in a large pot of water. Try a child's jacket draped around the back of a kitchen chair, just like the child would do at home. How about a woman's hat on top of a lamp shade? There is no limit to what can be done.

- Use movement to grab attention for a promotion, or to focus in on a major product. See the discussion on movement earlier in the chapter.

- Change your windows frequently. People will stop looking at the same old window if it is there too long.

- Develop a daily feature so that passers-by will be enticed to look in each day: A product of the day, a joke of the day, hide the stuffed Teddy bear mascot someplace else each day, trivia question of the day, special password of the day good for a surprise gift or discount.

- Keep your windows clean. Dirty, unwashed windows are a turn-off to customers and bad for your image.

Other ideas for window displays to support promotions, sales and special events will be found throughout the book.

Where to Find What You Need for Your Windows

If you are dressing your own windows, you should develop a relationship with a local distributor, designer, or producer of window display materials. Get on the mailing lists of some of the national companies in the field. You will be able to get just about anything you need to decorate a window including mannequins, mannequin parts, banners, turntables, oversized formed plastic products, seasonal displays, lights, classic columns, pedestals and platforms, and animated characters.

But don't confine yourself to the traditional window dressing materials. You can use just about anything in a window. Sometimes by simply repainting you can use a prop again and again.

Antique dealers, art galleries and furniture stores are ideal places from which to borrow materials for your window displays. You can usually get them to lend you what you need so long as you give them credit in the window.

You can make your mannequins more attractive by adding jewelry and other accessories. Borrow what you need from other merchants, giving them credit in the window.

If you are running a sports promotion, try borrowing equipment from local sports teams. (See Chapter Nine.) You can probably get old newspaper headlines from your local newspaper.

Your historical society and local library are good sources for display material. So are veterans' organizations, scouts, and garden clubs. Make contact with some local hobbyists and collectors who will probably be very happy to lend material for your windows. Finally, don't overlook local junk yards or the garbage dump. You would be amazed what you can sometimes find at these locations. All you need is a little paint and you have a first-class window prop.

GETTING THE MOST OUT OF YOUR FRONT DOOR

The "first impression" campaign should continue with your front door. It is only a small piece of the picture, but an important one which is all too often ignored.

How many retailers have a sign on that door which says, "Welcome," "Please Come In And Browse," or "Through These Doors Walk the Nicest People In The World?" Probably very few, yet such signs are inexpensive to have made and would probably bring in additional traffic.

Use the front door as a continuation of your window. If the windows are promoting a sale or special event, have a sign on, or over, the door saying, "Entrance to Our Spring Clearance Sale," or "Meet Jambo The Magician," etc. Sometimes a sign isn't necessary to serve as a bridge. If, for example, you are promoting St. Patrick's Day in the window, all you would need on the door are shamrocks.

Not only should you have a welcome sign of some type on the outside of the door, but you should have a "thank you" sign on the inside which the customer sees on the way out—such as "Thank You For Shopping With Us," "Thanks For Your Support," "Have A Safe Trip Home," "We Appreciate The Time You Spend With Us."

Other than a single sign, or the shamrocks, your front door should be clean and offer a clear view into the store. You want the passer-by who is turned on by the window to have a good view of the interior of the store as he or she approaches the door.

DESIGNING A CUSTOMER-FRIENDLY STORE

Designing a store requires special talents and is a job that should be done by a professional. Even if you do not have plans, or the money to renovate your store, it still might be a good idea to consult a store designer for suggestions on how you might improve the selling floor. You may also want to contact the local U. S. Government Small Business Administration office to see if any of its programs offer this form of consulting free. (See Chapter Two regarding how to get in touch with the Small Business Administration.)

A retailer should always be looking for ways to improve the interior of the store to make it easier for customers to shop and find the merchandise they came to buy. A designer can assist you in that area.

However, even without a designer there are many steps you can take to make shopping an easier and happier experience.

- Your merchandise should be organized in such a way that customers will quickly find it. One technique is to have the various sections of the store numbered, with directories up front, in the middle, and in the rear of the store identifying in which section specific products can be found.

- Always have an interesting product or display featured up front and visible from outside. It should be aimed at attracting the attention of passers-by, and at grabbing the interest of a customer walking through the front door.

- Whenever you have a limited sale, or if you have a regular sale table, it should always be in the rear of the store so that customers will have to pass all of your other product displays to get to the bargains. You'll never know how much additional business you will pick up this way.

- Cleanliness and neatness throughout the store should be a must. Your sales help should be trained to tidy up and replace product automatically when it is out of place. Customers react positively to a clean, neat environment, and negatively to a messy and dirty one.

- The aisles should be wide enough for customers to walk through without bumping into displays and counters, but not so wide that they cannot get a good look at the products on either side of them.

- Movement control within a store should be an important goal for all retailers. While it is not always easy to achieve, you want to develop a pattern of movement for your customers so that they will be exposed to key product areas as they move from Point A to Point B. You will probably have to study their movement habits before you can develop your plan. Indeed, in developing your plan you may discover that it is easier to move your key product areas within customers' existing shopping patterns than it is to change their habits.

- Avoid placing product higher than a five-foot tall person can comfortably reach (unless your clientele is all male—in that case you have an extra 7-8 inches). Also many people cannot or do not like to bend. Try not to place product less than one foot off the floor.

- Lighting is important, especially when fashions, home furnishings and other color-oriented products are sold.

- Sales help should wear name tags, and should be identified by their area of specialization when necessary. This would be particularly important when selling consumer electronics products, major appliances, etc.

- Cash registers should be placed very carefully with efficiency of staff in mind. If you have full-time cashiers, the registers can be near the front of the store. But if your sales help also handles the money, you might have the registers scattered around the store so that your people do not lose time away from their sections. Such placement will also enable them to keep an eye on the section while at the register.

- If your budget can afford it, you might want to consider having a host at the front door to greet customers as they walk in, and thank them on the way out. This person could also act as a plainclothes security man.

- Products should be grouped together where it makes sense, and can lead to additional sales. In a women's clothing store, for example, matching jackets, skirts and blouses should be displayed in the same cluster. In a men's store, ties and shirts should be inseparable.

- Some of the manufacturers of products you sell may provide displays for use with their merchandise. These may be permanent displays, or for short-term promotional use. They may be given to you free, at cost, or as part of a package if you purchase a certain amount of merchandise. In using these displays you must decide how and if they fit into the decorative environment of the store. If they overwhelm your other displays, you may opt not to accept them.

MAXIMIZING PRODUCT APPEAL OPPORTUNITIES

It is important that your products be displayed in order to maximize their appeal within the store. You must identify those with very strong eye appeal, and then use them as a major focal point.

You should also identify the impulse products in your line and place them in high traffic areas. That's where they can do the most good for you.

CREATING IN-STORE SIGNS THAT SELL MERCHANDISE

Very important to the success of the store is your use of interior signs. Just like everything else, your signs should not only contribute to the ambience and image of the store, but also to the sale of merchandise. Signs that don't help sell are really not doing their job.

There are many things that your signs can do:

- They provide pricing information.

- They provide product information.
- They direct or lure customers to particular products, specials, or sections of the store.
- They promote coming events.
- They complete the story you started to tell in the window.

Your signs can take on several forms:

- They may be neon and used on the walls to identify the various departments or sections of the store.
- They may be in the form of moving message boards and provide information on specials and sales items as well as upcoming events. The signs can range in size from a single line crawling message to a wall-mounted five-line-at-a-time display.
- They can be banners, appropriate for the season of the year, or heralding a specific sale, a special event, or a holiday.
- They can be distinctive price/size tags on the product, with the store logo or name.
- They can be price, sale price or percentage-off signs for your counters, display tables, or racks.
- They can be counter, display table or rack signs, with a series of one-line descriptions of the features of a specific product.
- They can be self-standing signs, with an easel backing so that they can be placed on counters.
- They can be "as seen" signs. Manufacturers will often supply point-of-purchase material of print ads, along with the tag line, "As Advertised in Time Magazine," etc. They may also offer P-O-P of the product with the line, "As Seen on Such-And-Such Show on NBC." These P-O-P displays are usually provided in easel format and are aimed at creating additional customer excitement and credibility for the product.
- They can be signs of all types, shapes and forms provided by your manufacturers and distributors. They all want to help you sell through to the customer and will provide all types of Point-Of-Purchase aids and signs.
- They can be odd-shaped signs like arrows, circles, stars or puffs. The odd shapes, along with color, are aimed at grabbing the attention of customers.

You should give a great deal of consideration to the type of Point-Of-Purchase signs you have made for your store since they should reflect its "look" and its other signage. If you have a featured color scheme throughout (the windows, walls, display cases, etc.), you should use those colors on your P-O-P materials too.

Printed signs or those professionally handmade are always preferable to the handwritten ones so often used. There are several ways to approach your signage needs:

- You can have the complete signs printed locally.
- You can purchase colorful stock signs, and have the pricing information and messages printed locally.
- You can use your computer or purchase a special signmaking system. Insignia Systems, Inc., for example, has a system which can make signs ranging from one-inch by three-inches to 11-inches by 14-inches. Its system costs around $2500.
- You can use local art students to create some of your special signs and/or hand-letter the stock signs you purchase.

There are talking signs, too. Push-button activated displays can feature audio or video point-of-purchase messages. Speak to your manufacturers or distributors to see if they have any available.

OTHER PARTS OF THE BIG PICTURE

There are several other steps which you might take to help enhance your in-store image among customers:

- Use only recyclable packaging materials. Most of your customers will have a favorable impression of the store if you do.
- Place a suggestion box in a prominent place within the store. Acknowledge every suggestion, and give gifts to those people whose suggestions you implement.
- If you have celebrities as customers, ask them for an autographed picture which you should display in a heavily traveled area. Many customers are impressed when they learn that they shop at the same store as celebrities do. It enhances their image of the store.
- If you can afford the space, you might have a small lounge/sitting area in the store for customers to take a brief break. You can serve

coffee. This will probably only work in certain types of stores, usually upscale. The danger of a lounge/sitting area is that it may become a hangout, attracting the same people all the time. So if you set one up let everyone know you are doing it on an experimental basis. This will give you an "out" in case you have to close it down.

- If you supply merchandise to prominent groups in the area (the ballet, theater company, orchestra, athletic team, school, etc.) try to get permission from them to let you call yourself the group's "Official Supplier." Then promote it in-store and externally. You could have signs on the store walls proclaiming "Official Shoe Supplier to Ourtown Ballet," "Official Post-Game Caterers to Ourtown Tigers," "Official Stationers to Ourtown College," etc.

- If you, or the store, receive awards from community, religious, business, government, educational, or professional organizations, prominently display them.

- Consider placing somewhere in the store a literature rack containing general consumerism material, as well as specific use and care information on products you sell. For example, if you sell clothing, you might have material on how to remove stains. If you sell electrical products, you might have literature on safety and how to avoid overloading circuits.

LOOK TO YOUR SUPPLIERS AS YOUR PARTNERS

Throughout this chapter retailers have been encouraged to seek out the manufacturers of the products they sell, or their distributors. Many will offer a variety of assistance packages to store owners in a broad range of categories including store design, marketing and merchandising, promotions, signage, special events, advertising, public relations, and training.

Let your suppliers know that you are very interested in promoting their products, and would appreciate any help they can give to you. Ask what support programs they can offer.

You might also encourage your suppliers to use your store to test promotions which they might want to try before rolling them out nationally.

RESOURCES

The following are contact points where you can obtain information for services mentioned in this chapter.

Display Materials (In-Store and Windows)

- Yellow Pages listings: "Display Designers & Producers—Counter, Windows, etc.," "Display Materials," "Display Fixtures," "Store Fixtures," and "Mannequins—Display Fixture."
- Trimco, 459 West 15th Street, New York, NY 10011 (212-989-1616). A comprehensive, 100-page catalog ("Display Basics Plus") of just about everything a retailer would need for in-store and window decorating. Free.
- The Creegan Company, 510 Washington Street, Steubenville, OH 43952 (614-283-3708). Manufacturer of animated characters and mascot costume figures for store windows and seasonal displays.
- Windsor Marketing Group, 2 Industrial Road, Windsor Locks, CT 06096 (1-800-243-2747). Stock Point-Of-Purchase signs.
- Insignia Systems, Inc., 10801 Red Circle Drive, Minnetonka, MN 55343 (1-800-874-4648). Markets a sign system which enables retailers to make print-shop quality signs in-store.
- National Association of Display Industries, 470 Park Avenue South, New York, NY 10016-6820. Will send copy of its show directory listing members, their addresses and types of products offered.
- Sunnywell Display System, 661 Brea Canyon Road, Suite 6, Walnut, CA 91789 (1-800-322-0938). Moving message boards.
- Bullock Communications, Inc., The Mark Building, 15 Phoenixville Pike, Malvern, PA 19355 (610-648-9300). Shopper-activated audio shelf-talkers.

CHAPTER 5

Creating Exciting Holiday and Seasonal Promotions

"What an exciting store!"

"The place comes alive!"

"It's theater!"

How often have you read or heard those comments used to describe retail operations?

While stores like Bloomingdale's, Macy's, and Neiman-Marcus may draw rave reviews like this from shoppers, you don't have to be a retail giant to generate this image or similar customer enthusiasm.

No matter what your size or product line may be, you can make your store an exciting place at which to shop, a place to which customers will want to hurry back and visit more frequently, buying more products and spending more money.

This can be accomplished through lively in-store promotions and entertainment, eye-catching displays, theme-related sales, and a warm, friendly atmosphere. The various holidays of the year, the four seasons, and several other commemorative dates are ideal vehicles to use to develop exciting storewide promotional events aimed at attracting more customers—and more business.

GETTING MAXIMUM EXPOSURE AND OPTIMUM RESULTS

In order to gain maximum exposure as well as optimum results for your in-store promotions, you should be very thorough in carrying out your themes so that they are evident throughout the store in your advertising, promotional publicity, and even by the way your sales staff dresses.

Windows   The store's windows should reflect the holiday or seasonal theme the customers will find once inside the store.

Front Door   Care should be taken to include some theme decor on the front door, too. This might include, for example, shamrocks on St. Patrick's Day, red hearts on Valentine's Day, Santas around Christmas, American flags on Independence Day, etc.

In-Store   In-store decorations should include the colors (if there are any) associated with the theme or holiday, posters, and other decorative materials which clearly tell the customer what the theme is all about.

But decorations should not be the only way you carry out the theme. Your sales staff should wear appropriate costumes and/or accessories which relate to the themed promotion. Tapes of songs associated with the holiday or seasonal theme should be played as background music. Drawing for prizes related to the theme can be held daily or weekly. Budget and space permitting, light refreshments should also be served. Again budget permitting, you might want to give away small favors related to the theme. Most important, and if appropriate, hold a sale keyed to the theme of the promotion. Ideas will be found in this chapter, as well as in Chapter Seven.

Here are some of the in-store promotional themes that should be considered, along with guidance for implementation. Many of the ideas presented in other chapters can also be adapted for use with these themes. Ideas and suggestions for getting publicity in local media for these promotions are presented throughout the chapter. Chapter 13 contains techniques for getting publicity, and Chapter 14 has sample press materials.

GETTING IT ON FROM JANUARY 1 THROUGH DECEMBER 31

The New Year

This is an ideal theme to run from the day after Christmas through the first week of the New Year. It will appeal to all people and age groups. The decor both in the windows and store should be that of a New Year's Eve party:

streamers, confetti, balloons, Happy New Year signs, pictures of the "New Year Baby," noisemakers and hats, formal wear and party dresses on mannequins. You might also consider including "fake" newspaper headlines "forecasting" events for the year ahead: "Local High School Basketball Team Wins State Championship"; "U. S. Government Finishes With Surplus; $1000 Dividend To Be Sent To All Taxpayers"; "Nation's Capital To Move To (Name Of Your City)" etc.

Sales help should be dressed in either formal or party wear and wear "Happy New Year" hats, and other party favors. Serve champagne and/or a non-alcoholic beverage. (Note: whenever you are serving alcoholic beverages during a promotion, *always* offer a non-alcoholic beverage too.) Background music should be New Year's Eve songs.

As far as merchandise goes, there are several options with products directly related to: New Year's Eve or the New Year; the winter season; post-Christmas clearance. Any can serve as the basis for a special sale. Some sales themes to use: "Start The New Year Off With A Bargain"; "Our New Year Resolution: To Keep You As A Happy Customer"; "First Sale of the Year"; "Ring In The New Year Sale"; "Make A Resolution To Shop And Save At (Name of store)"; "Our 1994 Sale—$19.94 Specials."

New year calendars or pocket diaries are ideal gifts to give to customers since they will be used throughout the year and each time a customer uses the calendar or diary, the store's name will be a reminder. If you have firmed up your promotion schedule in time, it should be included in the calendar or diary with each promotional event overprinted on the appropriate date. Prizes for drawings could include champagne, baskets of fruit and/or cheese, or some of the store's products. Always try to get prizes donated by offering the donor both in-store and in-window recognition for contributing the merchandise. Your suppliers should also be contacted about donating product for prizes. If you advertise a promotion and promise to include the donor's name in the ads, chances are that you will be able to get more expensive and attractive prizes donated.

Each evening during the last hour of business (or some other appropriate time of the day), you might actually stage a "New Year's Eve" celebration. Hold a countdown to "midnight," toss confetti and streamers, pass out noisemakers and hats to customers, serve champagne and other snacks and just have a good time. It will add another dimension to the promotion, and will probably help attract additional people to the store, as well as media coverage. If you have a mailing list, you might send formal invitations to your customers, inviting them down to celebrate "New Year's Eve" at their leisure during the week of the promotion. You might want to key this invitation as a "thank you" for supporting the store during the past year.

Both daily newspapers and television channels should be invited to cover your mock "New Year's Eve" party. Try to get them to cover it as early in the week as possible since it would help attract more customers to the store while the promotion is still on.

Elvis Presley's Birthday and Other Significant Dates

If you have a large customer base of people over 45 years old (especially women), you might want to hold a promotion in conjunction with Elvis Presley's birthday, January 8. Give the windows and store a 1950s and 1960s look. Play Elvis songs, and videotapes. Tie-in with local record stores and video rental shops. Encourage residents to loan you Elvis memorabilia for displays, also pictures of themselves back in the 1950s and 1960s. Have Elvis posters all over the store. Sponsor Elvis "look-a-like" and "sound-a-like" contests, perhaps co-sponsoring with a local radio station. Be sure to let radio, television and newspapers know about any Elvis promotions.

Elvis Presley's birthday is just one of the many celebrity birthdays with promotional potential. Others include Davy Crockett (August 17), Casey Jones of railroad fame (March 14), Charlie Brown and Snoopy (October 2), and Mark Twain (November 30).

Dates for these and hundreds of other holidays, birthdays, anniversaries, and proclaimed weeks and months can be found in *Chase's Annual Events,* published each year by Contemporary Books.

Winter

A theme to use anytime during January, February and March, it will appeal to all people and age groups. As with most promotional themes, it should not run more than ten days to two weeks.

The decor throughout the store and in the windows can be anything which depicts winter: ski posters, ski equipment, ice skates, hockey sticks, sleds, cold weather clothing on mannequins, snow shovels, potbelly stoves, artificial snow, blow-ups of pictures or posters of igloos and Eskimos, thermometers showing below zero readings, a fireplace, etc. The sales staff should be wearing ski sweaters, and other winter-type clothing. Refreshments, of course, should be hot drinks: coffee, tea, toddies, warm wine.

Feature winter and cold weather products in your more prominent displays. If you have the appropriate product mix and clientele, consider setting off a corner of the store as "Warm Weather Bound . . . " and display products customers would normally take with them when they vacation in a warm climate.

If you plan a sale around your winter promotion, you might want to consider these themes: "We've Thawed Our Prices," "Cold Weather Bargains," "It's Snowing Savings," "Winter Wonderland Of Savings," "Meltdown To Spring Sale," "The Thermometer And Our Prices Are Down." You might also institute "Snowy Days Sales," offering special discounts to all shoppers when it is snowing outside. For favors to give to customers, try to arrange for discount passes from a local ice skating rink and/or ski lift tickets from a nearby ski area. Other giveaways to consider might be auto window ice scrapers with your name on it, inexpensive room thermometers, plastic paperweights with snow scenes in them. Songs about winter will make excellent background music. Prize drawings might be for cold-weather products: mink earmuffs, thermal gloves, ski equipment, a weekend at a nearby ski resort.

To create additional excitement, if it snows during the promotion (or anytime during the winter), sponsor a "mini" snowman-building contest among a few youngsters just outside the store. Have them put funny hats and other clothing on the snowmen and contact the media about this photo opportunity.

Another way to attract attention to your winter promotion is to have a person dressed in a snowman's outfit handing out circulars outside the store, or in the area in which the store is located. However, before doing this, be certain that it fits in with the image of your store and does not violate any local ordinances. Another photo opportunity for local newspapers and television would be warm-weather vacation clothing—especially bathing suits—amid frigid winter displays. If you carry the product line, try to set it up during a snowy day and get live models in bathing suits.

Valentine's Day

Valentine's Day has broad public appeal, with probably more gifts purchased by younger people than older people. Gift purchases usually fall within a rather limited number of categories: sweets, flowers, jewelry, men's furnishings, lingerie and other more intimate products. However, this doesn't mean that a retailer carrying other products cannot capitalize on this gift-giving day through clever tie-in promotions.

The Valentine's promotion should run for a week to ten days, ending on February 14. The in-store and window decor should be hearts, Cupids and the color red. Also consider getting blow-ups of short love poems, Valentine's card verses, and/or "graffiti-like" statements on love (combinations of words and symbols which you might get local graffiti artists to prepare). Photographs and posters of lovers holding hands, embracing, walking down a beach together would also add to the decor. Sales help should wear as much red as possible, and have Valentine pins on their clothing. Female sales help who own necklaces or earrings with hearts on them should be encouraged to wear them. Sweets served from heart-shaped boxes, or heart-shaped cookies would make ideal refreshments. Background music? Love songs, of course.

If your store doesn't sell the traditional products people usually buy as Valentine gifts, try some unique approaches: hold a "Red Sale," offering special pricing on all red products in the store; offer gift certificates packaged with a small box of chocolate candy; take instant pictures of customers against a red, heart-shaped background and insert them into special Valentine cards which can accompany the gift or gift certificate. As a traffic builder, ask your regular customers to provide the name and address of their loved one(s) who, in turn, can be sent a special invitation for a Valentine's Day shopping event. (Make it a special event with refreshments, door prizes, etc.) In-store drawings might be for boxes of candy, bottles of wine, flowers, dinners for two at local restaurants. (Try to get dinners donated, offering in-store promotional exposure.) As favors, give heart-shaped key rings inscribed with the store's name, small packets of candy hearts, or other heart-shaped novelties.

Contests you might consider can include "An Ode To My Lover" poetry contest, or "Miss Valentine of 19XX." Such contests can lead to publicity in local media. If you set a "rule" that only people wearing something red will be admitted Valentine's Day, send a story about it to the local media at least one week before February 14.

Presidents' Day

Celebrated the third Monday in February, it combines the commemoration of Lincoln's (the 12th) and Washington's (the 22nd) birthdays and is traditionally a very big sales period. A retailer may want to celebrate Presidents' Day as a one-day event, a three-day weekend event, or run it from February 12-22. If a store is running a Valentine promotion, it can always start its extended Presidents' Day event on the 15th; its reputation as a sale day makes its promotions appealing to all people and all ages.

Traditional decor would include pictures of, and memorabilia associated with Lincoln and Washington: posters and jumbo postcards of the Lincoln Memorial, Washington Monument, Mount Vernon and the White House; American flags; stovepipe and tricornered hats; powdered wigs and Colonial costumes on mannequins. If there is a Lincoln and/or a Washington High School in the area, try to borrow banners and any display materials the schools have. While the focus on Presidents' Day is traditionally on Lincoln and Washington, there is no reason why you cannot use it as a tribute to all presidents of the United States.

Sales help can join in the spirit of the promotion by dressing in Colonial garb (powdered wigs, tricornered hats), the stovepipe hat and dress favored by Lincoln, or in patriotic red, white and blue outfits. You might also have an employee or actor dressed as Lincoln or Washington to greet customers and pose for instant pictures with them.

Cherry pie has been associated with George Washington (remember, he chopped down the cherry tree) and so you might serve it, along with coffee, to the customers. Try to get a local bakery to contribute the pies, or at least provide a very good discount. Patriotic songs will make excellent background music.

Since Presidents' Day sales usually offer tremendous savings, this is a good time to put on sale closeouts and other products that you can afford to offer at a significant markdown. Talk to your suppliers about any specials they may be able to provide. In holding such a sale, be certain that it does not degrade the image of the store. If you cater to an upscale audience and can command top price, it may be wise just to feature the decor without any sale. Themes which you might use: "Your Dollar Buys More," "Stretch Your Dollar Sale," "We're Chopping Our Prices," "Presidents' Day Values," "A Lincoln Penny Goes A Long Way," "One Cent Sale," "We're Cleaning Out The House." You might even give each customer a new Lincoln penny glued to a small card announcing that it is a "good luck penny from (name of store) guaranteed to bring the holder one year of good luck."

If you hold drawings, they might be for cherry pies. You might also try to get an airline, hotel chain or travel agent to donate a weekend trip to Washington as a grand prize. (Your chances for getting such a trip donated increase if you promise to advertise it in the media.) Special events which might attract media coverage would include the presence of Washington and/or Lincoln look-a-likes, the presence of Lincoln and/or Washington

High School bands, cheerleaders, drill teams, or authentic memorabilia (autographs, actual clothing worn by either, etc.). If you expect very large crowds for a Presidents' Day sale, or they develop before you open the doors that morning, alert the local newspapers, radio and television.

St. Patrick's Day

This is an important event if you have a large Irish population in the city, in the neighborhood in which you are located, or among your customers. An ideal period is from the weekend prior to March 17 through the day itself since, like most holiday-oriented promotions, it should not run beyond the day of the holiday. While this promotion will probably be most attractive to people of Irish ancestry, in many cities, everyone becomes Irish on March 17.

The window and in-store decor is green, green and more green. And don't forget the shamrocks, leprechauns, maps of Ireland, posters of Irish tourist attractions, posters announcing the local St. Patrick's Day parade, shillelagh, and other memorabilia.

Sales help should be wearing the green (dresses, ties, shirts, jackets, sweaters) and should top it off with green St. Patrick's Day hats, shamrocks, and St. Patrick's Day pins. You might also want to have an employee dressed in a leprechaun outfit greeting customers, and posing for instant photographs with them. This could also attract media interest as a pre-St. Patrick's Day photo opportunity. Try to get media coverage a couple of days prior to the event during a "dress rehearsal."

Any Irish-made merchandise should be featured, as well as green products. While it is not necessary to hold a St. Patrick's Day sale, you might consider a "Celebrate St. Patrick's Day Sale," "A Green Sale" featuring special pricing on all green products, or "Bargains From the Old Sod," featuring Irish-made products.

While Irish Coffee is an ideal refreshment to serve, also offer non-alcoholic beverages. Many people of Irish ancestry are very sensitive about the image of Irish people linked to heavy drinking so be careful not to promote alcoholic beverages during this event. If you have the budget, consider giving customers shamrocks (live or fake), St. Patrick's Day buttons, or green St. Patrick's Day hats as favors. There are great tapes of Irish music available to get into the swing of the promotion. You might also want to get a bagpiper to play at the store during certain hours. It should be a good drawing card, and could attract local television coverage.

If there are active groups in the community, you should consider setting up a special evening at the store for the local Hibernians, Irish Historical Society, etc. It could be a special sale, or just a social event with Irish entertainment, prominent Irish community leaders, and local government officials in a preview salute to St. Patrick's Day. An advance story should be sent to publications of the organizations involved.

If you decide to hold a drawing for prizes, offer products imported from Ireland. And, while it may be difficult to arrange, you might try to get an airline, hotel chain or travel agent to provide a trip to Ireland as a grand prize. Your best chances for arranging this would be if you will be backing the promotion with a big advertising campaign and will give prominent mention to the trip's sponsor.

If you will be featuring many products made in Ireland, you should try to get a feature in a local newspaper's lifestyle page. Also contact local magazines, weekly newspapers, mass-circulated Irish newspapers, radio and television. If you can get this publicity prior to St. Patrick's Day, it will bring people to the store.

Easter/Spring

An Easter display and/or promotion is almost a "must" for most retailers since it represents an important holiday, a change in season, appeals to all people and all age groups, and is often the first real shopping done by many people since the Christmas season. Easter displays work well for the 10-14 day period up until Easter Sunday. Then the theme can be converted into a pure spring promotion by taking out any symbols associated only with Easter.

Decor is spring and Easter: pastel colors, parasols, Easter eggs, tulips and other spring flowers, Easter bunnies (chocolate and stuffed), bonnets, jelly beans. The smell of spring in the air. Easter and spring songs will make good background music, and jelly beans are good promotion refreshments.

Easter and spring-oriented products should be featured as well as those associated with the outdoors, and rainwear. (Remember April showers bring May flowers.) Sales themes might include "Easter Savings," "Spring Savings," "Winter Close-outs," "Easter Egg Hunt Sale," "Savings from The Easter Rabbit," "Spring Ahead To Bigger And Better Bargains." Also consider an "April Showers Sale," which kicks in on rainy days. (See Chapter Seven for more information on sales.)

Gifts to give to customers would include chocolate Easter eggs, dyed eggs, spring bulbs ready for planting, flowers, small plants. If you have a drawing for customer prizes, consider Easter dinner for two or four (arranged through a local restaurant), large solid chocolate bunnies, stuffed bunnies, umbrellas, tickets to baseball games. (See Chapter Nine for sports promotion information.) Sales help should wear the light colors of spring: women wearing bonnets, men boaters. Having an employee in a rabbit's costume to greet customers, pose for instant photographs, and hand out jelly beans will add in-store excitement. The costumed character, standing outside the store or walking around the immediate neighborhood, could help draw traffic. It might also attract some media attention as would the sponsorship of an Easter egg roll for youngsters, and an "unusual" Easter bonnet competition among customers. One publicity idea would be to set up a photo opportunity at the local railroad station, bus depot or airport of the "rabbit arriving in town" about a week before the promotion starts. Contact local television channels, radio and newspapers.

Live chicks and bunnies should be on display only if they have been borrowed from a farm or educational organization, will be well cared for, and will be returned to the farm or organization at the end of the promotion. Touch base with the local humane organization to make certain such a display is not against the law. In most areas it is against the law to give away, or sell, chicks or bunnies; even if not illegal, such a practice might promote boycotts or demonstrations against your store by animal rights groups.

National Secretaries Week

National Secretaries Week, which encompasses National Secretaries Day (the fourth Wednesday of April) should be celebrated as a special tribute to secretaries and the valuable work they do for the business community. The promotion which should run the entire week, should emphasize the positive contribution secretaries make and avoid any stereotyping.

Decor should concentrate on banners or signs paying tribute to the area's secretaries. They might read, "We Salute (Name of city) Secretaries —Thanks For Everything You Do!" or "A Salute To (Name of city) Secretaries—Our Most Valuable Employees." You might also set up a display of pictures of secretaries from the area. (Try to obtain them directly from local companies.) Sales help might wear buttons reading, "We Salute Our Secretaries."

Offer a special discount to secretaries who purchase products during the week. You might also offer each one a rose, and enter them in a drawing for prizes. Promote the special discount through bulletin board posters which you send to the personnel departments of local companies, government offices, etc. Set up a special gift certificate for secretaries which employers can purchase. Package it with a small box of chocolates, or attached to a rose or other flower. If you carry appropriate products (flowers, sweets, gift baskets, wallets, etc.) which will appeal to all secretaries, contact the personnel departments of local companies and try to sell them on the idea of purchasing gifts for all their secretaries. Offer free gift wrapping. If you hold a drawing for prizes among secretaries, you might want to offer dinners at local restaurants, tickets to entertainment events, or even gift certificates to local beauty salons. You may even want to sponsor a local "Secretary Of The Year" competition, award or luncheon. It will attract good local media coverage.

Mother's Day/Father's Day

Mother's Day is the second Sunday of May, Father's Day the third Sunday of June. Both, of course, are important shopping periods for retailers who carry products that are appropriate gifts for mothers and/or fathers. Ideally, promotions for both days should run for about ten days so that two Saturdays are included.

Appropriate Mother's and/or Father's Day signs should be displayed. Some should be saluting parents, others should have some "sell" in them: "Don't Forget Mother On Mother's Day," "Happy Father's Day," "We Salute (Name of city) Mothers," "Thanks For Everything, Dad," "Every Day Should be Mother's Day!" A window or in-store display might feature a mother/father in a relaxed position and a sign reading, "Thanks Mom/Dad For Everything You Have Done For Us." You should also set up a display of photographs of area mothers and fathers during the appropriate promotions. Take instant photos of them when they shop at the store. It is an effective way to pay tribute to your customers.

You might also take snapshots against an appropriate backdrop ("Happy Mother's Day," etc.) of sons and daughters who purchase gifts for their mothers and/or fathers. The picture can then be enclosed with the gift. For those wanting to send gift certificates, develop a special gift wrapping (with a small box of sweets, a rose, etc.). With each gift purchased, enclose an invitation for the recipient to come by the store the following week to have her or his picture taken (to send to the purchaser of the gift). It is not only a nice gesture but can also result in an additional sale to the parent. Have each gift-giver enter his or her parent in a drawing for prizes, and also invite all parents shopping in the store to enter. The ideal prize would be a weekend at a nearby resort (try to get the resort to donate the prize), or dinners at local restaurants. You might also want to sponsor a local "Mother/Father of The Year" contest, award, or awards luncheon. You can get good media coverage through this type of sponsorship.

Armed Forces Week/Day

This occurs during the week of the third Saturday in May, a very important event in areas where there is a strong military presence (Active, reserve, retired military, National Guard, veterans), especially if there are military bases in the area.

Decor should be patriotic and military: American flags, recruiting posters, historic pictures and art, mannequins in uniforms, displays of medals and insignia, and even equipment. Contact the information office at military bases, as well as reserve, National Guard and ROTC units to see if they will loan to you display material and equipment. If you have an exterior area (parking lot, space in front of the store), you may want to borrow a larger piece of equipment (tank, vehicle, etc.). You may also want to include a special exhibit built around a local war hero, Medal of Honor winner, etc. Also contact the local posts of the American Legion, Veterans of Foreign Wars, Vietnam Veterans' Association, etc. They may have historic equipment or other display material to loan to you. Tapes of patriotic music should be played. It may even be possible to get a local military band to supply you with a tape it has made. Serve soda or a non-alcoholic punch and give customers American flag pins or key chains as gifts.

Sales help should be wearing as much red, white and blue as possible, as well as American flag pins.

As for merchandise, it is an ideal time to promote "Made in the USA" products. You might also offer special discounts to servicemen, reservists, and veterans. Or you can use the promotion as a sale for the general public: "Armed Forces Week Sale," "X-Percent Off All Made In The USA Products During Armed Forces Week," "Salute To The Military Sale." You may not want to hold a sale but rather give a percentage of profits earned during the week to the local USO chapter, a veteran's organization, or some other group connected to the military.

One of the ways to promote your armed forces event is through bulletin board fliers which should be sent to the local military units, reserve and National Guard units, and veterans' organizations. If you hold a drawing during this promotion, offer "Made In The USA" products or dinners at local restaurants as prizes. You may want to arrange with the local military base to honor the "May Soldier (or sailor, marine or airman) Of The Month" at the store with a merchandise prize. This could get good local publicity. (At least the local military newspaper will carry it.) An impressive display of military equipment, or an exhibit about one or more local war heroes will draw press interest. Holding a reception for military commanders (active, reserve, National Guard) and leaders of veterans' groups may also attract media. Don't forget to send material about these events to publications of the local veterans' organizations.

Graduation

The month of June is graduation month for virtually every type of school (college, high school, grade school, trade school, and even pre-kindergarten) and is, therefore, a significant gift-giving period. While adults are the givers, the products are for the students. If you carry products for any of the graduating age groups, you should consider promoting graduation gifts. Check and see when the schools in your area are holding their graduations, and run your promotion around those dates. A graduation promotion should run about two weeks.

Decor should include caps and gowns, diplomas, photographs of local schools, yearbooks, school logos, pennants and other items associated with schools. You might also feature class pictures, pictures of class leaders, pictures of the salutatorians and valedictorians. Banners and/or signs might read, "We Salute Our Graduates," "Best of Luck June Graduates," "Here's To Bigger and Better Things, Graduates!"

Merchandise to promote will include all products which will appeal to graduates. Since the bulk of the graduates will be from grade school through college, that means products which will appeal to ages 14-25. If you plan to have a sale as part of the promotion, a theme you might want to consider is "Hail To The Graduate Sale." You may want to invite customers purchasing gifts to enter the graduate's name in a drawing for prizes. Prizes might include savings bonds, athletic equipment, or tickets to local entertainment events.

You might also want to sponsor an award for a graduate at one or more of the local schools. (Check with the school(s) to see if it would be possible.) Another aspect of your graduation promotion might be to donate a portion of your profits toward a high school scholarship fund. This will work best in a city in which there is only one high school. It will also create a lot of goodwill for your store, and enable the store to get publicity in local media.

Independence Day/Summer

Sometime after summer begins is the time to set up your Independence Day/Summer display and event. Once the July 4th weekend has passed, you can drop the Independence Day-related materials and still have a good promotion for another ten days or so.

Decor is red, white and blue, patriotism, American flags, copies of the Declaration of Independence, replicas and pictures of the Liberty Bell. Also add summer clothing and products, picnic baskets and supplies, sand and shovels, beach umbrellas, replicas of firecrackers, banners from local day camps, summer schools, beach clubs—anything that quickly says "summer."

Sales help should be wearing a lot of red, white and blue (even Uncle Sam hats if you can get them) during the Independence Day phase. An employee dressed in an Uncle Sam outfit can greet customers, and pose for instant photographs with them. Then they can switch over to a summer look —even a casual "beachy" look if it doesn't compromise the image of your store.

Summer merchandise should be featured. Sales themes can include: "Firecracker of a Sale," "Fourth Of July Specials," "Summer Specials," "Summer Sparklers," "Beach Bargains," "Star-Spangled Sale," "Sun And Fun Sale," "Prices Are Bursting Out All Over." Favors might include small American flags, American flag key rings, or red, white and blue sun visors. If you play background music, make it patriotic marching band music until July 4, then switch over to summer songs. Drawing prizes can include tickets to summer activities (outdoor concerts, boat rides, amusement parks), red, white and blue beach coolers or blankets.

After July 4th weekend, encourage customers to display their beach and vacation pictures on a special exhibit wall in the store. You might even run a "Best Tans In Town Contest" for customers. It will probably get you some media coverage. You might also display "Letters From Camp," a collection of humorous letters from customers' children that would probably be covered by the local newspapers, radio and the television channels. If it fits within your product line, you might offer to stage fashion shows at area beach/swim clubs as a way to extend your reach into the community.

Labor Day/End of Summer/Back to School

The period between the last week of August and the second week of September presents an opportunity for several promotional themes. Labor Day weekend usually signals the end of the summer beach season (though fall doesn't start until late September), and the beginning of the "back to school" period. The "end of summer" theme will appeal to people of all ages, and "back to school" will appeal to a younger audience—those going back to school and their parents.

Decor can take on several forms: A last-fling-of-summer look with posters/photographs of empty beach scenes; signs saying "Farewell Summer of 'XX,'" and "Welcome Back from the Beach"; mannequins wearing lightweight jackets over beachwear. The "back-to-school" decor can include text books, school yearbooks, school banners and pennants, school varsity sweaters and jackets, blackboards, blownup photographs of local schools, mock-ups of report cards, school desks. Sales help can get into the swing of things by wearing varsity sweaters or baseball caps from local schools, or blazers with school crests. For "end of summer," casual wear (and a good tan) can be the dress. Background music can include both local school and well-known college songs.

For "end of summer," emphasis should be on fall products as well as close-outs and sales on summer merchandise. Themes could include "End Of Summer Specials," "September Savings," "Fall Preview," "Back From The Beach Bargains," and "First Look At Fall." For "back to school," themes might include "Back To School Savings," "Blackboard Specials," "Student Sales Corner," "Classroom Classics," "3Rs Sale." Any merchandise associated with going back to school (clothing, supplies, sports equipment, educational products, learning materials) should be emphasized.

Gifts to customers might be sand dollar key rings, or football schedules for all local school teams. For the "back to school" promotion, you might offer book covers (most schools require them and it is a way to get ongoing exposure for your store), rulers, or ball-point pens. You might have special gifts for students who received all "A's" on their June report cards. For both promotions, you can offer season tickets to local school football games, dinners at local restaurants, tickets to professional baseball games (if there is a major or minor league team in your city) as drawing prizes.

Among ways to attract media coverage would be to make a cash contribution to a local school (setting up a presentation picture with students and the principal); donating a percentage of profits during the "back to school" period to one or more schools; outfitting the local "teacher of the year," holding a party for students who had ended the school year in June with all "A's."

Fall/Columbus Day

Fall begins in late September, and Columbus Day is celebrated the second Monday in October. The latter is a traditional sales day (weekend, or even week). You might start off with a fall promotion, and lead into the Columbus Day event the Thursday or Friday prior to the holiday. Both fall and Columbus Day promotions usually attract a broad cross section of the population.

Decor includes the colors of fall, fall foliage, leaves, football (team uniforms, pennants, helmets, "game" balls—they have the scores on them —all obtainable from local schools), pictures and posters featuring Columbus and his ships, scale models of his ships. If baseball is a popular sport in your city and there is interest in the World Series, you might include World Series memorabilia as part of your fall window and in-store displays.

Sales help should wear fall clothing and/or local school football team jerseys. Buttons can promote your Columbus Day sale.

There is a variety of merchandise to promote during this period, and it all depends upon your customers, the merchandise you carry, and your approach to the traditional Columbus Day sale period. Fall products, of course, are a natural at this time. Some retailers promote their winter products in October; others may even use Columbus Day sales to unload summer products. In addition, products made in Spain and Italy (in honor of Columbus) can have special appeal. Themes include "1492 Sale" (with special selection of products at $14.92 or $14.92 price-off specials); "Fabulous Fall Buys"; "Discover Columbus Day Values"; "Discover A New World Of Values"; "October Extravaganza"; "Fall Values." Since it is also football season, fight songs from local and national schools will make good background music. Because of the crowd a Columbus Day sale can usually attract, it is not advisable to offer refreshments. During your fall promotion, however, you might want to serve coffee and tea.

If you plan to hold a prize drawing, you might offer dinners for two at local Italian restaurants. Be sure to try to get the restaurants to provide the dinners free in return for in-store and window promotion, as well as in your circulars and advertising.

An event which will attract media attention is one with ridiculous prices on a limited number of products (five television sets at five cents each). People will line up all night long and make a mad rush to the items when the doors open (a made-for-television news event). However, be certain such an event will not compromise the image you are trying to develop for the store. Another media possibility would be an announcement that a percentage of Columbus Day profits will go toward cleaning or rehabilitating the local statue of Columbus. (Both announcement and presentation of check can make news.) You can also have a descendant of Columbus or of a crew member "cut the ribbon" to open the store on Columbus Day (and be on hand to sign autographs), or you can hold a reception for the local Columbus Day parade committee.

If It's October, It Must Be . . . .

Virtually every day, week and month is designated as a salute to a worthwhile cause, to call attention to a commercial product, service or industry, or to focus on some offbeat event. While some are a result of official proclamation, others are by decree of a business association or an organization with a special interest in the event.

These special days, weeks and months include: "Adopt A Dog Month"; "National Bubble Gum Week"; "National Disc Jockey Day"; "National Muffin Week"; "Potato Lovers Month"; "According To Hoyle Day"; "National Hobby Month"; "National Asparagus Month"; "Ask A Stupid Question Day"; "Be Late For Something Day"; "National Cheerleading Month"; "National 4-H Week"; "National Home Decorating Month"; and "National Home Improvement Month."

Depending upon your product line (and your sense of humor), some of these events may make for an interesting promotion at your store.

Information about these and other dates, with the name and address of the appropriate sponsoring organization, can be found in *Chase's Annual Events*.

Halloween

Your "fall festival" can take on a new, and even more colorful look for Halloween. Start ten days to two weeks before "trick or treat" day. A Halloween promotion can be attractive to "children of all ages," meaning anyone from toddlers to seniors.

The traditional orange and black colors should reign along with pumpkins, witches, brooms, costumes and face masks of all shapes, sizes and colors. "Trick Or Treat" signs and other Halloween greetings should be scattered around the store and its windows. Serve punch but call it "Witches' Brew." You might also want to serve cookies resembling a pumpkin face, and even pumpkin pie (especially if you can get a local bakery to provide them).

Fall products are usually featured at Halloween, as well as anything which will appeal to children. It is also a good time to start fall sales and winter preview sales. Themes can include: "Trick Or Treat Sale"; "Broomstick Bargains"; "Orange and Black Sale" featuring products of both colors; "Halloween Headliners"; "FALLing Prices"; "A Peek At Winter"; "Fall Close Outs—Winter Previews." Sales help can be in Halloween costumes and even masks, as long as it doesn't detract from the image of the store. This is one promotion in which everyone can get involved and have some fun.

Give each customer a small "trick or treat" bag of candies. You might also provide large, empty "trick or treat" bags (with the store's name prominently displayed) for children to take on their rounds. It will give the store additional exposure in the community. If you are going to have a drawing, pumpkin pies are the ideal prizes.

All types of special events can be held in connection with Halloween: a "Witches' Brew" recipe contest; a pumpkin decorating event; a costume contest; art contest; storytelling contest. Have it broken into different age categories; you might even have some adult categories, especially for seniors. These contests can attract media attention. The media will also be interested if you have the largest pumpkin in town on display, or a large one which is uniquely decorated, or if you have a pumpkin pie baking contest (invite media personalities to judge it), or if one of your employees claims to be a witch or warlock. For this promotion as well as for publicity purposes, you might want to hire a "so-called witch or warlock." It may be well worth the investment since it will not only get the store good media exposure but also probably help attract new customers.

Election Day

If it is a Presidential election year, or an important well-publicized local election year, you might want to run an Election Day event. Ideal time for such a theme would be a week to ten days prior, ending on voting day (unless, of course, it is a very heated election campaign; in that case, you might want to run it a full two weeks). Even if voter turnout is usually light in your community, the colorful decor and memorabilia can make it an attractive event for a much larger segment of the population.

Decor is that of an election campaign. A lot of red, white and blue bunting, campaign posters from *all* the candidates (do not be partial to one!). Try also to get posters from historic campaigns; see if your local newspaper will provide front pages from past campaigns, and if local collectors, the local political organizations, or the local historical society will loan you other political memorabilia to display. If one specific organization provides most of the material, credit them as "sponsor." It will add credibility to the display, attract more people and probably media attention. Ideally, if the local newspaper will sponsor the display, you *will* get good promotional publicity. Your sales help should be wearing red, white and blue, campaign buttons from all candidates, or buttons which say "Vote." Since politicians are known for kissing babies, you might want to offer customers candy kisses. And if you have a drawing for prizes, offer Election night dinner for two. You might also arrange with the local political parties to give away invitations to their election night "victory" parties. Tapes of campaign songs and other tunes associated with Election Day ("Happy Days Are Here Again," etc.) will liven up the promotion.

Just about any merchandise can be featured. Sale emphasis might be placed on fall and winter products. Themes might include: "Election Day Specials"; "Vote For The Best Buys In Town"; "Cast Your Ballot For Savings"; "Our Platform: The Best Prices In Town"; "Your Election Ticket For Savings."

You might want to hold special "nights" for each political party, donating a percentage of profits for that night to the appropriate party. Each party will undoubtedly try to attract customers through its mailing list and other means. A way to have some fun (and get publicity) is to set up some sort of "election poll" among customers. Have certain products on two tables—one for each candidate—so that customers can express their opinions by taking product from the table of their candidate of choice; then announce the "election results." There are various other ways to conduct this poll, such as a separate cash register for each candidate, a ballot box, an actual voting machine, etc.).

Veterans Day

Celebrated November 11, it honors veterans from all wars and is a traditional sale day. It offers a retailer several possibilities: a traditional sale, or a sale which places special emphasis on attracting veterans. You might also aim it at active duty, reserve and National Guard members since they, too, in a sense, might be considered veterans.

Decor should include banners borrowed from all the veterans' organizations in the community such as American Legion, VFW, DAV, Vietnam War Veterans Association, Jewish War Veterans, Catholic War Veterans, etc. Also include uniforms from all the services and perhaps historic uniforms worn since World War I (which you might be able to borrow from local veterans' groups, or even individual veterans). Historic pictures and books about the military make great window display items and can probably be borrowed from a book store that you would acknowledge in the window. Sales help can again wear their patriotic colors of red, white and blue. Patriotic and military music should be playing in the background.

Emphasis might be on fall and winter products or any related to the military, as well as on anything red, white and blue. But just about any product can be featured during this promotion. Themes might include: "Veterans Day Specials"; "Red, White And Blue Sale"; "We Hail Those Who Served With This Special Sale"; "Salute To Veterans Of All Wars."

Special promotions should be developed with veterans' groups. Perhaps you should offer an extra ten percent off to members of these groups. (Work with the local veterans' organizations so that they will notify their members of this benefit.) Or hold special sale nights (or sale previews) for each group, donating a percentage of sales to the particular group on its night. (Again, the emphasis should be on having the local organization do a mailing to its members in order to attract as many people as possible since they stand to benefit by having large crowds attend on their night.) Give out patriotic favors (American flags, American flag key rings or lapel pins). If you plan to hold drawings for prizes, offer tickets to a local theater company, movie house, or dinners at local restaurants. Try to get these prizes donated in return for in-store promotional considerations.

Media might be interested if you have an interesting collection of military memorabilia or if you will donate a percentage of profits to repair or clean a local veteran's statue or memorial. Even more interest will be shown if the store's staff goes to the statue or memorial prior to Veterans Day and cleans it up, or cleans the surrounding area. Media will also be interested if you invite the oldest living veteran in the area, or a veteran from each of the wars from World War II to Desert Storm, to participate in some type of ceremony at the store.

Thanksgiving

With the Christmas selling season starting earlier each year, Thanksgiving promotions and events have become less popular among some retailers. However, for traditionalists who still start the Christmas season the day after "turkey day," a Thanksgiving promotion can be a viable event for about ten days. It can also serve as a "sub-promotion" for an early-starting Christmas promotion.

Decor is Thanksgiving turkeys and all of the holiday traditions, including Pilgrims, Indians and the Mayflower. Use "Happy Thanksgiving" and "Give Thanks For Everything" signs. Many of these materials can be purchased at local party stores. In portraying Indians, be certain to do so with accuracy and without exaggerating their physical appearance or dress. Employees can wear Pilgrim-styled clothing, or regular dress with a "turkey" button or a "Happy Thanksgiving" button.

If you serve refreshments, consider cranberry juice or chocolate turkeys. If you hold a drawing among customers, prizes should be turkeys (frozen or cooked). Try to get a local caterer, restaurant or deli to contribute.

A Thanksgiving promotion is a good time to clear off your shelves, especially of any fall products, prior to the Christmas selling season. Themes can include: "Pre-Christmas Specials"; "Turkey Day Clearance"; "Our THANKS For GIVING Us Your Support"; "Thanksgiving Specials." Turkey key rings and other small favors featuring turkeys can make ideal gifts to customers (all with the store's name, of course). Someone dressed in a turkey costume can add excitement to the promotion (greeting customers, posing for instant photographs with them), standing just outside the store or walking in the immediate area to attract traffic and customers. It might also attract media coverage.

Christmas

This is the season to pull out all stops. In recent years some retailers have started the Christmas selling season as early as the second week of November. Pricing strategy might be to start off with a pre-Christmas sale for a week or ten days, then go for full prices. In recent years, when product wasn't moving, some retailers cut prices a week or two prior to Christmas.

Decor is Christmas: Santas, Christmas trees and decorations, deer, elves, snow scenes, you name it. If you have a large Jewish clientele, you should also consider Chanukah decorations (a candelabra, signs saying "Happy Chanukah," etc.). Toys (operating electric trains, and dolls) also add to the Christmas decor even if you do not sell toys. Sales help should wear the traditional red, green and white Christmas colors, with women wearing Christmas pins and corsages. Men can wear Christmas ties. Santa hats can also be worn if they fit in with the image of the store. In addition to taped Christmas music, you may want to make arrangements—space permitting—to invite local church choirs, or school choral groups to sing carols at the store.

A live Santa can be used as a profit center: charge for photographs with him, also for special gifts he gives to children who visit his "throne." Or, if you prefer, you may want to use your live Santa as a goodwill ambassador to greet customers, pose for free instant photographs, pass out refreshments, and even make personal appearances in the community.

Turkeys and hams can be the prizes in a customer drawing. Candy Christmas canes, chocolate Santas and other treats can be given to all customers. Nonalcoholic eggnog may also be served. Develop a special wrapping for your Christmas gift certificates, perhaps with a small Christmas corsage or candy cane attached.

If your store has unique Christmas decorations or gifts, if your Santa is an unusual person, or if you plan a special philanthropic event (Christmas gifts or shopping sprees for the less fortunate), you may be able to get local media coverage. An excellent media-oriented idea is to set up a panel of a half-dozen young children and bring them in early in the Christmas selling season to "test" the new toys and games. Let them select what they think are the "top ten" of the season. You could hold a press conference at the store to let them make their announcement, and/or arrange special newspaper interviews and television appearances. This is an ideal promotion for a toy store.

BE SENSITIVE TO RELIGIOUS AND ETHNIC HOLIDAYS

When considering holiday and ethnic promotions, it is important to be sensitive to the traditions connected with them. For example, it would be inappropriate to run a sale in connection with Martin Luther King's birthday, the Muslim month of Ramadan, or the Jewish High Holidays of Rosh Hashana and Yom Kippur.

In-store and window displays that are non-commercial tributes to Dr. King would be an appropriate way to honor his memory on his birthday. For the Jewish holidays each fall, it would be appropriate to have one or more signs "Wishing Our Jewish Friends A Happy New Year."

You should become familiar with the many religious, ethnic, and foreign country holidays of your customers. Seek out the advice of local religious and ethnic leaders, as well as foreign consulates (or prominent representatives of foreign-born groups in the community) regarding what would be appropriate to do on such holidays. You may find that the holidays of some of the foreign countries of origin for large segments of your community can be developed into interesting promotions. This would include Chinese New Year, St. Patrick's Day, Fasching (Germany and Austria), Carnival (Brazil), etc.

FOR ADDITIONAL IDEAS TO CREATE EXCITING IN-STORE PROMOTIONS

Additional ideas for creating exciting in-store promotions and events can be found in other chapters throughout this book. See Chapter Six for in-store special events, Chapter Seven for unique sales ideas, Chapter Eight for contests designed to draw customer attention, and Chapter Nine for sports promotions. Chapter 13 explains how to get publicity coverage for your promotions, and Chapter 14 has samples of material which can be sent to the media to get that publicity.

RESOURCES

It is usually a good idea to find as many local resources as possible to fulfill your needs for promotional products and materials.

Sales Promotion Agencies

You may need the assistance of a sales promotion service or agency either on a full-time basis or from time to time to handle specific projects. Ask other retailers and businesses for recommendations. Also consult the Yellow Pages under "Sales Promotion Service."

Specialty Advertising Items

The ball-point pens, calendars, coffee mugs, key tags and other small, inexpensive items you would give away during promotions are called specialty advertising items. Distributors are located throughout the United States and can usually be found in the Yellow Pages under the listing "Advertising Specialties." For an expanded list of these distributors in your area, contact the Marketing Communications Department, Specialty Advertising Association International, 3125 Skyway Circle North, Irving, TX 75038-3526 (214-252-0404).

Decorative Items

Some decorative items can be purchased locally through fellow merchants, or distributors and wholesalers. Some national suppliers include:

- Bingo King, 1809 109th Street, Grand Prairie, TX 75050 (1-800-451-9986) sells theme decorations and accessories through its catalog . It has a good selection for New Years, Valentine's Day, St. Patrick's Day, Halloween, and Christmas as well as a red, white and blue patriotic decorating kit.
- U.S. Balloon Manufacturing Company, Inc., 140 58th Street, Brooklyn, NY 11220 (1-800-285-4000) has balloons of all sizes and shapes, including those which can be imprinted with your store's name.
- Balloon City U.S.A., Post Office Box 4397, Harrisburg, PA 17111-0397 (1-800-243-5486) is another resource for balloons.

Chase's Annual Events

Available from Contemporary Books, Two Prudential Plaza, Suite 1200, Chicago, IL 60601-6790.

CHAPTER 6

In-Store Special Events That Draw Customers

The name of the game for any retailer is to sell products. And while pricing, quality, styling, convenience and service may be the major factors which motivate a sale, don't overlook the in-store environment

People like entertainment whether they are sitting at home watching television, out on the town, or even shopping.

Holiday and seasonal promotions, already discussed, provide a happy ambience. But they represent only two of the promotional steps you can take to attract new customers, and keep old ones coming back.

In-store special events will also create that additional excitement so appealing to customers.

There is a whole range of special events you can conduct. They include an annual anniversary celebration, personal appearances by celebrities, entertainment, exhibits and displays, psychic readings, and international product promotions.

Before settling on a special event, there are several things you must consider:

- Will it appeal to your customers and potential customers? If your audience is the classical music set, do not schedule jazz musicians. If you sell sporting goods, do not schedule an exhibit of opera costumes.

- Will the event overshadow its purpose, to attract people to your store to make a purchase? If the event requires so much floor space that customers do not have full access to the merchandise, don't hold it.
- Will the event create too much noise or other distractions that will disturb shoppers?
- Will the event bring in enough additional money to cover its costs?

A special event should only be scheduled after you are convinced it meets your criteria and objectives.

MAKING THE MOST OF YOUR ANNIVERSARY EACH YEAR

Whether you have been in business one year, 11 years, or more than 100 years, pull out all stops to celebrate your anniversary each year. It offers you unlimited marketing opportunities, as well as a chance to create excitement and gain additional visibility for your store in the community.

Even though a one- or five-year anniversary may not appear to be impressive, it is in retail when you consider the turnover rate. *By focusing attention on your anniversary, you are demonstrating to your customers and the community that you have a stable, successful operation.*

While milestone anniversaries—your 100th, for example—might last an entire year, your annual celebration can run anywhere from a weekend to a month. It all depends on how long you want to celebrate and maintain the momentum.

The key theme of your anniversary celebration should be to thank your customers for making your store a success. Here are some ways in which to celebrate your annual anniversary.

An Annual Anniversary Sale

The easiest and most logical way to celebrate your anniversary each year is to hold a special "Anniversary Sale." It focuses on your success, and offers your customers the opportunity to share it with you. Use this "thank you" theme in your advertising, in your windows, and in your store. Make your customers feel they are part of the family, and you want to share your success with them. In planning the anniversary sale, contact your suppliers and see what support they might provide. It might be in pricing, special products, or some other area of marketing. You might start a tradition of rolling prices back to your founding year. If the business is more than 25 years old, the "rollback" concept might be too costly to do across the board. Instead, you might have just a select number of products at their original pricing, with smaller discounts on the rest of the products on sale. The "rollback" concept will probably work best across the board if you were founded less than 25 years ago. If you expect to have an anniversary sale every year, you might have an artist design a special anniversary logo which can be updated each year by just adding the new anniversary number.

Recreating Your Founding Year

If appropriate, you should recreate the atmosphere of your founding year. Have the sales help dressed in the styles worn during the founding year. Decorate the store and windows with memorabilia from the founding year. This could include newspaper front pages, clothing styles worn at the time, political campaign buttons from elections that year, etc. Contact the local historical society and local newspapers for help in locating these items.

Develop Special Collector's Item

You might consider developing a special collector's item as a giveaway for each anniversary. While it should be inexpensive, it should be something your customers will save. It could be some type of small commemorative pin with the store name and anniversary number. In addition to changing the number each year, you might also change the color. Another giveaway might be a commemorative drinking glass or mug. The design should be distinctive enough for customers to want to save them and build up a set. Other souvenirs to consider might include drink coasters or ash trays.

Special Anniversary Event for Customers, Employees

You could also pay special tribute to your customers and employees during your anniversary. Invite your customers to nominate the "employee of the year" and to select from among the finalists. Pick those with the most nominations for the finals and hold a special reception at the store for the winner. If you have a mailing list of your best customers, you might hold a special reception for them too. It could be at the store, or, if you are primarily a high-ticket retailer, you might want to have the reception at a local hotel or public hall. A third possibility, if you have a large outside area, is to have the reception there. If it is during a cold weather month, set up a tent. You should also serve birthday cake, and perhaps champagne to your customers at the store each year.

It is not necessary to get into an expensive event for your customers unless you are celebrating a milestone like your 25th or 50th anniversary. For a 25th or 50th anniversary, you might want to buy out a performance of a local theatre company and invite your best customers to attend, or reserve a section of seats at a sporting event or concert.

Launch a Significant New Program

An anniversary period is always a good time for a retailer to make a significant announcement regarding the business. It would be the ideal time to announce a new merchandising policy, an expansion program for the store, or even an expansion program into new product lines. You could also use the anniversary to introduce your own credit card, to announce a new credit policy, new hours, and even a new manager. Other significant programs to announce during your anniversary might include a "frequent buyer's program" (see Chapter Ten), a "product of the month" club (also see Chapter Ten), or a home delivery service.

Give Something Back to the Community

Your anniversary is always a good time to announce you are giving something back to the community for making your success possible. It could be a contribution to a charitable organization, the launching of a community involvement program, or the sponsorship of an award. Chapter 12 offers many ideas on how to get involved in your community by giving something back.

Get Official Government Recognition

For a milestone anniversary (usually in five-year increments), arrange to obtain public recognition. Ask the mayor and/or local city government legislature to issue a proclamation or legislative resolution honoring the store.

Arrange for the presentation at the store, and invite the media. Chances are the mayor's office will contact the media. Also ask the state legislators who represent your district to arrange for recognition. If it is a 25th, 50th, 75th, or 100th anniversary, they might be able to get the governor to issue a proclamation, and arrange a presentation ceremony. Also ask your congressman's office to insert a statement honoring your store in the *Congressional Record.*

Anniversary Publicity

If you are celebrating a milestone anniversary, you can probably get good media coverage: a newspaper feature story and/or business page story, and perhaps a segment on a local television magazine show. Anniversary events which should be pitched to the media include sales help dressed in the clothing of the founding year, the store redecorated to look as it did when it was founded (ideal for a 75th or 100th anniversary), the rollback of prices, the selection of the "employee of the year."

CREATING SPECIAL EVENTS FEATURING LIVE ENTERTAINMENT

Special events are usually one-day promotions, but some may last a weekend or even a week. And some can become recurring events, or part of a series of events.

Live entertainment, ranging from robots and musicians to psychics and magicians, can provide an exciting shopping experience for your customers.

Costumed Characters

Costumed characters have already been suggested for some of the holiday and seasonal promotions in Chapter Five. They can also be used anytime during the year to generate in-store excitement.

There are several approaches to take:

- Rent a "generic" one from a local theatrical costume house. Most offer a variety of costumes, ranging from animals and clowns to knights in armor and astronauts. Use one of your employees, or hire a local performer to wear the outfit during the event. Needless to say, the person should relate well to people and exhibit a "little ham".

- It is also possible to rent costumes depicting various comic book characters. Again, check with a local theatrical costume rental house. Since this type of costume will have instant recognition, it will probably be very effective in attracting traffic.

- Arrange to have one of the costumed mascots from a local sports team appear. You might be able to get him at no cost if you develop a joint promotion with the team. It might involve distributing ticket information in-store, a mailing to customers, or an agreement to advertise the appearance.

- Check with your suppliers to see if they have any licensing agreements to use cartoon characters. If they do, they may be able to arrange an appearance.

Get maximum use out of these costumed characters:

- Have them right near the front door (or just outside the entrance) so that they can greet customers and attract passers-by.

- If city ordinances permit, you might have the costumed character walking along neighborhood streets, "leading" passers-by back to the store in a "Pied Piper" effect.

- If you use a team mascot or well-known character, consider taking instant pictures of them with customers who make a purchase. Also encourage autograph signing for customers.

- One function the costumed character can perform is to keep shoppers' children entertained while their parents are browsing through the store.

- If your budget will permit, hold a drawing among all who visit the store during the costumed character's appearance. The prize: a free appearance at any event the winner selects. It could be a child's birthday party, or even an adult's surprise party.

- You might also have an auction among your customers for an appearance by the character. The proceeds would go to a local charity.

- If you have a unique costumed character, inform newspapers and television. They may want to cover. Any costumed character provides a good photo opportunity, especially with a young child.

Rent a Robot

Robots draw traffic and develop a happy and attentive audience. There are two types of robots: those with an individual in them, and those controlled by an individual hidden from view. The robot you use should be entertaining, as well as adept at promoting your store, specific products, or a sale. The person manning it should be thoroughly trained and rehearsed on what you want said. Be certain to audition the robot. Either watch him in action at another job, or screen video tapes of previous performances.

The robot can be used in various situations:

- In the window talking to passers-by, trying to lure them into the store.
- Right outside the front door to attract a crowd. Once a crowd has gathered, the robot then leads it into the store and then around the store, acting as a "guide." In smaller stores, the robot can lead the customers to the sale area, or to the special products being promoted.
- In the store itself, with a sign in the window announcing its appearance or with a video set in the window showing the robot in action inside.

Television stations usually like to cover robot appearances. So invite the local station(s) to come down and do an interview. Even suggest that they let the robot do the weather on the news show. A remote from the store with the robot and regular weatherman could be a good live segment for the channel.

Live Music

Depending upon your available space and customer base, you might want to feature live music in the store. But before considering it, you should be convinced it will enhance business, and not divert attention from the selling floor. It could be on a regular schedule (Tuesday nights, Saturday afternoons, etc.), or just on special occasions. An advantage for having it regularly scheduled is that you may be able to develop a loyal group of "music night" customers. You could have a pianist, cellist, accordionist, or even a small combo if you have the space. While most retailers will probably want soft background music, those who cater to young audiences may want to feature louder music. By billing "music night" as a showcase, you might be able to get a local music school to provide student talent. While you will be getting amateur talent, the school will recognize this as an opportunity to enhance its image and will undoubtedly provide its best talent at no cost to you. Let local disk jockeys know about your live music plans. If you try the "music night" approach, see if you can get local music critics to drop by and review the talent. Only invite them, of course, when you know you will be having good talent.

A Magician

Magicians fascinate people and should be used to draw customers not only to a store, but also to specific products.

The performance should be carefully choreographed so that customers are "forced" to move around the store, and are given time to shop. Otherwise, they will stick with the magician and you will end up losing sales. One effective scenario is for a brief performance in the window, with an announcement that it will continue inside in 5-10 minutes. Inside, the magician should again perform and announce the show will continue in a different section of the store in another ten minutes. The magician should be instructed to include plugs for various products and specials in his act. He should also use some of your products, if possible, as props during his performance.

Try to develop a unique news angle for the magician's appearance and try to get media coverage. For example, perhaps the magician will "saw his (or her) 1000th person in half" at your store, or will be retiring the rabbit that has been a major attraction for ten years, etc.

Before hiring a magician, watch a live performance. Make certain this is the right person for your clientele.

A Caricaturist

An artist drawing caricatures of customers will be a popular attraction. Many people enjoy being the subject of caricatures and will display the finished product at home or at work. You may want to have a caricaturist on hand on a regular basis, during special promotions, or just every once in a while. If you offer them on a regular basis, pick a slow day or time period. Offer them only when a purchase is made. Somewhere on the caricature, the artist should work in the store's name. This will give you additional exposure if the subject keeps it on display. Work out the best possible price with the artist. Estimate the number of caricatures to be drawn; then determine whether you should hire the artist by the day, hour, or per caricature.

To add fun to the event, ask customers for permission to display the caricatures in the store or window that week. Display them under a banner, "Saluting Our Customers—Thanks For Your Support." Promote the appearance of the caricaturist with a sign in the window and a caricature of a famous person. The sign might read, "Come In And Have A Caricature of Yourself Drawn by (Artist's Name). Free with Purchase."

Free Psychic Readings

A favorite attraction for stores with a large female clientele to consider would be free psychic readings.

You could have a special one-day event, a monthly event or even more frequently if it draws customers. You might schedule it for a slow afternoon each week. You could have a tarot card reader, handwriting analyst, palm reader, tea leaf reader, etc. If it is a one-time event, you might even have all of them at the same time. If it is a regular monthly or weekly event you might have a different psychic each time. Readings should be offered only when a purchase is made. An exception should be made for your best customers. You might send them an invitation to "drop by" at a specific time for a free reading. If they "drop by," they may end up making a purchase. Determine how many readings the psychic can do in an hour. That will give you a better idea as to whether you should negotiate a per-customer or a full-day rate. Promote with signage in your window prior to and on the day of the event. Also advertise in-store a week prior to the appearance. You may be able to get some media coverage on these appearances if you position them properly. Try to arrange to have the psychic make his or her predictions for the coming year, or forecast what's in the stars for several celebrities, the economy, etc. An advance release to the media promising these forecasts might bring out camera crews and reporters.

Balloon Sculptor, Origami Artist, Juggler, Mime, Puppeteer

There are a variety of other entertainers you might consider scheduling for in-store promotions. The list is almost unlimited. It is just a question of finding talented people in your city who might include:

- Balloon sculptors. They are great fun at parties, and will be an ideal in-store event, especially if many children accompany their parents shopping. The sculptor makes all kinds of things with balloons (hats, toys, animals, etc.), and then gives them away.

- Origami artists make all types of novelty items out of color paper. Use one who will not only demonstrate this Japanese art, but also conduct a workshop and show your customers how to do it.

- Jugglers are fun to watch, too. If you have the space, and room height, you might consider bringing one in for a one-day appearance.

- Mimes fascinate people. Retailers have successfully used them in their windows, as well as in their stores. They hold people spellbound as they go through their routines slowly.

- A puppeteer can perform in your window and lure people into the store to see the rest of the show—and shop. The technique should be similar to that of magicians. Or the performance can be inside the store, and promoted via signage in the window.

One way to find these performers is to check out who is entertaining at local children's parties, women's clubs and other organizations. The other way is the Yellow Pages.

There may be some interest from television channels to cover some of these appearances, especially if it is a slow day for news, or if there is a need for some light features that day. You may get coverage if you build up the performer. If the juggler is going for the *Guinness Book of World Records* for most consecutive performances without dropping anything, or is going to try something never before attempted locally, television and even newspapers may cover.

Pets Are a Customer's Best Friend

Most people are very attracted to pets, even if they do not have any at home. A smart retailer will consider conducting in-store pet promotions to help build traffic. If you have space, and it will not inconvenience your customers, occasionally let the Humane Society bring in kittens and puppies available for adoption. Advance publicity by the Human Society, as well as window and in-store signage will attract people to the store.

Once a year you may want to stage a dog and/or cat show so that customers can show off their pets. Hold it in-store or in your parking lot if you have one. Award ribbons or prizes to the winners. Set up some "fun" categories: "Biggest Smiler," "Least Obedient Dog," "Worst Dining Habits," etc. Local media enjoys covering such events.

You may also want to invite your customers to display pictures of their pets along a wall in the store. You can award prizes in such categories as "Most Unusual Pose," "Nicest Costume On A Pet," "Cat With The Widest Eyes," and "Most Unusual Pet," etc.

You would be surprised how much attention such pet activity will receive from customers, potential customers, and the media.

ARRANGING CELEBRITY PERSONAL APPEARANCES

Personal appearances by celebrities will always create excitement and attract traffic. However, before you book a celebrity, you should evaluate the expected results, and weigh them against the cost of the promotion.

Will the appearance sell products, gain new customers, and build incremental sales? Will it gain important positive exposure for your store in the community?

Tips for Getting Celebrities

Celebrity appearances usually involve a fee. However, there are times when you may be able to arrange a celebrity appearance gratis, or at a greatly reduced fee. Check with your suppliers to see if they have any celebrities under contract for personal appearances. Contact local entertainment promoters to see if they have any celebrities coming into town to perform. They may be able to arrange a free appearance if it will help promote the celebrity's performance, or if the celebrity is promoting a book or product you sell. If your product line appeals to the celebrity, you may be able to give products in lieu of a cash fee. This will save you money since the product value will be calculated on the basis of the retail price. Contact local charitable organizations that may have a working relationship with celebrities. Offer a percentage of sales completed while the celebrity is in the store to any organization which arranges a free appearance.

Using the Celebrity

Celebrities can be used in a variety of situations:

- Signing autographs.
- Doing sales pitches or demonstrations of products they endorse.
- Holding question and answer period with customers.
- Modeling clothing.
- Conducting a drawing for door prizes.
- Having their pictures taken with customers.

Autographs or pictures should necessitate a purchase, or even the purchase of a specific product.

Be sure to read Chapter Nine for information concerning the use of sports personalities. Some of the ideas can apply to non-sports personalities, too.

Publicizing a Celebrity's Appearance

Whenever you will have an in-store appearance by a celebrity, send out an advance story as well as a media advisory inviting coverage. If it is a show business personality, send the material to the entertainment page editors and columnists, the entertainment reporters on radio and television, and disc jockeys. Try to get a disc jockey to do a live interview with the celebrity from your store.

PERSONAL APPEARANCES BY DESIGNERS AND SUPPLIER PRESIDENTS

Depending upon your product lines, you may be able to develop exciting special events featuring designers, and presidents of supplier companies.

Designers

Customers like to meet and talk with the designers of the dresses, jewelry, scarves, furniture, suits, or even appliances they purchase.

Some designers are very well-known celebrities and will attract large crowds. However, even unknown designers will draw people to your store. A designer's appearance should be in connection with a promotion for his or her product and should be arranged through your supplier. The appearance may require an advertising commitment on your part, a significant product order, and/or the designer's transportation expenses. Local media will probably be interested in covering the event, especially if it is an appearance by a fashion designer. Contact the lifestyle and/or fashion editors at newspapers, and producers or hosts of women's programs on radio and television. Send advance information stories as well as invitations to cover.

Company Presidents

Some stores run "Presidents Day" promotions, inviting supplier presidents to appear at the store to greet customers and/or demonstrate their products. Of course, the greater the volume you do with a company, the better the chance you have of getting its president.

You might want to hold a single "Presidents Day" for all of your suppliers. This probably has the most promotional impact. Or you may want to invite each on an individual basis, setting aside one afternoon or evening a month for each president. Logistically, the latter will be easier to handle and more suited for smaller-sized stores.

When a president will appear, his or her company may spend some money in local media to promote the appearance. Chances are, however, they will probably try to get you to pay the costs. You should agree to arrange publicity interviews for the chief executive with local media while he or she is in your city. Business page editors should be contacted, as well as radio and television news desks. If there are any local business programs, or business reporters at local stations or channels, contact them. If you hold a single "Presidents Day" promotion, you will probably have to plan it a year in advance to assure everyone's availability.

During the promotion, each president should be stationed at a booth, table or section where his products are displayed. A sign should identify the company and its president who should wear a name tag. Space permitting, you may want to have a central assembly point for formal presentations by each president. This isn't necessary, however, if there is enough space at each company table.

DEVELOPING EVENTS WHICH EMPHASIZE PRODUCT SALES

It is vital to your business to hold special events that specifically target sales of your merchandise.

Private Shopping Nights

Set aside special nights for groups you are trying to cultivate as customers, as well as for regular customers during various holiday seasons.

Serve champagne and other refreshments, have door prizes, and perhaps distribute with the invitation one or more coupons for single-item discounts. Have your sales help primed to offer special attention to the customers.

Hold special nights for singles, husbands (before Valentine's Day and Christmas), wives (also before Christmas, Valentine's Day), seniors, police officers, firefighters, etc. You can set aside a night of personal shopping for just about any group you think has customer potential.

There are several story ideas you should propose to local media in order to get coverage for the special nights: "How men meet women at Singles Night," "How women interact with one another as they shop for Valentine's Day gifts for their husbands"; "How men go about shopping for Christmas gifts for their wives or girl friends." These might appeal to newspapers, radio and television.

"Welcome Back Party" for Former Customers

Once a year, you should consider holding a "Welcome Back" event for former customers. Select from your mailing list the names of the customers who have not been in the store for more than six months and invite them back for an evening of refreshments, champagne, and special discounts.

Promoting Products from Different Countries or States

Special events developed around products made in a foreign country, or a particular state or region of the United States, offer unlimited promotional opportunities.

If, for example, you carry many French-made products, consider holding a "French Week" or "French Month" promotion. The entire store should take on a French atmosphere, focusing in on the French-made products. Display travel posters and other scenic pictures of France. Serve French wines and cheeses, show French travel video tapes, and play French music. Contact the French Consulate or trade commissioner (if one is located in your city), or the French Embassy in Washington. Outline your plans and try to get them to offer assistance. They may be able to arrange for a French trade association to cooperate, and/or be able to provide posters, refreshments, gifts, etc. Also ask the firms supplying you with French products to provide money for the promotion, as well as other support. They may even be able to finance a door prize like a round trip to France. You may also be able to arrange for some French entertainers to appear at the store.

To launch the promotion, arrange a special reception with the French consulate or Embassy whose ranking officials may co-host the function. Invite city officials, leaders of any local French societies, key customers, and representatives from supplier companies. The latter should be approached to pick up the bill for the event.

This French promotion is just an example of the elements of a foreign country promotion you might conduct. Concentrate such promotions on countries from which you carry a substantial number of products.

Similar promotions might focus in on states or regions of the United States from which you carry significant product. You should discuss arranging these domestic promotions with the manufacturers as well as the various state trade and industrial promotion divisions.

Publicity opportunities for this type of promotion are numerous. If food, fashion or wine are involved, the lifestyle sections of newspapers will probably be interested in covering your event. Send to the lifestyle editors an outline of what will be featured, and the times of any special events. Try to get an on-air radio personality to do a show live from your store. Television news programs might also be interested in covering, especially if they can do an interview with an authority on the subject (French wine expert, French Government trade official, etc.). You might also put together a small basket of samples of some of the products on display to send to on-air radio personalities, disc jockeys, and hosts of local daytime television programs.

Fashion Shows

If you sell clothing, jewelry, hats, bathing suits, or shoes, you might consider holding fashion shows during the year. The ideal time is at the start of the selling season for the fashions you plan to show. Jewelry can be shown just about any time during the year.

There are several ways to schedule a fashion show. Ideally it should be held in the store. However, if you do not have the space, you might rent a hotel ballroom, an auditorium, or some other hall. It should be located near the store, and customers should be encouraged to visit the store right after the show, perhaps for refreshments. Try to get the manufacturers to underwrite the show, or pick up some of the expenses.

It is always best to use professional models. However, sometimes it is very effective to use sales staff or even customers to whom attendees may relate better. Moreover, customers who are asked to model will be flattered.

The show can be held during a slow time of the day, or in the evening after the store has closed. Another possibility is to stage mini-fashion shows several times during the day. Each show would last 10-15 minutes. They could be informal, with the models walking through the aisles and showing the fashions when they came upon customers.

Invite the local fashion writers at newspapers and magazines to cover your shows. Television news, and the television magazine shows may also want to cover. And don't forget to invite the hosts of women's radio programs.

Product Previews

Similar to fashion shows, these can be held whenever a new product line, or significant products are introduced. Some examples might be the new Christmas toys just as the Christmas selling season is to begin; new consumer electronics products when they come to market (usually after the Consumer Electronics Shows); new appliances and new furniture.

These product previews should consist of demonstrations by representatives of the manufacturer, or your sales staff. Customers can then inspect the products, try them, and ask questions. These product previews can also be held during slow periods, just after the store is closing, or even as a day-long event with a preview/demonstration every hour on the hour.

Inform media about these previews. If the product is unique, and offers good visual opportunities, television might cover. Lifestyle editors at newspapers and sometimes business editors might be interested, too.

Play "Let's Make a Sale"

If it does not conflict with the image of your store, every so often you might want to play "Let's Make A Sale."

How is it played? When a customer seems interested in a product, a sales person springs into action: "If you have a five dollar bill with any two same digits, we will take five dollars off the price tag." Other offers might be to ask a man to take off his hat and, if he is bald, give him a discount or gift. If someone trying on shoes has a hole in his sock, give him a gift (a shoe horn, or spool of thread), or a cash discount. Ask a customer if she has anything red on her (for a cash discount), etc. There is an endless number of things to ask for. Just use your imagination, but make certain that your requests will not offend any of your customers.

"Let's Make A Sale" is just another way to inject some fun into your customer's shopping experience.

A Tethered Balloon Ride

If you have the outdoor space, you might offer balloon rides to customers. Few have probably ever taken one, and the adventure associated with ballooning might make the ride a big attraction.

The balloon is tied down, and only rises a short distance into the air. However, this short trip becomes something special to someone who has never experienced it, particularly if you also take a picture of each customer in the balloon gondola. They should only be available to customers who make a minimum purchase.

It is a tradition after a balloon ride to drink champagne. If your budget can afford it, you might give each customer a split of domestic champagne. Or perhaps you can get a local liquor store to cooperate in the promotion and provide the champagne.

Balloon rides will probably attract media coverage. In addition to an advance story announcing the event, try to get radio, television, and newspapers to cover it. Also invite columnists, on-air radio personalities, and local television show hosts to take a ride. A disc jockey may even want to broadcast from the balloon.

Children's Story Hour

This could be a weekly, or even daily event—especially if you have many customers who shop with young children. Have a story teller keep the children occupied while the parents shop. Arrange this special feature for a two-hour period daily, or on Saturdays. Schedule it for the period when you are now getting the heaviest concentration of mothers-with-children traffic. By promoting this convenience, you may find that many more mothers with children will become your new customers during those hours. Try to hire a local school teacher or college student to be the story teller.

FEATURING CROWD-PLEASING SPECIAL EXHIBITS AND DISPLAYS

Exciting in-store exhibits and displays should be an important part of your special events schedule. If they are unique and well done, they will not only attract your regular customers but also new faces.

Memorabilia of All Kinds

This might include movie posters and pictures of old-time stars, old dolls and doll houses, toys from the '20s, '30s, and '40s, old newspaper headlines, historical pictures and materials about your city, old advertisements, World's Fair items, old opera costumes, and theatrical and other entertainment posters. The material can probably be borrowed from local collectors, the historical society and museums, the local newspaper(s), advertising agencies, the opera company, and theater company. You could have one big memorabilia exhibit, an exhibit covering an era (the '20s, '30s, etc.), or individual exhibits in each category.

One method of collecting the material would be to ask local media to help you find collectors who will loan display items to you. They might run a small story about what you are seeking. If there is a hobby page editor, seek out his, or her, assistance. You might ask local disc jockeys to request help from their listeners. This can result in good publicity months before the exhibit. And, of course, such an exhibit will probably get good press coverage, too.

Art

This can include artwork and handicrafts by local school children, scouts, the handicapped and senior citizens. Exhibit as well paintings by local artists or members of the art students' league, wood carvings, sculptures, and photographs. Shows might be organized with just one group, or be open to everyone. You might get better media attention if each was scheduled with a different group: the local school system, senior citizen centers, art students' league, etc. If you plan to give awards, have the local art critics from newspapers as well as museum curators do the judging. If might result in media coverage. Send stories about the exhibitors to the weekly newspapers which cover the areas in which they live.

Other Old Collectibles

You will be amazed at what people collect, and what other people will be interested in seeing on display. Consider exhibiting some of these products, especially if you sell their modern day counterparts: household products including old irons and other small appliances, stoves, washing machines, wash tubs; personal products including old razors, women's hair curling and straightening devices, shaving mugs. How about barbed wire? It is very popular out west.

Because of the uniqueness of these collectibles, the local media will probably give good coverage to such exhibits. Just let them know in advance of the event that you have something which warrants coverage. Also send stories about the event 10–14 days before it will start and ask that information be included in "Events" listings and announcements.

Joint Exhibits

Some local libraries and museums may cooperate by loaning exhibit materials for display at your store. Sometimes they may loan you several pieces which relate to a current exhibition at the museum as a means for drawing attention to that exhibit. This will not only help promote the museum, but will also draw people to your store to see the rest of the exhibit.

Always have an opening ceremony, inviting the key curator of the museum or chief librarian to "cut the ribbon." Invite media coverage, including art critics to review the "mini-show." Also try to get the exhibit listed in the "Events" columns of publications, on radio and television, and in library and museum publications.

Remember that if you display art borrowed from museums, you will have to provide security so that the material is not stolen.

The purpose of any special exhibit or display is to get people to come into the store. So, while you should promote the exhibit in the store window, only show a few examples of what can be seen inside the store. Use that window to tease people into entering the store.

PROMOTING YOUR SPECIAL EVENTS

The success of your special events program will depend upon how well it is promoted.

If it is an ongoing program, with different events scheduled weekly or monthly, chances are knowledge of it will spread via "word of mouth."

But that may not be enough to assure its success.

You should strongly promote special events through your store windows, as well as in the store, through fliers, bill stuffers, and advertising.

And don't forget publicity!

Many of your events will be newsworthy, and the local media may run advance information about them. See Chapters 13 and 14.

You should also reach out to groups in the community that may have a special interest in a specific event. This could include hobbyists, pet owners, amateur artists, etc.

RESOURCES

Many of the resources for the special events in this chapter can be found in your local area.

Costumes

- First check your Yellow Pages under "Costumes—Masquerade & Theatrical."

- Broadway Costumes, Inc., 954 West Washington Boulevard, Chicago, IL 60607 (312-829-6400).

Entertainment

- Check the Yellow Pages under the following listings: "Entertainers," "Clowns," "Puppets & Marionettes," "Magicians," "Psychic Life Readings."

Robots

- JCL Robots, 13961 Fernwood Drive, Garden Grove, CA 92643.
- Robot Entertainment, Inc., 1276 Holiday Park Drive, Wantagh, NY 11793 (516-783-5450).
- Sally Industries, 803 Price Street, Jacksonville, FL 32204 (904-353-5051).
- The Robot Factory, Post Office Box 112, Cascade, CO 80809 (719-687-6244).

Miscellaneous

- For television personalities, contact your local affiliate of the network and see if it can help. Perhaps it might jointly sponsor a local appearance.
- For hot air balloons, look in the Yellow Pages under "Balloons—Manned," or "Balloons Hot Air—Manned."
- Also see the Resources section in Chapter Five.

CHAPTER 7

Sales That Will Build Business

"Hold a sale and they will come . . . ."

Sales days rank among the top traffic builders in virtually every segment of retail. They bring in customers, and move merchandise.

In recent years, sales have become an even more significant factor in retail marketing. The depressed economy has made consumers more price-conscious and sales-oriented, and has forced retailers to take more aggressive action to reduce inventories.

Just how active you are in developing and conducting sales will depend upon your pricing strategy.

You will probably have a low sales profile:

- If it is necessary to maintain a strong profit margin.
- If you have a strong customer base willing to pay your regular prices.
- If your store has a very upscale image.
- If you are following a "low everyday pricing" strategy.

You will probably have a high sales profile:

- If stores in your immediate vicinity are sales-oriented.
- If sales are an integral part of your direct competitors' marketing programs.

- If you are willing to accept lower profit margins, and make it up in volume.
- If you want to build business during slow selling periods or reduce inventories.
- If there are many layoffs in your area, or the economy is particularly bad.
- If you carry product lines which have traditional seasonal sales periods.
- If you want to attract new customers by offering special sales items as a means for introducing them to your full line.

No matter how creative a sale is, no matter the number of customers it attracts, it is not successful unless merchandise moves. And merchandise will not move during a sale unless the customers *perceive* they are receiving a good buy.

A sale should be heavily promoted in order to reach out and attract the widest possible audience. Among the methods to consider when promoting your sales are:

- Advertising
- Mailings to customers and groups
- Window signs and displays
- In-store signage
- Handbills and fliers
- Bill stuffers
- Publicity in media
- Bulletin board posters

There are two important things to remember when holding a sale: first, if specific products are on sale, have plenty in stock. Second, offer rain checks to customers if you run short so that they can still get the item at the sale price.

Chapter Five carried information on how to create exciting in-store promotions around holidays, seasons of the year, and other annual events. Included were ideas for conducting sales in connection with these promotions.

There are many other sales events which can both mark special occasions and attract customers to the store.

TEN EXCITING SALES WHICH YOU CAN RUN THROUGHOUT THE YEAR

There are many "ongoing" sales which you can run throughout the year. Among them are:

The "Slack Time" Sale

Every retailer experiences slow periods of the day or week when customers just don't seem to be around. It could be the first two hours each morning, sometime in mid-afternoon or perhaps every Thursday morning. One way to counteract slow periods is to run specials, or sales during those hours. The sale can be on specific products, or a straight percentage discount on anything in the store. The "Slack Time" sale should be promoted via window and in-store placards, mailings to senior citizen centers, PTAs, and other groups whose members may have the time to do "off-hour" shopping.

The Rainy/Snowy Day Sale

Since business is usually slow during inclement weather, institute a policy that when it is raining or snowing outside, prices automatically come down inside. Establish a firm rainy/snowy day sale discount and promote it throughout the year. Use window and in-store signage, direct mail to customers and groups, and some advertising. An ideal promotion is through the sponsorship of one or more local radio or television weather reports. You may even be able to arrange, in advance, to purchase time on these weather reports whenever it is raining or snowing. A good way to announce the sale to media is through a release, "Store gears up for snowy winter, less profits." It should cite the *Farmer's Almanac* snow prediction, and how you will be cutting prices when it snows. This could also be a good item to send to disc jockeys.

"Your" Birthday Sale

Offer a special discount to any customer shopping on his or her birthday, or perhaps during the birthday week. The discount might be on all products purchased, or off the first $100 of purchases, or on any one product purchased. This "sale" is aimed at creating goodwill among customers, as well as at moving merchandise. Promote the concept through in-store signage, a flier stapled to cash register receipts, bill stuffers, and occasionally in your advertising.

You may also want to invite customers to "join" your Birthday Club. A member fills out a card listing his or her birthday. Then a week or so before the day, you can send an invitation to drop by the store for a special discount.

You might be able to get a local newspaper columnist to do a column about how he or she celebrated a birthday by going out and purchasing a personal gift as a result of your special discount. This might also make a good television news feature. Remind the writer or the television personality about your program ten days or so before his or her birthday. At the end of the year, you might also send out a story about which "birthday days" drew the largest number of customers.

Sale Based on the Date

You may want to feature a different product on sale each day, with the selling price based on that date. On January 15, for example, the price might be $1.15, $1.15 off or 15 percent off. On March 3, the product offered might be on sale for $33, or 33 percent off. It all depends upon your product line and pricing.

A variation would be to offer a different product each day throughout the year at a set price based on the year. For example, during 1994, have a different product on sale each day for $19.94. During 1995, the sale-priced product each day would be $19.95. A promotion among New York City restaurants offering a fixed luncheon price based on the year has been very successful.

This type of sale can be expanded beyond a single product or run as a storewide promotion any time during the year. You may want to try it over a weekend, or even for an entire week. As a daily sale, it should be promoted with window and in-store signage, as well as on any promotional materials you distribute. The key phrase to use in your promotional materials is, "Every Day Is A *Special* Day At (Name Of Store)."

Temperature of the Day Sale

Whenever the temperature dips below, or rises above, a certain level, the sale kicks in. The exact temperature will depend upon your climate and your objectives. The sale can kick in when the temperature tops 90 degrees in the summer and dips below freezing in the winter. Call your summer sale "A Torrid Sale," "The Hottest Prices In Town," or "Cool Prices On A Hot Day." Ideal cold weather themes could be "Come In And Watch Our Prices Melt," "Warm Up To Our Cold Day Specials," or "Our Prices Drop With The Temperature."

Heavily promote this "temperature" concept just before and during the winter and summer seasons. Use in-store and window placards, bulletin board mailers to nearby businesses, fliers at the cash register, mailings to customers, and advertising. On days when the sale kicks in, be sure to have a banner or sign in the window announcing that it is "on." Budget permitting, you should try to purchase radio spots on days when the temperature reaches the "sales" point. This promotion can also be conducted during other seasons by setting appropriate temperature parameters. After a heat spell, you might send a press release to the local media about how your customers saved over X-dollars as a result of your unique hot weather sale. Or consider a story on how certain people hope that the temperature gets real cold this winter so that they can go on a buying spree at your store.

Product of the Week Sale

Each week feature a different product at a special sale price. This promotion should offer interesting and exciting products so that it will draw customers back to the store week after week. It can be a tremendous traffic builder. Promote it as your "Surprise Special of The Week," without ever advertising the exact product. Make the customers walk into the store to see what is on sale. A placard in the window can tease passers-by to "Come In And See This Week's Surprise Special."

Weekly Senior Citizen Sale Day

Many retailers offer special discounts to senior citizens, often setting aside a slow period (one morning each week) for them. Since seniors are usually flexible with their time, it enables retailers to build traffic during a period when they need more business. Seniors are reachable through senior clubs, centers and housing; newsletters and other publications; and special programs. Contact your local governmental Senior Citizen office to provide you with information on how to reach this important audience.

In addition to weekly discounts, many retailers hold special sales and promotions during Senior Citizens Month each May.

Night Sales

From time to time during the year, you may want to hold a "Night Sale," dropping all prices after 5 or 6 P.M. During these "Night Sales" you may also want to extend your store hours until midnight, or even later. Post-midnight hours can be very important if there are many night workers in the area who finish work at 12. If you are located in or near a downtown business district, or an industrial area, promote these sales through company bulletin boards. Send the posters to the personnel (or human resources) departments of local businesses and ask them to post. You may also want to buy radio time on late night shows to advertise these special sales.

"If Your Name Is . . ." Sale

Periodically, pick a first name out of a hat and run a sale entitling anyone with that first name to a percent-off discount. Ideally, this type of sale should last one day, or one weekend. You may want to run it on a weekly basis, two times a month, or once a month. You may also want to just advertise the concept and dates, and let the customers come down to see if it is "their day." Or your can promote the names in advance. If you run the promotion on a limited basis, you may want to pick three to five names for each date.

You might try to get a daily newspaper columnist with a sense of humor to write a column about this promotion, complaining why his or her name hasn't come up. It could be a very humorous piece which would draw attention to the sale. Whenever the first name of a local disc jockey is a winning name for the discount, send a humorous letter of congratulations informing the deejay that "together with 4897 other local women named Alice," she's a winner. You may get air time. A third possibility is to arrange for all of the winners with the same first name to be available for a photo opportunity for newspapers and television. Pick a day when there is a considerable number of people with that same first name. A newspaper might even do a story to accompany any photographs it runs.

Full Moon/Half Moon/New Moon Sales

The positions of the moon provide you with a good theme to run sales. You might run one or several different "moon" theme sales each year during appropriate phases. The featured phase should be displayed in the window and throughout the store, down to full-, half-, and new moon-shaped price tags. Theme lines might include "Take A Full Moon (10 Percent) Discount," or "Half Moon Sale . . . Buy One And Half Off The Second." A good place to advertise this sale is on the same page as the horoscopes in newspapers, and also on radio and television weather forecasts.

SPECIAL SALES FOR SPECIAL OCCASIONS

While the previous sales may be conducted often throughout the year, the following sales would ordinarily be conducted only once during a year.

Christmas in August (CIA) Sale

The hot days of August are a wonderful time to bring out your Christmas decorations, Santa, and even some ice carvings and fake snow. "Christmas in August" sales almost always create excitement and fun and can even attract media coverage. The only difference between December and August is that you should feature your current product line, and not your Christmas line. Arrange for media coverage of Santa Claus arriving (have fake snow on the sidewalk), the lighting of the tree, photo opportunities with children and Santa, etc.

The Lottery Sale

Playing state lotteries has become a favorite pastime with people of all economic tiers. You can conduct a "Lottery Sale" in which everyone is a winner. After a purchase, the customer gets a scratch-off ticket which determines how much he or she gets off on a purchase. While everyone gets something off, some get a bigger discount than others. To make this sale even more interesting, you might have one or two getting 100 percent off.

Blood Donor Discount

In conjunction with the local blood bank, offer a special discount to anyone who donates blood during a set period of time. Plan this event with the blood bank's marketing and public relations people since they probably have good contacts with the media. They may be able to get free public service time on radio and television to promote this "Give Blood And Save Sale." An ideal time for this promotion is during a slow donor period and/or a shortage of blood in the area.

In addition to publicity done by the blood bank, you should also promote the sale. Try to get a popular disc jockey to donate blood. Chances are he or she will talk about it on the air and might even do a live remote from the blood bank.

Private Sales for Special Groups

A very effective way to attract special groups of new customers is to hold a private sale strictly for them. Keep the store open exclusively for this group, and offer an across-the-board discount or special sale prices. Such private sales could be for people who work or live in the store's building or complex or one nearby, or for employees of a firm that just moved in. Other groups might include the members of the local medical and dental societies and/or their wives, local chapters of other professional societies, teachers, civil service workers, etc.

Arrange the event with companies' human resources departments or the program chairperson at private organizations. Prepare invitations for the group to include in its next mailing, or you can get the list and do your own mailing. Ask companies to post the invitation on the bulletin board or distribute to each employee. Send press releases to each group's publication.

Customer Appreciation Day/Week

Once a year, it is a good idea to run a "Customer Appreciation Day (or Week) Sale." It is your way of saying "thank you" to your customers for their support. Go all out on this sale. Serve refreshments, give small me-

mentos (calendars, address books, pens, etc.), and personally thank each customer for his or her support.

Promote this sale with in-store and window signage, invitation letters to customers, advertising, and fliers at the cash register for several weeks prior to the sale date. You might be able to get a business page story about your philosophy that merchants must never forget the importance of the customer, must never take him or her for granted, and must never forget to show their appreciation to customers for their patronage.

Tax Time Savings Sale

A good sale to run just before April 15th tax deadline, the theme of this sale is "We're Cutting Our Prices To Help You Through The Tax Season." Your in-store and window displays may include blow-ups of Internal Revenue forms with the sale announcement superimposed. You may also try to cross-promote by asking local tax preparers to permit you to leave sale fliers at their locations. You may even hire someone to distribute fliers outside of the local Internal Revenue Service office. Media usually does all types of tax savings stories around this time of the year. You might try to get your sale included as an anecdote.

"Get to Know Us" Sale

Once a year, consider holding a "get acquainted" sale. Its purpose is to attract new customers. Try promoting it via direct mail, bulletin board posters, and through advertising in media you normally do not use. You may be able to obtain names and addresses of new residents through your county clerk's office, or some other governmental agency.

The Diet Sale

This is a two-part promotion. The first part is "Sign Up For Our Diet Sale —The More You Lose, The More You Save." During the one- or two-week period, customers weigh in and sign up for the sale which will actually be a month later. The enrolled customers weigh in again and get a percentage savings based on the pounds lost. (Eight pounds lost means an eight percent savings, etc.) This can be promoted through advertising, publicity, fliers, and in-store and window signage. Try also to tie in with various dieting groups in the community, asking if you could distribute fliers among their members. Attempt to get media to interview a few customers during the initial weigh-in. They could talk about how they plan to lose their weight, what product they have their eyes on and how much they hope to lose to save on the price.

Invite media back to cover the second part of the promotion and follow up with the customers they initially interviewed as well as with other participants. You might also issue a press release at the end of the second part, announcing total poundage lost.

Another possibility is to sponsor a competition among disc jockeys, donating one dollar to a charity for every pound taken off by the participants, with one hundred dollars a pound given to charity in honor of the deejay who loses the most during the month.

Reduce the Deficit Sale

Just about every city government has a deficit. Your "Reduce The Deficit Sale" is aimed at demonstrating both good citizenship and good pricing for your customers. You might offer a five-percent-off sale to your customers, and donate an equal five percent to the city treasury. Or you might run the sale and donate a percentage of the revenues taken in to the city treasury. This type of sale will get good media coverage. Hold a press conference to announce it, and arrange a City Hall ceremony when you present a check to the mayor.

Carload/Truckload Sale

Park a large truck in your lot, and around it have cartons of product piled on top of pallets. Have demonstration models in the store. When a customer purchases a product, he or she has to go to the truck area to pick it up. A huge sign could keep a running tally of the number of sales that day, or of the number left of each product. The public perception is that the store probably got a good price on its purchase because it bought a truckload, and is passing the savings on to the customer.

Leap Year Sale

This happens only once every four years, but it can be very effective. It should be a one-day sale on February 29. Make a special effort to invite, and offer special gifts to, people born on February 29. Publicize this search for leap year birthday celebrants by asking local media to run stories about it. Promote the sale via window and in-store signage, and small space advertisements on the horoscope page of newspapers. Invite media to cover. Try to arrange for a large group of birthday celebrants to be at the store together so that the media can get a better photo opportunity as well as a variety of interviews.

Rollback the Prices Sale

Rolling back your prices to your founding year was covered in Chapter Six. You can also conduct a "rollback" sale for any year you want. It might be for a historic year (the end of World War II), or one tied to a show business personality (the year of Elvis' first hit record). It could even be the store owner's birth year.

The "Good Old Days Sale"

Like the "Rollback Sale," "The Good Old Days Sale" is aimed at bringing back the memories and pricing of past years. Examples of "Good Old Days Sales" might be a "Gay Nineties Sale," recreating the last years of the 1800's; a "Fifties Sale," or a "Roaring '20s Sale." Decorate the store to recreate the image of the era, with sales help wearing clothing of the period. And try to drop prices (some, if not all) to what they might have been in those "good old days." Your windows should also reflect the period you are featuring. In planning the promotion, you might contact the local historical society or a local museum for assistance. They may be able to loan to you costumes or other material to exhibit in-store or in the windows.

Special Student Sales

There are a variety of sales you can conduct for students from local schools. They include a special "Graduating Seniors Sale," a "Students With Perfect Attendance Sale," and "An All A's Sale" for students with perfect report cards. Try to arrange and promote these sales with schools in the area, and even advertise them in the school newspapers. Also try to arrange publicity about them in local media.

In conjunction with these sales, you may even sponsor a competition among area schools. Offer a special prize for the school with the most "all 'A' students," and the school with the most "perfect attendance students." These prizes will focus additional attention on your sales, as well as promote goodwill in the community. In addition to your in-school efforts, use your regular promotional channels to get the word out to the public.

Flip of the Coin Sale

This is a very simple sale. There is an announced percentage off on all purchases, or sale items. For each purchase, the sales person flips a coin. If the customer has the right call, the percent off on the product is doubled; if not, the customer gets it at the announced sale price. A second variation is more dramatic but can result in some very unhappy customers (as well as happy ones). In this scenario, the customer has the choice of flipping the coin for double the percent off if he or she wins. Regular presale prices prevail for a loser.

The Confusion Sale

That's the name "Flights Of Fancy," a New York gift shop, gives to its annual sale. On each day of this month-long sale, a different product or product series is on sale for 20 percent off. On the last day of the sale everything previously on sale and not purchased is reduced by 35 percent. Typical daily sale items include: "Hearts And Anything Pink," "Boxes And Anything Blue," "Anything You Can See Your Reflection In." "Flights of Fancy" issues a calendar for the month listing its daily sales.

Cheaper by the Dozen (More or Less)

Quantity is the name of the game here. This is an ideal sale for lower- and medium-priced product. The more you buy of an item, or series of items, the less you pay. You might set 6, 12, or even 18 units as the requirement to get a discount.

The Daily Knockdown Sale

This is aimed at close-outs, irregulars and damaged goods. You have an announced policy that each day, or every third day, you reduce the prices on these items displayed in a special area. Each time you knock them down another 10-20 percent. If you can't sell a product at the end of the set period, hold a drawing among customers and give it away.

Two for the Price of One Sale

Purchase one and get the second one free. Only you know on which products your profit structure will allow you to do it. A variation is the "One Cent Sale." The customer pays full price for the first unit, and only one cent for the second one.

Grandparents Day/Mother-In-Law Day, Etc.

Grandparents Day (the first Sunday in September after Labor Day) and Mother-In-Law Day (the fourth Sunday in October) provide sales opportunities. In September, during that week, offer special discounts for grandparents. And in October, around "Mother-In-Law Day," offer discounts to anyone who comes into the store with a son-, or daughter-in-law. Send material about these sales to media. Be certain to send the mother-in-law material to disc jockeys. They will have a lot of fun with it, and you will get good publicity.

Bonus Buys

If local companies award year-end or mid-year bonuses to their employees, run a "Bonus Buys" sale. Anyone who shows a bonus pay stub is entitled to a special discount. Or, if bonuses are so common among your customers, just hold the sale around the time they receive their bonus checks, without requiring the stub.

A second type of "Bonus Buys" sale would feature specials which a customer could purchase *only* after buying a specific product at regular price.

Dog Days of August Sale

An ideal sale for mid-August when people are away on vacation. Hold it and promote it, aiming to introduce new customers to your store and product line. Invite them to drop in for a cool glass of iced tea, and see the "cool specials" you are serving up during these dog days of August.

Discover France Sale

The name of the country can be changed; even a state's name can be substituted. The idea is to hold a sale which focuses in on all of your products from that particular country or state. You really do not even need to have a large selection of products from the area being promoted. You can use the sale products as a means of building business during the promotion. (See Chapter 6.)

Trade-In Your Old Products

This is an effective promotion with higher-priced items, and has been very successful in the major appliance area. What you do is offer individuals the opportunity to get a trade-in allowance for their old product when they purchase a new one. You do not run any sales during this period, and the only savings the customer gets is the trade-in allowance. This is particularly appealing to the person whose appliance or other product is "on its last legs."

The "Next Season" Sale

When a customer purchases a product in the fall at full price, he or she gets a discount coupon good toward a winter purchase. Run this sale each season, offering discounts for shopping the next season.

Marathon Sale

Once a year you might run this type of sale that keeps the store open for a 48-72 hour period. It conveys that you are anxious to sell as much product as possible, and consumer perception will be that prices are good.

Sales, Sales, And More Sales

The types of sales you can conduct are almost endless. In addition to the more than 100 sales themes in this chapter and Chapter 5, there are countless others you can develop by using your imagination. Here is a list of what some of those sales might be called. All you have to do is structure a sale to the name:

- Price Crusher
- Hot Prices—Hot Values
- Carnival Of Savings
- Mid-Summer Madness
- Clear The Shelves Sale
- XX Percent-Off Sale
- Our Prices Make You Smile
- One-Day Sale
- Sell-A-Thon
- Everything Out Of The Store
- Price Busters
- Sale Of Sales
- January Jamboree
- March Markdown
- May Madness
- July Jumbo Bargains
- September Super Savings
- November Nostalgia Sale

- December Dollar Days
- Price Break
- Dollar And Sense Sale
- Vacation Sale
- The American Dream Sale
- Best Buys In Town
- Rock Bottom Savings
- (Season) Sellout
- Three-Day Sale
- It All Gotta Go Sale
- Shopper Stoppers
- Warehouse Sale
- Volumes Of Value Sale
- February Fantasy Sale
- April Action Sale
- June Jubilee
- August Accessory Sale
- October Out-Of-The-World Sale

PROMOTING THE VALUE OF YOUR SALES PROGRAM

If you have an aggressive year-round sales program with significant savings for your customers, there are several novel ways to promote it.

- Compute the amount of money customers can collectively save during the year as a result of your sales. Then get that amount in money or gold and display it for a day in your window or in-store. Have armed guards all over the place. Contact the media to cover the event. It will draw people and you will get very good publicity exposure. Most important, you will be getting across your point about the huge savings customers realize by shopping at your store.

- Display a huge bankbook listing each of the year's sales, and next to each the amount of money customers collectively saved. On the bottom line, run the total. This can be used throughout the year, each time highlighting the savings of that particular sale. Again, the purpose is to focus on the value your customers receive by shopping at your store.

- Business page editors may be interested in a story on the value of shopping during sales periods. This could also be a good subject to discuss on talk shows, using your collective figures as the example.

CUSTOMER PROMOTION CALENDAR

If you can plan your promotions well in advance, it would be advantageous to provide your customers with some type of sale calendar.

It could be a full 12-month calendar, with sale days imprinted on the appropriate dates. Or, if you do not plan that far in advance, you might issue a quarterly calendar.

Another way is to provide customers each quarter with a sheet of self-sticking circles, each imprinted with another sales event. They can then place them on their own calendars.

RESOURCES

Resources for the promotional and support materials to conduct these sales can be found in Chapters Four, Five, Six and Eight.

CHAPTER 8

Contests That Will Attract Traffic to Your Store

Just about everyone loves a contest. They enjoy participating and, of course, the anticipation of winning.

A carefully structured contest, offering meaningful prizes, will not only create excitement among existing customers but will also build additional store traffic. Even people who ordinarily do not enter contests will participate if the prizes are perceived to be valuable, or something they want.

Before conducting a contest, be certain to consult with your attorney since there are various rules and regulations governing them.

There are several types of contests retailers might consider:

- A sweepstakes. No skills are required. A person just enters his or her name and a drawing is held to pick the winner(s).

- Games of chance. Again, no skills are required. A person spins a wheel, scratches off a game card, or picks a capsule from a drum.

- A skills contest. The customer does something to win. It may require guessing something, or a special talent.

EVERYTHING YOU NEED TO KNOW ABOUT RUNNING A SWEEPSTAKES

Sweepstakes contests can be held in connection with promotions (see Chapter Five), sales (see Chapter Seven), other special events (see Chapter Six), or by themselves. The more expensive the top prizes are, the more interest and entries there will be in the sweepstakes.

To keep costs down, try to get suppliers, other merchants, and companies to provide the prizes, or at least give you a good price on them. In turn, you will have to offer good window and in-store promotional support.

The more you agree to spend to advertise and promote a sweepstakes, the better cooperation you will receive in obtaining prizes. A local merchant, or a travel destination, will only provide expensive gifts if there is going to be good exposure.

Let your imagination take over when naming the sweepstakes. Name it after the promotion or sale ("Trick Or Treater," "Cold Weather," "Summer Ender," etc.). Name it after the grand prize ("Holiday In France," "A Night Out On The Town," "Shopping Spree Madness," "Dress To The Nines," etc.). Name it after anything else ("Lucky Days," "Dreams Come True," "Reach for The Sky," "The Big Win," "A Needle in The Haystack," "Customer Appreciation," etc.).

A sweepstakes can take on several formats: Customers can enter by writing their name, address, and telephone number on an entry form, or slip of paper. They can enter by submitting their business card (use this format if business people and firms make up your customer base.). Also customers can be automatically entered each time they make a purchase. However, remember that a purchase cannot be a condition for entering a sweepstakes.

A modified form of sweepstakes is the daily drawings for prizes you might hold during your holiday and seasonal promotions and special events. The daily drawings would be from among customers who had registered that day at the store. You might then save each day's registration slips for a grand drawing at the end of the promotion.

If any of your suppliers is running a national sweepstakes, you might run a local version. Right next to the national contest information and entry forms, promote your own contest. Have a special form which customers can use to enter. Posters promoting your version might read, "Enter XYZ Company's Automobile Sweepstakes, And Our Local Drawing For Six Months Of Free Gasoline." While your prizes may be more modest than the national sweepstakes prizes, they should relate to them. If the national contest is for a trip, you might offer a set of luggage. If the national grand prize is a house, you might offer maid service for a year. Be sure to touch base with the supplier holding the national sweepstakes before announcing your local tie-in.

For all sweepstakes, require that entries be dropped off at your store. The names and addresses from the entries should be used to develop a mailing list and/or to track where your customers live. This information will help you develop your marketing plans (see Chapters Two and Fifteen).

MAKING GAMES OF CHANCE PAY OFF WITH INCREASED SALES

Games of chance can work effectively in connection with special sales. They can determine how much discount a customer gets on a purchase. They can also work well on customer appreciation days and with other give-away promotions, determining which prizes an individual gets.

There are several ways to run games of chance:

- Rent a carnival or roulette wheel, or one-armed bandit and invite customers to try their luck. What number or combination comes up determines the percentage-off discount. You can have customers try it for each product purchased, or just for the total bill. Make the highest odds numbers or combinations, the highest discount figures (50–75 percent) in order to enhance interest in the promotion.

- Use lottery type scratch-off tickets to determine discounts or prizes. They can be printed to meet your specifications, or you may be able to buy stock cards. See the Resources section at the end of this chapter.

- You might also encourage customers to bring in their losing state lottery tickets for a "second chance" prize. Develop a discount structure based on the lottery serial number printed on each ticket. Perhaps the third digit from the right determines the discount. If you plan to run a "second chance" contest, be certain that you check to see if it must be cleared with your state's Lottery Commission. If you run such a promotion, contact area shops that sell lottery tickets and offer to provide a sign: "Your Losing Tickets Are Worth Money At (name and address of your store)."

- You can also have numbers in capsules or on tickets and let customers pick one from a large container. This is the easiest and least expensive way for a "game of chance" drawing. It also gives you greater control over the amount of the discounts to be offered since you place the numbers in the container.

- You might consider using a "Treasure Chest." A customer is given a key and if it opens the chest, he or she is a winner. The customer then selects one of the envelopes in the Treasure Chest to determine which prize has been won. Another way: if the key opens the Treasure Chest, the person becomes a finalist for a big grand prize. Then have all the finalists come back to get another key with only one fitting the lock. The person getting the lucky key is the big prize winner. If the prize is a very big one, local television might cover the finals in order to capture the reactions of the winner.

- Several one-, five-, and ten-dollar bills can be circulated around the city as "Special Prize Money." Post the winning numbers inside the store so people have to come in to see if they have a winner. Each winning bill should have a value which can be applied toward the purchase of products.

- For the Chinese New Year, serve tea and fortune cookies to your customers. While most of the cookies will have the customary fortune, some should contain the good news that the customer has won a prize. Among the prizes can be merchandise from your store, dinners for two at local Chinese restaurants, and various inexpensive Chinese-made products (fans, chopstick holders, decorative soup-spoons, etc.). Contact some Chinese restaurants in the area to see if they will provide the meals free in return for promotional signage at the store. This contest is an example of how a retailer can get involved in a holiday promotion at relatively little cost. The surest way to get publicity for a sweepstakes or game of chance is to come up with a spectacular *big* prize. Three months rent, or mortgage payments, is one prize which might draw media attention. Another would be having the winner "own" the store for half a day, keeping all profits.

HOW TO USE SKILLS CONTESTS TO DRAW CUSTOMERS

These contests generate a lot of fun and interest because they require a customer to use skills or talent. They range from guessing and costume contests, to poetry writing and photography competitions.

"Guess the Number of . . ."

Guessing the number of items in a bowl or cylinder has challenged Americans of all ages, and has long been a popular retail contest that is easy to conduct. The winner is the person who comes closest to guessing the exact number of items in the bowl.

You can run such a contest from time to time or on a regular monthly basis.

If you run it monthly, consider awarding a grand prize for the year in addition to the prize for each contest. It would go to the customer who comes up with the closest correct guess for the cumulative number of items displayed over the year. Run this cumulative contest during the last quarter of the year. Let everyone know the correct numbers for the first nine months so all they have to do is add in their guess for the last three months. Set mid-December as the closing date for the cumulative contest.

Different items you might consider for your guessing contests include:

- January: Ping pong balls
- February: Chocolate Kisses
- March: M & M's
- April: Jelly beans
- May: Golf balls
- June: Pennies
- July: Peanuts (in their shells)
- August: Dimes
- September: Quarters
- October: Halloween candies
- November: Bubble gum
- December: Candy canes

Initially, you might have the container in your window, inviting passers-by to come into the store to enter the contest. Then, if the space permits, move it inside the store, keeping the sign in the window. If you run this contest throughout the year, you might be able to get a newspaper or television channel to run a picture of the bowl each month. It is the type of light "sign-off" a news show might do. A newspaper might look at it as "It's that time of the month again . . . ." If this is a one-shot contest and you have an oddball item to guess (how many worms in the pail?), media may also cover.

Costumes and Fashions

During the year, you might run a "Costume Day" or "Costume Night" contest, inviting your customers to shop in costume and compete for prizes. You might have awards for "Best," "Most Original," etc. Take instant photographs or videotape everyone so that they don't have to hang around for the preliminary judging. However, have the finalists come back for the grand finale judging. Other "fashion" contests might include "Easter Hat Preview," "Trick Or Treat Chaperon Wear," "Sloppy Wear," etc. These contests are designed to draw media coverage. Because it is such a visual event, television may be very interested, as well as the lifestyle pages of newspapers.

Poetry Contests

These can be fun and attract good media coverage. Invite your customers to write a poem about the store, their favorite sales person, or a particular product ("An Ode To My Jeans," "The Sneakers I Love," etc.). You should establish the theme for the contest so that all poems will be about the same subject. To judge the poetry, arrange a panel to include an English professor or high school English teacher, a disc jockey, a newspaper columnist, a critic from a local television station, and a librarian. Have a read-off of the best ones at the store. Try to get media to cover, and see if a local disc jockey will carry the read-off live.

Groundhog Day Shadow Game

For a week prior to Groundhog Day (February 2), invite customers to guess whether or not the local groundhog will see its shadow. On a tote board in the window, provide a running total of the vote. After the groundhog has made its appearance, conduct a drawing among those who correctly guessed whether or not he saw his shadow. If you do not have a local groundhog, use "Punxsutawney Phil" to determine your contest. His "shadow search" results are always well-publicized on network television news programs and in daily newspapers. Furnish media, especially disc jockeys, with daily updates on the voting. Try to get a newspaper to run a daily tally box near its weather forecast. Also try to get a television weatherman to give daily updates.

Look Alike Contests

"Look Alike" contests will create in-store excitement and probably result in good media exposure. There are two types of contests: one open to all "look alikes" of famous people, the other just for "look alikes" of a specific famous person (Elvis Presley, Jackie Gleason, Lucille Ball, etc.). If you open it up to all famous people, you might have specific categories for judging (television, motion pictures, sports, politics, etc.).

Try to get a local television personality, a disc jockey, newspaper entertainment editor, and a locally elected official as judges. To attract candidates, contact local modeling schools, send material to radio, television, and newspapers, and place small classified ads in appropriate media. One of the look-alikes you should seek would be a double for a popular local radio or television personality. Invite media coverage of the finals.

Halloween Art Contest

When Halloween rolls around, invite your customers' children to participate in an art contest. Have them submit their work and display it in the store, as well as in the windows. Set up a prize structure based on age brackets (Under 6, 6–8, 9–11, etc.).

Pumpkin Decorating Contest

The Halloween season also lends itself to a pumpkin decorating contest. Invite everyone, young and old, to participate. Display the pumpkins at the store, and give prizes to the winners. Have three categories of judging: subteens, teens, and 20-plus.

Cherry Pie Contest

Since cherry pies are so often connected with George Washington, sponsor a cherry pie baking contest around Presidents' Day. After you have picked the winners, serve the pies to your customers.

Calendar Contest

If you have the budget to produce an annual customer calendar, consider illustrating it with art by area youngsters. Sponsor a contest inviting them to submit art on a specific subject (their pet, the street they live on, their teacher, their room, the city, etc.). Pick the 12 best and use each to illustrate a different month. A savings bond prize should be given to each winner. Send press releases to media announcing the contest and encouraging entries. Have a press conference to unveil the winning entries. Try to arrange to have several local artists and art teachers as judges.

Do-It-Yourself Greeting Card Contest

This contest is designed to bring out the talent in your customers. Invite them to design a greeting card for a special holiday promotion. It might be for Valentine's Day, Christmas, Halloween, Thanksgiving—you pick the holiday. Display all the entries in the store, and award prizes to the best ones. Chances are a newspaper may run a picture story on the winning cards. Television might also be interested.

Vacation Picture Contest

In a great "end of the summer" event, invite customers to display their favorite vacation photographs. Establish several judging categories: scenery, on the water, at the beach, the city, etc. Award prizes in each category and set up a special display area for the winners. To judge the contest, get the photo editor from the local daily newspaper, a local professional photographer, and a photography instructor.

Shopping Spree Contest

These are always fun, and usually are covered by media. The most popular version, usually conducted by supermarkets or food manufacturers, gives the winner a fixed amount of time (usually 5–10 minutes) to shop. He or she can keep everything brought to the cash register during that period. This version will work if you have smaller ticket items. If you have higher-priced items, you might cut the time down to 2–3 minutes, or set parameters: only one of each item (tie, shirt, slacks, suit, jacket, etc.).

Another version allocates a budget for the spree. If the winner goes over the amount, he or she has to give double the overage back (i.e., if $100 over a $2000 budget, a $200 return in merchandise). If the winner is under, double that amount is donated to the winner's favorite charity.

To enter the contest, have people write in 25 words or less "Why I Like To Shop At (name of store)." Or you might just have them answer a question in one word: "The first thing I'll take during my shopping spree will be _____." This is a natural for television because it is so visual.

Super Savings Guessing Contest

From time to time when you have a sale, you might want to reinforce the value of that sale through a unique contest. Let each customer estimate the total savings by customers during the sale. The person who comes the closest to the correct amount is the winner.

"Best Tan in Town" Contest

As the name implies, customers compete for the "Best Tan in Town" title in this contest, ideal for mid or late August. While just about any store can sponsor one, it is especially appropriate if you sell bathing suits, sportswear, health foods, cosmetics.

Sand Castle Building Contest

Bring piles of sand to your parking lot and invite customers to compete. The concept is that "since you couldn't get to the beach today, we brought it to you". A great July event, you might also try to run this contest sometime during the winter. The winter version will be a natural for media coverage, especially television.

Snowman/Ice Sculpture Contests

If you have the space, you might hold a snowman contest in front of the store or in the parking lot. You can limit it to children, adults, or even a family competition.

A second winter contest is for the best ice sculptures. This might also work during your "Christmas in August Sale." (See Chapter Seven.) Since it requires certain skills, it might be a "by invitation only" contest. If hotels in the area have ice carvers on their staffs, try to set it up as a competition among them. This will attract media coverage because of their professionalism (and especially in August because it is a cool story for a hot day).

Home Video Contest

Invite your customers to enter your home video contest. Let them submit 3-5 minute tapes. Invite a local television producer to select ten finalists. Show them in-store and let customers pick the three best. You might also run all the submitted tapes over a special weekend "Ourtown Home Video Festival" at the store. Local television channels might be interested in running the winning entries on a news show.

RESOURCES

Games of Chance

- Scratch-It Promotions, 1763 Barnum Avenue, Post Office Box 5318, Bridgeport, CT 06610 (800-966-WINS). Scratch-off cards for lucky numbers.
- Bingo King, 1809 109th Street, Grand Prairie, TX 75050 (800-451-9986). Breakopens for lucky numbers. Instead of scratching off numbers, customers "break open" five windows.
- Duro Sales, Inc., 20 East Industry Court, Deer Park, NY 11729 (516-595-2151). Win and spin wheels.

CHAPTER 9

Using Sports as a Promotional Vehicle

If appropriate and properly selected and conducted, there is probably no more exciting or glamorous vehicle to use in marketing your business than sports.

What makes sports so appealing is both the great public interest and the variety of promotions and sports available. There are men's and women's sports. Professional, college, high school, semi-professional and amateur down to Little League. Team sports like baseball, football, basketball, hockey, soccer, volleyball, lacrosse, and softball. Individual sports like boxing, horse racing, tennis, golf, swimming, hunting, fishing, bowling, ping-pong, ice skating and gymnastics. The list is endless.

However, because of the glamour and personal emotions connected with sports, you *must* be certain that a sports promotion is appropriate for your store and audience, and will be the *most cost effective* way to reach that audience.

Thus, before deciding upon a sports promotion, you should carefully evaluate it and determine whether or not it will bring you the desired results. It is time to ask "The Five Promotional Criteria Questions" found in Chapter Three.

Furthermore, you *must* take into consideration the sports atmosphere in your community. What are the favorite sports and teams of your cus-

tomers and potential customers? Who are their favorite athletes? You may find that a semi-professional or amateur team has a very strong following. Or a retired athlete might be the most respected sports figure in the area.

Most important, make your decisions on what is going to help business, and not on what you personally like!!!

Here are some of the ways you can use sports to promote traffic, sales and recognition for your store.

HAVING SPORTS FIGURES MAKE PERSONAL IN-STORE APPEARANCES

Personal appearances by athletes, coaches, team trainers, and even sportscasters can be a very effective way to attract traffic and increase sales.

However, such personal appearances should be carefully scheduled and programmed so that you can achieve your objectives. What you want to avoid is a mass invasion of people who want to meet the personality, or get an autograph, without any thought of making a purchase. Customers *not* interested in meeting the celebrity should always be able to shop without fighting their way through a mob.

Thus, personal appearances by athletes should be connected with the sale of a specific product, or dollar amount. Only those who make the required purchase should get the chance to meet the athlete and get an autograph.

If you are interested *only* in an adult audience, you should try to schedule the appearance at a time when children are in school or in the evening. It is always a good idea to require that children be accompanied by an adult at such promotions.

Who to Schedule for a Personal Appearance

That's a decision which you have to make yourself. You must determine which person will attract the greatest number of potential customers, and meet the marketing goals of your store. It might be a professional athlete, a long-time retired athlete (ideal for the retailer who is looking to attract an older audience), or even a team trainer.

Here is a list of possibilities:

• Professional athletes from teams in your area.

- Professional athletes from visiting teams in town for a game.
- Professional athletes during their off-season, especially if they live in the area.
- Retired professional athletes, or former college greats.
- Team managers and coaches (professional and college).
- Individual performance athletes (boxers, jockeys, golfers, tennis players, auto racing drivers, etc.).
- Trainers from both professional or college teams (ideal for certain types of retailers including shoe/athletic shoe stores, sporting goods stores, drug and medical supply stores, etc.).
- Team broadcasters.
- Team executives if they have a very high profile in the area.

When a Personal Appearance Fee May Not Be Necessary

In order to get one of these personalities to appear, you will probably have to pay an appearance fee. Sometimes you might be able to pay them in merchandise instead of money. But there are exceptions to fee arrangements:

- When the athlete's appearance is in connection with a book he or she has written.
- When the appearance is in connection with a product he or she endorses. It is important for every retailer to determine what personalities its suppliers have under contract for in-store appearances. Use them whenever possible.
- If there is a connection with an upcoming sports event. Promoters often bring athletes connected with the event into a city on an advance promotion trip. Try to strike a deal by offering promotional windows, in-store promotions or other activities calling attention to the event in exchange for providing the athletes at no cost. The appearance can be during the advance trip, or even during the event itself. These events might include tennis matches, golf tournaments, rodeos, auto races, gymnastics competitions, ice shows, etc.
- If they feel it will help ticket sales, some professional teams might arrange appearances by their players or coaching staff. They may also cooperate if you purchase a very large block of tickets for games or a significant number of season tickets.

- By tying in with charitable organizations. Many have access to professional athletes who will make special appearances on behalf of the charity providing funds are raised. You may be able to arrange this by agreeing to give a percentage of sales that day to the charitable organization.

How to Use the Athlete at Personal Appearances

It is very important to program appearances carefully so that they fulfill your marketing objectives.

Some of the activities athletes can engage in during an appearance include:

- Signing autographs. You might set this up so that a person who makes a minimum purchase receives an autograph on a card. A larger purchase might bring an autographed picture. A still larger purchase may earn a customer an autographed baseball, football, basketball, or hockey puck. Sometimes, the athlete might autograph the product with which he is connected.
- Posing for pictures. You might have a Polaroid™ camera on hand so that customers can have their pictures taken with the athlete. Since this is costly, require the purchase of a specific product or a minimum dollar purchase.
- Conducting a drawing for prizes. If you have sponsored a sweepstakes or drawing for prizes, have the athlete pick the winners.
- Holding a question and answer period, letting the athlete answer customer questions.
- Using the appearance as a fund raiser. Charge a nominal fee for all autographs, donating *all* of the money to a local charity.
- Conducting a clinic in your store if you have the space.
- Using the athlete to model clothing or fashion accessories if those products are sold in the store.
- Involving certain athletes in skills competitions. For example, set up a basketball net outside your store and have a basketball player shoot 10 foul shots. Then invite your customers to try to top his record. If any do, give them a certificate that says, "I outshot (name of player)." The athlete doesn't have to be present after he takes his shots. This "competition" may attract media interest.

Whenever an athlete is to appear at your store, send advance press releases to the sports pages and sports columnists and invite media coverage.

TICKET GIVEAWAYS FOR YOUR CUSTOMERS

A sports promotion that always creates excitement is a ticket giveaway or drawing. There are several different types. To enter a drawing, a person has to visit the store and register. (Note: The law usually requires that a purchase is not necessary to enter a sweepstakes.) The drawing may be for a specific game, or a series of games. Or you might purchase season tickets and hold drawings for each game on a regular basis.

Some giveaways are tied to purchases. A ticket is given to each customer who purchases a specific high-priced item, or more than a certain dollar amount. You can usually purchase blocks of tickets at discount so the perceived value of the gift is more than your costs. You may be able to trade off space in your ads if you advertise, or trade off window display space for tickets to the event.

A third type is a major sweepstakes to an important out-of-town event such as a professional team sports event (Super Bowl), the Kentucky Derby, the Indy 500, the Masters, etc. A minor league baseball team in your city might sponsor a trip to see its big league team play. A professional team might sponsor a trip to one of its road games. You should also approach airlines, hotels, and local travel agents to see if they will co-sponsor the prize. They may if you will heavily advertise and promote the sweepstakes and their participation in your ads, fliers, and store windows.

ATTRACTING CUSTOMERS WITH SPORTS EXHIBITS

Interesting sports exhibits will attract traffic to your store, as well as media coverage. For example, prior to an auto race, have one or more of the race cars on display in your parking lot. Or, if it will fit, place one in your window or inside the store. Perhaps even have the driver appear for a few hours. Consider taking Polaroid™ pictures of customers who make a purchase. How about having a thoroughbred, or trotter in your parking area, along with a jockey or trainer who can answer questions? Take Polaroid™ pictures of customers with the horse. Contact a local track to arrange this promotion.

Another idea is to feature a display of newspaper headlines of famous sporting events of the past (national, international, and/or local). Exhibit them in the windows as well as throughout the store. Arrange the exhibit through your local daily newspaper, listing it as co-sponsor.

Consider also a display of sports memorabilia. You might invite customers to display theirs, or find a single collector in the city who would be willing to show his or her collection. Display both in-store and in your windows.

Sports art provides an excellent display opportunity. Offer local artists the chance to display their works at the store. Contact the local art students' league, other art schools, local galleries and even a local museum which might agree to a loan. The local newspaper art critic should be invited to review this exhibit.

You can arrange to display material from local teams. Local professional and college teams might loan you uniforms and equipment, trophies, memorabilia and other material. In turn, they might ask that you make available to your customers their schedules and ticket information. Local team displays will probably generate their greatest interest at the start of the season, and during play-offs and tournaments. You may also want to consider displays for local high school, semiprofessional, and amateur teams if they have strong support or are heading to state tournaments. Same with your Little League teams if they generate wide community interest.

Often you can build a display or exhibit around a single athlete. It might be a local team's current star, or a retired athlete who lives in the area. He or she might loan you trophies, clippings, equipment, and other memorabilia. Hold a preview reception for your best customers, featuring the athlete. Also invite the local newspapers and radio and television stations.

When you hold a display, always send relevant material to the local media so that they might run announcement stories. The media should also be encouraged to cover the exhibits. Try to hold an opening event in connection with each display, inviting local sports personalities as well as your best customers. (See Chapter 13 for more information on how to get publicity.)

CREATE A "SPORTING EVENT" ATMOSPHERE

An upcoming major sporting event provides just about every retailer with the opportunity to recreate the atmosphere of that event in store.

Whether it is the World Series, Super Bowl, Kentucky Derby, or Indy 500, you can bring the event to your customers. Decorate your store with banners and memorabilia from the event as well as newspaper headlines and coverage from past years. You may be able to obtain uniforms of the participating teams, or racing helmets and silks. Have your sales people wearing the caps of the teams and/or other parts of the uniforms.

Use videotape machines to show previous years' competitions. Run an in-store "guess the final score or winner" contest. This will create a lot of excitement within the store and attract customers.

GETTING INVOLVED IN THE ARENA OR STADIUM

There are many ways a retailer can get involved in promotions at sporting events. While most usually involve professional sports, you might also develop them in conjunction with college and amateur teams.

Sponsor a race at a local race track or trotting track. The track will name the race after your store. Let your customers know when it will take place. Perhaps hold a drawing, and invite the winners to be your guests at the track. Also try to arrange discount tickets for your customers, as well as special seating.

You might sponsor a skills competition for fans. Some basketball teams invite one or more fans to take a half-time half-court shot. If the ball goes through the hoop, he or she wins a car or some other expensive prize. If you sponsor the shot, you can purchase an insurance policy to cover the cost of the big prizes. Another basketball competition is to see if a fan can sink ten consecutive free throws. Still another is a season-long dribbling relay competition. At each game, teams representing a cross-section of the community (families, police, firemen, schools, law firms, doctors, women, etc.) compete. The round robin tournament concludes with the finals on the evening of the last home game of the season. Fan skills competition in other sports include throwing a baseball from behind home plate into a basket at second base; also a distance throw, and a team relay race around the bases.

In football, it might involve trying to throw a football into a target, or punting onto one.

Teams usually solicit local firms to underwrite these types of competition, as well as other sponsorship packages. There are several ways in which the participating fans are selected. Sometimes lucky seat numbers are drawn; often a lucky number is selected from the game program. And sometimes fans must register at a locale away from the arena or stadium in advance of the game.

If you underwrite any competition, try to get the team to agree that all sign-ups must take place at your store. It is a good way to build traffic and gain exposure. To sponsor this type of competition, contact the marketing department of the local professional team. You might also want to check local college teams to see if they offer such opportunities.

Consider sponsoring a giveaway day or night for one or more teams if you have the budget. The giveaways—all imprinted with your store's name—can range from T-shirts, hats or bats, to travel bags, umbrellas and sunglasses. Since they also have the team's logo, most giveaways are kept and used, giving your store's name good exposure, too.

Sponsor lucky number prizes in game programs. Some team programs list lucky numbers with drawings held during games for cash prizes and/or merchandise. It will get you exposure among fans at the games. Offer merchandise or gift certificates. Contact the local team(s) for further information. Or you can sponsor the team mascot. Many teams now have costumed mascots who entertain in the stands and/or field and arena floor. Some are sponsored by local merchants. It is an idea you might discuss with your local teams.

A POTPOURRI OF SPORTS ACTIVITIES TO CONSIDER SPONSORING

A One-Million Dollar Hole-In-One Competition

Since it is possible to cover it by insurance, you might sponsor a one-million dollar hole-in-one competition. It is an excellent way to secure publicity for your store in local media as well as to raise money for local charities.

The National Hole-In-One Association, which sells hole-in-one insurance, has developed an exciting shoot-out format. A special green is created on a golf range and for several days, balls are sold for one dollar each to golfers. It is estimated that as much as $30,000–$50,000 can be raised for charity this way. Any golfer who makes a hole-in-one and all hourly "closest-to-the-pin" winners advance to the finals. They then have the opportunity to shoot for the big prize. (See the Resources section at the end of the chapter for information on how to contact the association.)

An In-Store Sports Trivia Contest

Using photographs and other nostalgic items for visual identification, conduct an in-store trivia contest. Shoppers who participate receive an entry form on which to write the answers to the questions posted at each item. Since the items and questions are scattered throughout the store, participants will be exposed to your entire product line. Give merchandise prizes to the winners. Invite local radio and television sportscasters and writers either to compete in a special category or to act as judges. If there is a local all-sports station in the area, perhaps you could ask it to be a cosponsor.

Promote this with teaser questions in your window, ads, and fliers. Also send teaser questions to sports columnists at newspapers, and sportscasters on radio and television. Try to arrange media interviews for the winner. Invite sportscasters to try to stump him or her at a press conference at the store.

Player Awards

It may be possible for your store to sponsor one or more of the various awards given to local team players. This might include "Player of The Week," "Player of The Month," "Rookie of The Year," "Most Valuable Player," "Most Improved Player," etc. These awards can be structured for professional teams as well as for school and amateur teams. Or you may want to sponsor them for an entire league in which amateur (or Little League) players participate.

If you sponsor the award, be certain to name it after your store. Plaques and trophies are the appropriate awards for amateur teams and players and can be presented at games (if they draw big crowds), or at an annual awards banquet. Store merchandise and gift certificates might be given to professionals and presented at games so that your store will receive good exposure before many fans.

You might also sponsor a "Most Popular Player" contest with fans casting their ballots at your store. The contest might be among players on a professional team, or on a college or high school team. It could also be among all of the professional athletes on the city's teams or all of the high school, college, or amateur athletes in the city.

To make arrangements to sponsor player or team awards, contact the local team and/or league. In sponsoring college or high school team or player awards, ask the schools to make certain they do not violate amateur rules.

Teams and Leagues

In almost every city there are opportunities to sponsor amateur teams and get your store's name on their uniforms. These teams include softball, bowling, baseball, basketball, and football, as well as Little League. There may also be opportunities to sponsor an entire league. Sponsorship costs will vary from city to city. It might require paying for uniforms, equipment, field or arena rent, and officiating fees. It might also include travel expenses to tournaments and other incidentals. If you become a sponsor, make certain that you promote it in-store. You might be able to get your customers to become fans, go to the games, and get involved.

If local media cover Little League and other amateur sports leagues, you will get publicity on the sports pages. And, if your team goes all the way to the state tournament, interest will mount and your exposure will increase.

Check with the local amateur leagues to find out how you can become a team or league sponsor.

A Bicycle, Walking or Foot Race

Individual recreational competition is becoming more popular throughout the United States among people of all ages. Most of these events are held locally or regionally and seek sponsors. Sponsorship (part or whole) offers retailers a good opportunity for positive community exposure. These events are already organized and sponsors are asked to donate money, prizes and giveaways for competitors (T-shirts, sun visors, hats, etc.). Giveaways have the event and sponsor's name on them, and are used after the competition so that you get long-term exposure.

Some of the events you might sponsor are bicycle races and Bike-A-Thons, walking races and Walk-A-Thons, road races (from short ones to marathons), triathalons, and three-on-three basketball (team event).

Try to get the organizers to agree that all competitors must pick up or drop off their entry forms at your store. If you are the only sponsor, insist that your store name be part of the event title.

A Player Achievement Contest

Sponsor season-long player achievement contests among the major teams in your city. For example, in baseball: the longest home run hit by a home team player, most consecutive strikeouts by a pitcher, the longest hitting streak. In basketball it could be the most points scored by a home team player in a game, most blocked shots, and assists in a game. The football competition could be based on longest punt or pass, or most yardage gained in a game.

Try to get the local media to keep a running scoreboard on these achievements. Also keep a scoreboard in your store, or window. At the end of the year, present the winners with appropriate prizes: merchandise, gift certificates, trophies or plaques. An alternate prize might be to donate a sum of money to the favorite charity of each of the winning athletes. By donating money instead of awarding prizes, the contest will probably draw greater media attention.

Weekly "Pick the Winners" Contest

You can create excitement by sponsoring a weekly "Pick The Winners" contest. Require that all entries must be picked up and or dropped off at your store. For baseball, contestants might have to pick the local team's cumulative runs and hits for the week. For football, they would have to figure out the scores for 10-15 games, or the cumulative scores for five games. For basketball, contestants would pick cumulative scores for the week for an area team, or for several teams. For hockey, they would select the high scorer of the week and the number of goals. Offer merchandise or gift certificates as prizes.

An alternative would be to co-sponsor the contest with a local newspaper or radio station. In that case, the newspaper might publish the entry form; however, you should insist that entries must be dropped off at your store (unless you are located in a very large city).

A Sale Tied to Sports Scores

You might want to run sales tied to the scores of various local sports teams. Promote sales based on the outcome of specific games. The winning point spread of a basketball game could determine the percentage savings for your sale. Announce the sale before the game, and how the savings will be computed. Be sure also to announce a ceiling, in case of a huge point difference. For baseball, base it on the number of runs or hits the home team scores, also with a ceiling. The point spread may also work for football (with a ceiling). Or you could offer one percent off for each touchdown, and a half-percent off for each field goal.

Ticket Stub Promotion

A good ongoing promotion involves special discounts to fans who present ticket stubs at your store 24-48 hours following the game. There are several offers you can make: the same discount no matter who wins, or the score; a discount if the home team wins; a discount based on the point spread; or a discount if the team scores over a certain number of points, or runs. Your discounts can be across the board on all products, or on a special selection of products. Fast food outlets have run such offers as two hamburgers or franks for the price of one if the team wins. Sometimes there is a consolation prize when it loses: a free soda or French fries. Others offer a free slice of pizza if the basketball team scores above a certain number of points or holds the visiting team under a set number of points.

If you conduct a ticket stub promotion, tie in with the team so that the offer may be printed on the back of the tickets. Try to arrange for the public address announcer to call attention to the offer during games. Both will involve some costs.

"Nights" at Games

Most baseball and basketball teams promote special "nights" at games for which a company can purchase large blocks of tickets at discount. Consider sponsoring such a "night," either underwriting the entire event for your best customers, or passing along the discount to them. "(Name Of Store) Night" can be a fun customer event. Most teams will usually acknowledge groups on the scoreboard, over the public address system and sometimes also on their broadcasts and telecasts. Some teams have special dining or picnic areas for groups that purchase a certain number of tickets.

This "night" will have some perceived value to your customers since you can pass along the discounted ticket price. If you purchase enough tickets, you may also be able to negotiate a free souvenir or game program for your customers. Promote this "night" through fliers at the store and mailings to key customers. You may be able to develop this "night" into an annual event which customers will look forward to attending each year.

A Players' Wives Fashion Show

If you sell fashions or accessories, you might want to hold an annual fashion show using professional athletes' wives as models. To get the most out of the event, tie in with a local charity and run the show as a fund raiser. Charge admission and give *all* proceeds to a local charity. Invite the media to cover the event. Most such shows get good newspaper and television coverage.

Programs from National Sporting Events as Premiums

Often it is possible to purchase programs in bulk from major sporting events such as the Super Bowl, World Series, All-Star Games, etc. Since they are collector's items, you might want to obtain some and offer them as premiums to customers who make certain purchases. Contact the professional league's marketing department.

TAKE ADVANTAGE OF YOUR SUPPLIERS' CONNECTIONS

Check with the manufacturers who supply your merchandise to determine if they are tied in with any athletes, teams or sports promotions.

If they are, examine how you can get your store involved. They may also have former professional athletes working for them and you may be able to arrange their appearance at your store.

If you have ideas for sports promotions, or tie-ins which you would like to conduct, invite your suppliers to participate. Perhaps an idea you present may be adopted by a supplier as part of its marketing support program. Your store may be the place selected to try it out, since it was your suggestion, before rolling it out nationally.

RESOURCES

To arrange the appearance of local professional athletes, or marketing tie-ins with the teams, contact the team's marketing department. It may suggest you contact the athlete himself or his agent. For college cooperation, contact the athletic director at the school.

Non-Local Athletes

- Contact the player at the team address. Team addresses for Major League Baseball, the National Football League, National Basketball Association and the National Hockey League can be found in the *World Almanac*. Or, write to the League offices and they will send you a list.
- American League, 350 Park Avenue, New York, NY 10022
- National League, 350 Park Avenue, New York, NY 10022
- National Football League, 410 Park Avenue, New York, NY 10022
- National Hockey League, 650 Fifth Avenue, New York, NY 10019
- National Basketball Association, 645 Fifth Avenue, New York, NY 10022
- Sports Illustrated Speaker's Bureau, 1271 Avenue of The Americas, New York, NY 10020 (212-522-1427). It can arrange appearances for professional and retired athletes.

Hole-In-One Association

- National Hole-In-One Association, 730 Campbell Center, Dallas, TX 75206 (800-527-6944).

CHAPTER 10

Building Repeat Business and Incremental Sales

Two key elements of the formula for success for any retail establishment are to get its present customers to keep coming back to purchase more goods and products, and to increase the amount of each sales transaction in the store. This is true whether you run a department store, women's clothing store, boutique, supermarket, sporting goods store, stationery store, or even a bakery.

It is true that a combination of factors will normally be responsible for attracting the repeat customers: satisfaction with purchases, quality of merchandise, pricing, treatment by sales help, store ambience, the location and store hours, etc. But specific programs can also be developed in order both to generate and accelerate this repeat business and incremental sales.

INTRODUCING A FREQUENT BUYER'S PROGRAM

Probably one of the most effective techniques for encouraging both the repeat business and incremental sales is through the establishment of a frequent buyer's program.

Airlines may have started it but there is no reason why virtually any retailer cannot set up its own program to reward its frequent customers.

There are a variety of ways to develop and conduct a frequent buyer's program. Only you know your profitability structure and how much you can invest in such a program. To make this determination, factor in all costs including administratı ve, promotional, and awards. Your goal should be to realize initially a profit as good, or nearly as good, as your current profit. Once the program gets off the ground and you have covered your start-up expenses, your profits should increase as your volume increases. A well-promoted frequent buyer's program will not only attract repeat business from present customers but also attract new customers to the store.

However, you should monitor your program very closely on an ongoing basis in order to make certain that it is meeting its objectives and not becoming a drain on your profits. In order to protect yourself in case the program is not meeting its objectives, have your attorney include a disclaimer in the rules given to all participating customers. It should state that the program can be canceled at any time, and without prior notice, by the store. Your rules should also contain an ending date for the promotion. You can always extend that ending date once you see the promotion is working to your satisfaction.

STRUCTURING YOUR FREQUENT BUYER'S PROGRAM

There are several different ways to organize a frequent buyer's program:

Formally Structured

It can be formally structured with a membership card, a personal score sheet to track points earned, printed rules, and redemption information and/or a catalog. Numbered membership cards should be given to customers who register for the program. The registration application should be signed by the customer, and include a release statement (drafted by your attorney) in which the customer indicates he or she understands and agrees to abide by the rules of the program.

Stores which carry higher priced items will probably find it advantageous to run such a formally structured program.

Informally Structured

It can be an informally structured program in which customers are required to save their cash register receipts for redemption purposes. This is an ideal structure for stores which generate a very large number of customers who make relatively small purchases (supermarkets, bakeries, newsstands, greeting card and drug stores, etc.). While a membership card is not necessary, copies of rules and redemption information should be made available. This is a very simple program to conduct since customers are not required to register, and the retailer does not have to track any points. The proofs-of-sale are the register receipts which remain with the customer. It is even possible for the retailer to set up the redemption process through an outside fulfillment firm. That way it is not directly involved at all, other than by promoting it as its frequent buyer's program.

Specific Product Program

A third type of program is aimed at promoting repeat business by targeting the sale of one or more specific products: if you purchase a half-dozen pairs of shoes over a set period of time, you get a seventh pair free; buy 11 quarts of milk in one month and get the 12th free; after purchasing ten shirts, get the 11th free.

Each customer is given a special card when making his or her first purchase of the item. Subsequent purchases are recorded on the card and when the required number has been made, a customer turns it in for his or her free product. (Stores may also require that sales slips be shown when turning in the card.) This "special product recognition" program is ideal for specialty shops (shoe stores, dry cleaners, shoe repair stores, haberdashers), as well as for retailers who want to run a program requiring little administration or who are interested in creating additional sales in one or more specific product areas.

IMPORTANT GUIDELINES TO FOLLOW IN SETTING UP YOUR PROGRAM

Never lose sight of the objectives of your frequent buyer's program: to develop repeat business and incremental sales. You want customers to come into the store more frequently than they have in the past, and you want each cash register transaction to be higher than before the program started. In order to accomplish these objectives, and gain immediate impact, you may want to consider including several conditions in the rules.

- A specific number of points must be earned, or purchases made, each quarter in order for the membership to remain active.

- All of a customer's points must be redeemed within a certain time frame. In the formal program, it might be within 12 months of being awarded. In the register receipt program, it might be every quarter. In the "free product" program, it might be every six-to-nine months. The purpose of this rule is to motivate your customers to increase the number of purchases they make during a period of time so that they can step up to a higher prize plateau, or not lose points.

- Require that a certain amount of points must be accumulated before the customer's first redemption (though the customer will be able to redeem all of the earned points at the end of the program). This may encourage some customers to expedite making additional purchases so that they can reach the necessary redemption plateau. You can also control redemptions by initially offering merchandise awards which require high numbers of points. You can then add lower point merchandise at the end of the program.

- Make certain that your attorney approves all elements of your frequent buyer's program, including the rules, its structure, and printed materials.

Awarding Points

An effective way to set up a program is to award one point for every dollar spent. This "point per dollar" system can be used for either the formal or the register receipts programs. In the formal program, when a sale is made, the points should be entered on the frequent buyer's score sheet (as well as into your computer if you have set it up that way). Each score sheet entry should be signed by a store employee, and certified with a special stamp in order to prevent the false allocation of points.

It is to the store's advantage, for several reasons, to have the scoring system computerized. You can exert better budget control since you can quickly determine the number of customers who are active in the program, and the number of outstanding redeemable points. You have the ability to identify customers who have not visited the store recently. In those cases, you might drop them a note letting them know how many additional points they need in order to reach a higher plateau. There is also an opportunity to send a monthly statement to customers informing them of their up-to-date point total, along with information about bonus points for the coming months, special sales and promotions, and other news about the store.

Since the cash register tapes serve as the only official documents in that frequent buyer's program, it is important that the store's name, and date of sale be imprinted on all register receipts issued. The tapes should be totaled when they are redeemed.

Purchases made in the "special product recognition program" should be recorded on the score card given to each customer at the time of the first purchase. Each subsequent product purchase should be entered and certified with an official stamp (have a unique rubber stamp made), as well as by a salesperson's signature. After the customer has made the required number of purchases for the free product, the card is turned in.

Bonus Points

In order to motivate additional store visits and purchases, consider offering bonus points from time to time. They might be awarded to encourage members to purchase certain slow-moving products, during certain special promotions, or at the introduction of a new product line. Contact suppliers and try to set up these special promotions for your frequent buyer's program members. Ask the manufacturer to absorb the cost.

Bonus points can also be awarded immediately to a "sponsoring" member who brings in a new member or after a new member reaches a certain plateau. Also, a combination of both: award some points to the "sponsor" at the time of the first purchase, and additional points after the new member reaches a certain plateau.

During very slow periods (when most people are away on vacation, or during a very cold winter when people are staying home, etc.), bonus points can provide a needed incentive.

In the cash register receipt program, program your machine so that every 50th or 60th tape has a "lucky star" printed on it, entitling the holder to a set number of bonus points. When issuing bonus points for product purchases, use a special stamp on the register receipts.

Since every point that you award costs money when it is redeemed, be certain that when you offer bonus points the additional business generated will more than make up the costs. It is not necessary to offer double or triple bonus points (unless you have a supplier picking up the costs). Instead, offer a 25 or 50 percent bonus.

The Awards

The award structure should be based on your profit margins, promotional budget, and the other factors discussed earlier in this chapter. There can be a great deal of flexibility on what you offer as awards, and how you handle the redemption of the points for prizes.

After a customer reaches a certain point level (for example 1000 points), he or she receives a percentage discount on all purchases during the next six months or year. At the next plateau (perhaps 1500 points), the percentage discount or even the time frame increases. The only award in this program is discounts on all future purchases. The redemption procedure is simple to handle at the store level. You can also place point values on some or all of your products. Customers select their awards from among this merchandise. This can be very cost efficient to you since you compute the redemption value on the retail price of a product for which you paid wholesale. A possible negative is that you may be taking a sale away from the store since the customer might have purchased it anyway. This redemption technique is also simple to handle.

Let the frequent buyer select an award from a fulfillment house catalog. Your store would issue certificates to customers confirming the number of points. Customers would send the certificates, along with their orders, directly to the fulfillment house, which would then bill the store.

Another way to offer awards is to contact resort hotels within 200 miles of your city that are trying to attract guests from the same economic bracket as your customers. They may be willing to offer heavily discounted rooms, or even free rooms for your program, especially if you agree to promote both the program and the hotel through media advertising and direct mail. You could then position your frequent buyer's program as a "vacation program," offering the hotel stay each time a member reaches a certain plateau. By signing up a number of resorts in the area, you can make your program even more appealing to your customers. Redemption would be done at the store, with a certificate given to the frequent buyer, who would have to make his or her own arrangements with the resort. In setting up such a program, be certain your attorney draws up a formal agreement with the resort(s) spelling out exactly what each member will get free-of-charge, and make sure that each member understands what the stay includes.

It is also possible to set up similar travel arrangements with resorts in other sections of the nation. However, there have been some problems in certain areas of the country with fulfillment of the promised program. Your attorney should check out these promotional offers with the appropriate Better Business Bureau and the state attorney general.

Special events (the circus, ice shows, rodeo, theatrical productions, etc.), as well as sports teams, usually offer discount tickets to groups. Often the more you buy, the greater the discount. Tickets to these events might serve as awards for your frequent buyer's program. You could purchase them at the special group rate and redeem them for earned points based on the box office price. Discuss this program with the box office managers so that they will give you the flexibility of returning any tickets which are not claimed by your customers. These ticket awards would work well for cash register receipt programs.

Savings bonds can also be effective frequent buyer awards since their value is usually perceived to be the redemption price, while the cost to the store is actually half. Award winners would have to fill out the bond application form and the store would have to arrange for the bond to be issued through a local bank.

You may also let frequent buyers redeem their points for store gift certificates, or for certificates which can be used at local restaurants. The restaurants should give you a good discount on the certificates (half price) in return for the promotional exposure, as well as the new customers who may be introduced to them through the program. This, too, is an ideal award to use in the cash register tape program.

Setting Up a Program in Conjunction with Other Stores

A frequent buyer's program can also be organized in conjunction with other stores in the area (mall, neighborhood, or city), enabling customers to accumulate points whenever they make purchases at any of the participating stores.

Ideally, the program works best among non-competing stores that are trying to attract the same type of customers (see Chapter Eleven regarding cross-promoting). An example of such a combination of shops appealing to an upscale clientele would include a high-end jeweler, a furrier, an expensive hair salon, an expensive shoe store, a gourmet food store, a florist, a high-end boutique, and a four-star restaurant. This is an excellent technique through which to build both new and repeat business among a target group of customers

A formal type membership card program is probably the most effective way to conduct this multi-store promotion. However, it could also be set up similar to the "special product recognition program," requiring that a purchase be made at each participating store in order to redeem the card for an award. This latter method will work as a "sampler" but there is no real incentive for the customer to return to any of the stores for repeat purchases.

In establishing a joint program, it is important to cost it out carefully so that each store pays its fair share based on the business generated. Careful records must be kept in order to determine how many points have been earned from each store so that the redemption costs per point can be charged back to the individual stores. It will probably be necessary to have an impartial accountant administer this program, and/or conduct an audit for all of the participating stores.

Promoting Your Frequent Buyer's Program

For a frequent buyer's program to be successful, it must be publicized among your customers and potential customers as well. You should promote enrollment and the program's value to customers, as well as incentives to make more purchases in order to collect more points.

There are many ways to accomplish this:

- Media advertising. Its themes might include: "Customers Save Money And Earn Merchandise Through (Store's Name) Frequent Buyer's Program," "Frequent Buyers Earn Merchandise And Gifts At (Store's Name)," etc.
- Direct mail to current and potential customers.
- In-store and window signage.
- Allow charitable/non-profit organizations to encourage their members and supporters to donate their earned points to them so that they can be redeemed for products needed to support their activities. Each charity will undoubtedly promote your frequent buyer's program among its members and supporters, resulting in additional business for you. To make this an even more attractive promotion for charitable and non-profit organizations, use a special fulfillment catalog offering business-oriented products (office supplies, etc.). Local media should be notified if you are permitting customers to donate their points to charitable groups. Arrange for a picture of a prominent com-

munity citizen who is involved with one of the cooperating charities and the director of the organization when he or she obtains a frequent buyer's program card and pledges x-number of points. Another media opportunity is when the organization redeems its points for products.

- Monthly mailing of point statement to each member.
- Promotional incentive program among members: award a special prize (merchandise or bonus points) to the member who records the most points each month. Also a prize for the most points recorded in a year. If you can afford it, or arrange to have it donated, offer a trip to a popular resort area. Another special prize should be awarded to the first customer who reaches a certain plateau (perhaps 1000 points). It should be an amount within reach of a considerable number of customers so that many of them might be motivated by the promotion to expedite purchases or go on a shopping spree. Once the initial plateau is reached, rerun the promotion at a second plateau (perhaps 2000 points). Promote your incentive programs through your monthly point statements, circulars distributed in the store, and in-store signage.
- If you accept bank credit cards, try to arrange for publicity about the program in the local bank's bill stuffer. In conjunction with the bank, you may want to offer cardholders bonus points if they sign up for the frequent buyer's program and use the card for their first purchase. You may be able to get the bank to pay for the bonus points.

Hitchhiking on Someone Else's Frequent Buyer's Program

Even if you do not have your own frequent buyer's program, it is possible to hitchhike on an already existing program, and at no cost to you!

Several credit card companies award points to their cardholders for every purchase they make. The points can then be redeemed for all types of gifts.

If the credit cards you accept are among those offering such a program, you should take advantage of it and promote the fact that customers making their purchases with the card earn valuable points. For example, American Express cardholders can earn points which are applied to their frequent flier programs. Your in-store signage can read, "Make Your Purchase With The American Express Card And Earn Frequent Flier Miles."

It is one way of capitalizing on an existing program without any investment on your part.

OTHER METHODS FOR BUILDING REPEAT BUSINESS AND INCREMENTAL SALES

There are many other techniques which can be used to develop repeat business and incremental sales. All of the items listed within this section can be employed either as part of a store's frequent buyer's program, or on an individual basis.

Customer Communications

It is important to maintain good communications with your most frequent customers, letting them know you are thinking of them.

Send birthday and/or anniversary cards. Obtain these dates when the customer enrolls in your formal frequent buyer's program, signs up for your mailing list, or applies for a store credit card. In addition to the store's name, the card should also include the signature of the owner and/or the sales person who usually takes care of the customer. Futhermore, invite frequent customers to visit the store for a special gift during birthday week. If you have accurate records on each frequent buyer, you can base the gift on the amount of purchases made over the past year. If only a moderate customer, give the person a gift of modest value; if it is someone who spends several thousand dollars a year, give a much more expensive gift. The invitation to visit the store should be sent along with the birthday card.

After a customer makes a significantly large purchase, send him or her a personal handwritten thank-you note.

Each December send your frequent customers a letter, thanking them for their patronage, and wishing them and their families holiday greetings. In addition to the letter coming from the store owner, the sales person who takes care of the customer can send an appropriate holiday card.

Institute a monthly newsletter. It can include the usual information about store events, coming sales, and promotions, but it can also include news about customers (new children, grandchildren, milestone anniversaries, job promotions, special awards and honors, unusual vacation trips). Each issue might also contain a short item about one of the sales people (biographical sketch, hobbies, etc.). The purpose of the newsletter should be to develop a closer relationship between the customers and the store. It can be mailed to customers, or distributed at the store.

Special Customer Services

Additional recognition can be given to your better customers by providing special services for them. It is another way of saying "thank you for your patronage." At the same time, you are making it easier for them to shop at your store.

Should the store's ratio of salespeople to customers permit it, assign a specific personal salesperson to each one of your frequent customers. This will probably make your customer very happy since he and she will perceive this to be VIP treatment. The salesperson should, from time to time, drop a note to the customer about a coming sale, a product in which he or she might be interested, a special promotion, etc. Each salesperson should get to know the preferences of his or her VIP customers in order to expedite their visits to the store. Appointments can also be set up with the customer, assuring faster and more personal service.

Hold special frequent customer days or nights, running promotions, sales previews and other events exclusively for them. The functions should be held at a time when the store is not open to the general public. Serve wine and cheese or other refreshments. Special events can include the preview of a new line, product demonstrations, the introduction of a spectacular new product, fashion shows, a reception for a noted designer or author, or even a "thank you" reception for the frequent customers.

Develop special offers for your frequent customers: a few additional percentage points off on sales merchandise, a coupon book which provides for a special discount on a different product or product category each month, discounts for shopping on special days or hours, free alterations, free delivery, etc.

Establish an exclusive telephone number for frequent customers to call to learn about the latest sales, newly arrived merchandise, special offers and promotions and other news about the store. Change the taped message at least once a week.

If space is available in the store, set up a frequent customer lounge. Furnish a telephone so that customers may make free local calls; provide lockers so that they may check their bags while shopping in the area; serve coffee or other light refreshments; have lounge chairs and a television set.

Try to arrange discounts for your frequent customers at non-competitive shops in the area, local restaurants, and other establishments that might want to do business with them.

DRAWINGS FOR GIFTS AND OTHER CUSTOMER RECOGNITION

Another form of recognition, and a means of encouraging continued support from your frequent customers, is through drawings for prizes, and other gestures of appreciation.

Select a "Customer of The Month" through a drawing of names from among all shoppers who visit the store. Let every customer submit one entry each time he or she shops at the store; the more frequent the visits, the better the chances of winning. Your frequent customers should be automatically entered each month in addition to their in-store registrations. Each "Customer of The Month" should receive a gift valued in the $25-$50 range.

Purchase season tickets for local sports teams, theater companies, and other special events and give them away on an individual game/event basis through regular drawings among customers. Automatically enter all your frequent customers in each drawing. (Require other customers to enter at the store.)

Hold a drawing each month for a different product you carry, inviting customers to register each time they are in the store. Automatically enter your frequent customers in all 12 drawings. Not only is this a goodwill gesture, but it also allows you to focus attention on a different product each month that you are trying to promote.

If you sell food, or cooking related products, invite your customers to contribute their favorite original recipes for a cookbook. When completed, give a copy to anyone whose recipe is in the book, as well as to all of your frequent customers. In addition, sell copies of the book in the store, giving all profits to a local charity in the name of the recipe authors.

Share something "philanthropic" with your frequent customers. Perhaps sponsor one or more children in their name through the "Save The Children Federation," or make a contribution in their honor to a local charitable organization. When you present the check, be certain to invite your frequent customers to attend the ceremony. And, of course, notify the media.

You might consider inviting your customers to an annual picnic which would be another way of saying "thank you." At the same time, it would give your sales staff an opportunity to get better acquainted with them.

You might also establish a customer advisory council to meet with you and key employees a few times a year. It not only demonstrates your recognition of the importance of the customer to the store, but will also provide valuable input from the customer standpoint.

DEVELOPING NEW AVENUES FOR REPEAT BUSINESS

By creating attractive new sales "packages," and by also targeting several special audiences, it is possible for a retailer to build significant additional repeat business.

Offer an automatic gift service. Customers provide a list of people to whom they want to send birthday, anniversary, and other gifts during the year. Let them select the gifts at the start of the year, or set it up so that the store will contact them several weeks before each event, at which time they can decide upon the present. Have the customers provide a rough price range and areas of interest of each gift recipient so that you can offer suggestions when you contact them. Provide cards for the customer to sign and send with the gift. The store should handle the gift wrapping and shipping. You should also offer this service during the Christmas gift-giving season to local companies, as well as to individual customers.

Consider starting one or more "product of the month clubs," with a different item sent to members each month. The type of club and products should be based on your product lines. It might be a tie or shirt each month, a blouse or sweater, a special cake every 30 days, a different wine, a three-pack of socks, a plant, etc. Take a long look at the products you sell and try to develop an interesting year-long program. This is an excellent gift-giving program; you may even find people who will want to rotate the monthly products among several different individuals. It is also a program to sell to local business firms, especially around Christmas.

You may want to establish a gift registry so that your customers may list key information about themselves (sizes, favorite colors, patterns, products needed, etc.). Thus, when friends and relatives come into the store to buy gifts for them, they have all the vital information necessary to complete the purchase. A person listed in the registry would have to inform friends and relatives about it. The store might provide "cute" cards for the individual to use: "I May Not Be In 'Who's Who In America' But (Name Of Store) Has My Numbers." Because this is a sensitive matter, it is really up to the individual to tell his or her friends about the listing. During the pre-Christmas season, however, store advertising could suggest that residents might want to check and see if people on their gift list are registered with the store. One of the advertising themes might be "If You're Looking To Buy A Christmas Gift For Your Favorite Person, Check Our Registry. Chances Are We Have Their Numbers."

There are a number of special audiences retailers should seek as regular customers. For one, stores that sell "sized" products might want to set up a service for people who require non-conventional sizes. It can be done several ways: customers register their sizes and the store contacts them when products in their size arrive; setting up a telephone hot line (live or taped) for customers to call for latest information on non-conventional sizes; posting a current list of these sizes somewhere in the store, or mailing such a list on a monthly basis to interested customers. Through this service the store might also try to match customers who wear two-sized articles (different size gloves on each hand, different size shoes). If you offer this service, you can get good publicity exposure in the local media. Contact the lifestyle editors at newspapers, disc jockeys, radio women's show hosts, and television news and magazine programs.

Many city and state laws require equal access for the handicapped and disabled. However, the retailer who goes all out to make them feel welcome will undoubtedly earn their loyalty and get their business. The same with customers who may be blind or hard of hearing. Develop a program aimed at these audiences in conjunction with the local professional groups which represent them. Find out what, if any, special assistance the store should provide to help them shop. During the individual meetings with each organization, ask that a meeting be arranged with some of their members, or people they serve, preferably at the store, in order to gain further insight. If there is a city government agency involved with the handicapped, consult it also.

It is very important that you not only be sensitive to the needs of the handicapped, but also sensitive to their feelings. Most do not want special privileges (like special hours or days for shopping) but rather want to be part of the mainstream. The blind, for example, might appreciate receiving sales circulars, a description of the store (including its layout), and other product information in Braille. The hard-of-hearing might appreciate having a salesperson (or even a volunteer) who can sign. This is what you should determine during your meetings. Check to see if these organizations or the appropriate city department can help you implement your program, locate individuals or foundations who might be able to help, or even assist financially with some start-up funds. When you do launch such a program, ask the organizations to publicize it among their members, and the people they serve. Also notify local media.

If you sell merchandise which comes in different colors, especially men's clothing, you may want to consult with local ophthalmologists regarding what special services you might provide for the color blind. This might include tags identifying the color and/or tags which identify colors which will match the tie, shirt, jacket, pants or socks being purchased.

If you offer this service, call it to the attention of the local media, and also prepare a simple, single-page promotional piece on the service and provide copies to local ophthalmologists to give to their color-blind patients.

SAMPLE LETTERS TO SEND TO FREQUENT CUSTOMERS

Several times within this chapter, recommendations were made that personal letters be sent to your frequent customers. Here are samples of letters which might be sent.

WHEN A FREQUENT BUYER HASN'T MADE A PURCHASE IN SOME TIME

Dear Ms. (or Mr.) Jones:

We miss you!

It has been three months since any frequent buyer points have been credited to your personal account, leaving you 210 points short of the second plateau of prizes. (Name some of the prizes at that plateau.)

We hope that this recent inactivity in our program does not reflect any dissatisfaction on your part with our merchandise or service. If it does, please call me immediately at (telephone number) so that we can discuss the matter.

We appreciate the confidence you have shown in us through your past purchases, and hope to see you back at the store in the near future.

Thank you.

Sincerely,

INVITE FREQUENT BUYERS TO VISIT STORE FOR BIRTHDAY GIFT

Dear Ms. (or Mr. Jones):

Happy birthday!

We hope that not only will your birthday be a happy day but also that each of the next 364 days will be equally happy, healthy, and prosperous.

As a token of our appreciation for your loyalty and continued support, we have put aside a little birthday gift for you. Next time you are in the neighborhood, please drop in so that we may give it to you.

We look forward to seeing you and wishing you a happy birthday in person.

Sincerely,

WHEN A CUSTOMER MAKES A SIGNIFICANT PURCHASE

Dear Ms. (or Mr.) Jones:

We hope that you will be very happy with the (name of product) you purchased (day of week). If, for any reason, you have any questions about it, or problems, please contact me immediately. My number is (telephone number).

We want to thank you for shopping at (name of store), and hope you will be in to see us again soon.

Sincerely,

Note: This note should be handwritten

END OF THE YEAR THANK YOU/SEASONS GREETINGS LETTER

Dear Ms. (or Mr.) Jones:

As we approach the Holiday Season, I want to take this opportunity to thank you for your business during the past year. A store can only be successful if it has the support and loyalty of such customers as you.

We pledge that we will continue to offer you quality merchandise at competitive prices, and provide the professional sales services you should expect when shopping.

In closing, we would like to wish you and your loved ones a very wonderful holiday season and a healthy, happy and prosperous New Year.

Sincerely,

EARLY IN THE NEW YEAR

Dear Ms. (or Mr.) Jones:

Our computer, in its new year burst of enthusiasm, just told us something we wanted to pass along to you.

In 19XX, our customers saved over $1.2 million through purchases made during our seasonal sales.

This is almost double the savings from the previous year!

And, we were able to do this without compromising the quality of our products or our services to you.

We hope that our savings to you will grow even larger during the coming year.

Thanks for your continued support.

Sincerely,

RESOURCES

Companies which conduct incentive programs are usually listed in the Yellow Pages under the heading "Incentive Programs."

Two national companies you might contact:

- Marden Kane, Inc., 36 Maples Place, Manhasset, NY 11030 (516-365-3999).

- Maritz Performance Improvement Company, 1400 South Highway Drive, Fenton, MO 63099 (314-827-4000).

A source for specially designed barcoded frequent buyer program membership cards:

- Vanguard ID Systems, 436 Creamery Way, Exton PA 19341 (800-323-7432).

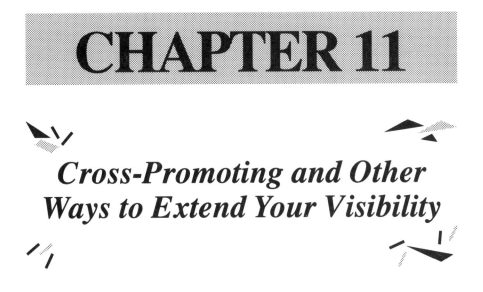

CHAPTER 11

Cross-Promoting and Other Ways to Extend Your Visibility

It is important for you to seek expanded exposure for your product lines and store at other locations throughout the area. A unique, carefully planned program will enable you to extend this visibility in the community and attract new customers.

Here are some of the techniques which will help you achieve this.

CROSS-PROMOTE WITH OTHER STORES

Cross-promoting with non-competing stores can be a very effective technique to build traffic and sales. In choosing partners, select stores which appeal to the same economic segment of the population as your store does. The stores might be close to you (the same block, neighborhood, or shopping mall), or some distance away.

Examples of cross-promoting "partners" might be:

- An expensive dress shop, furrier, jeweler, hair salon, florist, and cosmetics store.
- A men's clothing store, sporting goods store, shoe store, liquor store, and hair stylist.

- A children's clothing store, shoe store, toy store, book store and fast food restaurant.

There should be a signed agreement among the cooperating stores covering all elements of the promotion. During its initial stages, the program should be frequently reviewed so that, if necessary, it can be strengthened, and problems eliminated.

Techniques for Cross-Promoting

Feature products from the other stores in your windows, as well as inside in a special display area. While the other retailers' merchandise should not be sold at your store, it should be used to enhance and/or accessorize your products. For example, the expensive dress shop's mannequin might also have on a stole from the furrier and accessories from the jeweler. Its wig should be set by the hair salon. On a table should be flowers or a plant from the florist, and make-up from the cosmetics shop. A placard with the other stores' names, addresses, and hours of operation should always be included with the product displays.

Give customers an "introduction card," entitling them to a special discount on their first purchase at each of the other stores. In addition, when used at all participating stores, the card should then be entered into a drawing for prizes. From time to time, distribute to customers discount coupons good for a 30-day period at any of the other participating stores. This type of promotion is designed to spur sales during slow periods.

Try a "combination ticket," good for a rebate or special gift *after* purchases have been made at each of the co-promoting stores. All promotions requiring multiple store purchases should have an expiration date.

Cross-promoting stores should also consider holding joint sales, advertising programs, and special promotions (contests, fashion shows, community events, etc.). For special promotions, you might even want to hire a shuttle bus to carry customers between stores.

Another promotional vehicle would be to set up a frequent buyer's club among the participating stores, awarding points for all purchases (see Chapter Ten).

Short-Term Cross-Promotions

There are also short-term cross-promotions you might conduct with just a single partner. A shoe store might offer a discount toward the first pair of heels or soles at a local shoe repair shop. In turn, the shoe repair shop might give its customers a percent-off discount coupon good at the shoe store. A men's clothing store could offer a free pressing or cleaning at a local cleaner when a customer buys a suit. The cleaner could offer its customers a discount coupon for the clothing store. A store might tie in with a local movie theater, giving away tickets to customers for a special preview performance. That same week, the movie theater could give all ticket buyers a discount card for the store.

There are other instances where you can just try to get promotional exposure in other stores. If you do couponing or sell products backed by national promotional weeks or months, other stores may be happy to distribute your materials without asking for anything in return. For example, florists might offer a free rose to each patron of a nearby beauty salon, along with a discount coupon good toward the customer's next purchase of flowers. A restaurant might offer two-meals-for-the-price-of-one coupons at upscale clothing stores in the area. A fast-food outlet might distribute coupons through neighboring stores good for discounts on hot dogs purchased during "National Hot Dog Month." A sporting good store might arrange for a men's clothing store to hold a drawing among its customers for a tennis racket. All of these "one-sided" promotions are aimed at getting you exposure in other stores in the community with "no strings attached."

EXTENDING YOUR VISIBILITY TO OTHER LOCATIONS

The objective for extending your visibility is to get exposure for your products and your store name at locations away from your store.

Fairs, Block Parties, Special Events

Participate in promotions and events which large numbers of potential customers will attend. This includes events in the neighborhood in which your store is located, as well as in other parts of the city. The types of events would include block parties, fairs, charitable bazaars and fundraising functions.

How you participate will depend upon the event, and what you hope to accomplish. You might set up a display and offer some products for sale, and take orders for others. You might run a promotional booth designed to familiarize attendees with your product line, and not have anything for sale. Rather, invite guests to register for your mailing list. You might also offer an inexpensive gift imprinted with the store name (ball-point pen, key ring, etc.). Or hold an hourly drawing for prizes among those who registered for your mailing list. In addition to a product display, have an ongoing "fun" skills contest. Set up a one-hole putting green, a basketball net, or a ring toss game. Make it easy for people to win a small gift (ball-point pen, key ring, etc.) and qualify for the finals sweepstakes. Hold the drawing for prizes at your store, inviting all finalists to attend.

Product Shows Open to the Public

In many cities, there are a variety of special consumer product-oriented shows held each year. They include home, kitchen and bath, auto, art, sportsmen, ski and antiques shows. If your products fit into any of the shows' categories, you might consider exhibiting and selling your products.

Before committing your store's participation, obtain as much information as possible:

- What were attendance figures for the past three years?
- What are the demographics of those who attended those shows?
- Are the ticket prices too high for your target audience?
- Will the show's promoters offer discount tickets for you to pass along to your customers? Will they offer such discount tickets through other sources?
- How much money will be spent promoting the event, and how will it be spent? Where will advertising appear?
- What other events are scheduled for that same period in your city?
- Will participation at the show disrupt the normal conduct of business at your store?
- Are products usually sold, or is it basically a show in which products are displayed and leads developed?

The answers to these questions should provide you with enough data to make a decision on whether you should participate in the show.

If you do not take exhibit space, you may still be able to participate in the show. Contact the various manufacturers whose products you carry and see if they plan to exhibit. If they will, arrange to have sales people from your store at their booth to help visitors. Contact other exhibitors and offer to loan them any of your products which might help complete their displays. For example, if you sell kitchenware, an appliance store may want to use your pots on the ranges they are displaying. Loan the products if you will get credit on a placard at the booth. Also get permission to have your literature on display.

Model Homes

If you have the appropriate products, consider conducting an active program of furnishing the model homes of major builders in your area. Appropriate products will include furniture and furnishings, decorative accessories, appliances, china and silverware, and anything else found in the home. Make a deal with builders to sell them, at cost, the products for the home. In turn, insist that they display a placard crediting your store, along with its address. Also try to negotiate credit mentions in their real estate ads and brochures. If you have product literature, ask that they permit you to have some on display. Request that they notify you when they sell any homes in the development. You should then send a letter of congratulations to the new homeowner. Inform him or her of your role in the model home, and offer the services of your store. You might also issue an invitation to come by for a small gift.

In return, offer the builders some in-store recognition. You might promote products being shown at the model homes with tags saying, "Featured At (the name of the development)."

The model homes program is important. Many people who are not even in the market for a house will visit them in order to get decorating ideas. Others who purchase a house in a development often try to duplicate the decorating ideas they saw in the model home.

Empty Store Windows

An excellent way to extend visibility is to get property owners to permit you to display your products in vacant store windows. An attractive window display in an otherwise empty store will probably make the location even more appealing to a potential lessee. So there is something in it for the landlord, too.

When you see a suitable vacant store, offer the owner a nominal fee for permission to place a display in the window. Explain how this attractive display will enhance the location, and probably expedite the rental of the store. Arrange to occupy the window until the store is rented. Obviously you would select stores in areas from where you want to attract new customers. But you should also select some locations near your store. This would enable you to gain additional exposure for your merchandise among people already in your immediate shopping area. All window displays should include a placard with the address of the store and directions how to reach it from that location. Perhaps offer a free gift (or discount) to customers mentioning they saw the window.

Reaching Out for Tourists and Business Visitors

If you are located near major hotels and/or sell products with tourist and business visitor appeal, consider reaching out to this audience. Try promoting your store and product line in the glass display cases found in many hotel lobbies. They are very effective since they are usually strategically located in areas of the lobby frequented by guests. Carefully plan your display so that a guest can quickly determine your product line. The store address, telephone number, and travel directions from the hotel to the store should be on a placard in the display.

If local hotels provide visitors with room directories of local shops, try to have information about your store included. Also, if hotels permit, try to arrange the placement of table tent cards in each guest room. This probably will involve some costs.

Provide the front desk and/or concierge with printed brochures about your store and product line. If your city attracts large numbers of foreign tourists, consider printing these brochures in the principal languages of the visitors. Moreover, you should have sales help who speak these languages. Visit the concierges on a regular basis to fill them in on your product line. Invite them to visit the store to familiarize themselves with what you can offer visitors. Also consider holding a special reception at the store for all the concierges in the city. They, and the front desks, are in a position to refer business to your store. So, cultivate them!

Join your local Convention and Visitors' Bureau. Work closely with it and take advantage of its various visitor promotion programs. You will find that membership will usually give you an entree to the key hospitality and convention planners in the area.

Consider advertising in the various tourist publications which are distributed to vistors. Also, if one airline brings most of the visitors to your city, you may want to advertise in its in-flight publication. You should also contact the airline and see if it would be possible to develop an in-flight promotion with it. Perhaps on each incoming flight you would give away a $25 gift certificate to someone sitting in a "lucky" seat. Or perhaps special discount coupons to all arriving passengers. An effective promotional message to visitors would be an invitation to visit the store for a free souvenir of their trip. Many will drop by for the souvenir and end up making a purchase.

Airport displays can also be used to promote your store and products. However, incoming passengers usually leave and airport as quickly as possible and may not pay enough attention to your display to justify its cost.

If local sightseeing company buses carry advertising, consider purchasing space on them. If the sightseeing companies recommend shops to visitors, see if your store can be added to the list. Perhaps you can offer a small souvenir, or a discount to anyone visiting the store and showing a receipt from the sightseeing company.

Trade Shows and Conventions

Trade shows and conventions bring visitors to town. With the right product line, you might be able to generate business from this audience. Pick the shows and conventions very carefully, and make certain that your products will appeal to the attendees and/or their spouses. If you locate an appropriate event, take a booth at the convention to sell suitable products, and promote visits to your store to see the full line. Advertise in the convention/trade show program, or daily publication. Offer a discount to those who bring the ad to your store. Provide shuttle buses between the convention hall and the store.

Many conventions provide free shuttle bus service between the various hotels and the convention center. Consider advertising on these buses.

Develop a program for spouses. It might be a fashion show at the convention hall or at a nearby hotel. Try a wine tasting/shopping trip to your store, or a visit to a museum with a stop back at the store for refreshments. Since spouse programs are expensive, be certain that they will generate sales. Focus on sponsoring programs for upscale professional groups (state medical society convention, bar association meeting, Young President's Association, etc.).

Free Shuttle Bus

To attract customers from different sections of the city, consider sponsoring a free shuttle bus. It could run along a regular route, picking up customers at specified stops. Or, each day it could run between a different area of the city and your store. Monday could be "Near East Side Day," Tuesday "Uptown Day," Thursday "West Yourtown Day," etc. If there is a nearby office or industrial park, you might run a "lunch hour" shuttle. Employees could work in some shopping during lunch.

Be certain that any shuttle bus you use has a distinct look. It should carry your store name on the outside, with perhaps some advertising posters. Inside, advertise your specials and other products from your line. Some stores use British double-decker buses. Others paint their buses a bright color, or the store's colors. Still others rent or purchase buses which resemble cable or trolley cars.

Since a bus represents a large investment, make certain it will pay off in additional customers and sales. Perhaps you might want to try using a rented shuttle bus for special promotions and sales to see how it works out. Or you might want to use the shuttle to spur weekend business. If you decide to use a bus, examine carefully the options of renting vs. leasing or owning. You may also want to consider running such a shuttle bus in conjunction with some neighboring stores. While the promotional value of having an exclusive bus will decrease, you will save quite a bit of money.

Major Credit Card Promotions

If you accept major credit cards, speak to the bank or credit card company about tying in with their promotions. Ask how you might get publicity in the newsletter/bill stuffers they send to their customers each month. You might participate in any discount coupon mailings they may be planning. Offer store gift certificates as part of any point accumulation promotions they sponsor. Promote within the store any customer sweepstakes they may conduct.

If any of your suppliers are participating in a national or regional credit card promotion, participate as a local outlet. Display promotional material, and ask the supplier for input on what it would like you to do.

Try to arrange special shopping nights for specific card holders. Those invited receive VIP treatment, are served refreshments, and make payments with their card.

Visibility through Supplier and Vendor Advertising

Another method for extending your visibility is by endorsing your suppliers and vendors in any testimonial advertising they might run locally.

This might include your interior designer, lighting specialist, florist, accountant, bank, employment agency, insurance agent, etc.

While such advertising will not carry a hard product sell, it will give your store name additional visibility at no cost to you.

Before cooperating with a supplier or vendor, insist upon the following:

- Approval of the final copy of any endorsements or other statements attributed to you, as well as anything written about the store.

- Approval of all photographs of you and the store which will be used in the advertising.

- Information about others who will appear in the endorsement ad or series of ads. If these other endorsers, in your judgment, lack the prestige your business has earned, you should not cooperate.

Your Logo on Shopping Bags, T-Shirts and Hats

A very effective way to gain ongoing exposure for your store is to have its name prominently displayed on your shopping bags. Customers, especially women, save and reuse these bags. Each time they carry the bag, they are promoting the store's name. The more attractive the bag, the more exposure it is going to get.

T-shirts, hats, and various cloth bags with your logo will also serve as "walking billboards" for your store. By developing a program to get these products into the hands of your customers, you will be getting extended recognition for your store.

Consider offering these products as goodwill gifts to your better customers, as premiums for purchasing certain high-ticket products, or as prizes in contests. Have your sales staff wear them when away from the store. The T-shirts draw a good deal of attention when worn at beaches and parks.

CHAPTER 12

Developing Community Involvement Programs to Create Awareness

By developing an active community outreach program, you will be able to achieve even greater visibility for your store, and greatly enhance its image among your potential customers.

Moreover, participation in community outreach programs can have a very significant impact on your sales, as many of the ideas in this chapter will show you.

How can you get involved in the community?

• By working closely with charitable and non-profit organizations

• Through the sponsorship of events

• By sponsoring awards

• By becoming an active member and participant in the activities of one or more organizations

• *By showing that your store cares*

GETTING INVOLVED IN CHARITABLE AND NON-PROFIT ORGANIZATIONS

One of the more effective ways of participation is through your involvement, and your store's, with charitable and non-profit organizations. Only you are in a position to decide the degree of involvement, and with which organization(s) to become involved. Much will depend upon your marketing program, your budget, the amount of time you and your staff can devote to it, and what you hope to achieve.

Selecting the Organization(s)

As to which organization(s) to work with, there are several types to consider:

- The local affiliates of the national health-related education and research organizations (American Heart Association, American Cancer Society, Multiple Sclerosis, Cerebral Palsy, etc.).
- Local non-profit hospitals and health care facilities.
- Local educational facilities.
- Local cultural facilities.
- Local non-profit social services facilities.
- Local tourism, economic development, business promotion organizations.
- Senior citizens, scouting, and youth organizations.

In selecting the organization(s) with which to get involved, make sure it meets certain criteria:

- It has an excellent reputation in the community.
- It should be nondenominational, unless your clientele is predominantly of one religion or nationality. Or become involved with several organizations which represent the major religions and nationalities in the area.
- It should have an active and aggressive group of volunteers.
- It has a good public relations and promotional support staff or capability.
- It has entree to celebrities.
- It has a good mailing list which, under certain circumstances, it will let you use.

Once you have chosen the organization(s), what are some of the ways in which you can work with it (them)?

Donate Percentage of Receipts

Consider developing a promotion in which one or more charitable organizations receives a contribution based on your profits. It could be a one-day-a-year event, billed as "Give Something Back Day," "We Care Day," or "(Name of charity) Day." Perhaps an afternoon or evening event. A variation would be to run it as a month-long promotion, giving a percentage of all profits to charity. You could donate them to a single charity, or to a group of charitable organizations. Or, you might designate a different charity for each day of the month, with each charity receiving its day's percentage of profits. Have the charity (or charities) do a mailing to its list of contributors and friends, inviting them to shop that day. It's an excellent way to raise money. It is also an effective way to introduce new customers to your store. To encourage them to come back, give each shopper a coupon good for a discount on his or her next visit to your store. If the charitable organization(s) has access to any celebrities, ask if it could arrange an appearance at your store as part of the fundraising promotion. You might set up an autograph table, or have a photographer take pictures of the celebrity with customers. Charge customers a fee, giving the money to the charity.

Provide Products

Providing products to an organization is another way to gain visibility for your store and its product line. You can contribute products for charity auctions, or as door prizes for meetings and events. Among them can be promotional products such as T-shirts, hats, and canvas bags with the store's logo. If you contribute product for a charity auction, feature them in your store window in a special display promoting the auction. It is a way to get some credit for something good you are doing.

People attending fundraising luncheons and dinners are usually given a "goody bag" of small gifts to take away with them. If you have the appropriate product line and budget, and this is an important audience to reach, consider donating gifts for the bags. Or ask your suppliers for any overruns or samples they may want to donate.

If there is a product very much in demand and in back order with the manufacturer, you might save the last one and conduct a "sealed bid" auction among customers. Feature it in your window and invite bids, with the amount above the purchase price donated to a charity.

Fashion Shows and Other Special Events

Offer to produce a fashion show or some other special event appropriate to your product line for a charitable institution, with all proceeds going to the group. Instead of a fashion show, it might be a preview of Christmas toys, an author luncheon, a lecture, a cooking demonstration, a wine or champagne tasting, etc. It could be held at the store, or at some other location. The charitable organization should have the sole responsibility for the invitations and for selling the admission tickets. It should also pay for the rental of the hall if it is held away from the store. If feasible, you might even be able to sell products at the event, though you would probably have to give a percentage of the profits to the charity.

You might also just loan your store to an organization for a fundraising party. Perhaps an ideal time would be to preview your Christmas decorations.

Credit Card Solicitation

If your store has its own credit card, ask local charitable organizations if you could use their mailing lists to solicit new cardholders. Offer to pay a fee to each charity for each person on its list who signs up for the card. You may also offer a bonus to the charity at the end of the first year based on the amount of sales charged to the card by its members. This should offer an incentive to the charitable organizations to encourage use of your card.

The solicitation letters to potential cardholders should identify the organization which provided their names, and should explain how you will be contributing to it. Keep reminding these cardholders in their monthly billing statement about the annual contribution. If the contributions are significant, at the end of the year present a blow-up check of the amount to the organization(s). Local media might run a picture of it. You can also display the blow-up in your window.

Assist Organizations in Recruiting Volunteers

Help one or more charitable groups recruit volunteers. Kick off the recruiting program by announcing that your employees have pledged X-number of volunteer hours during the coming year. This will get media attention. If you advertise, consider running an ad urging local residents to become volunteers, and list the organizations which need them. Included in the ad should be a statement about your store's commitment to reach out and help the community. If your employees are volunteers, mention that also in the ad. You might give the number of volunteer hours they spend each year, and/or their names. It would make a good image-building advertisement for your store. If you cannot devote a full ad to the subject, try to include a paragraph or two soliciting volunteers.

As an incentive to volunteer, offer a one-time discount to all residents who sign up with the organization during a set period. If you have the space, you may want to let the group set up a table in your store to recruit volunteers.

Rewarding Volunteers

Working with one or more organizations, you can salute its volunteers in several ways. Annually sponsor a "Volunteer Appreciation" night at the store. Residents who have volunteered a certain amount of hours during the year would be invited to the party. Offer some door prizes, refreshments, entertainment, and small gifts. While nothing will be on sale, it is a good way to introduce these people to your store. Underwrite the cost of certificates of appreciation to be given to volunteers who fulfill a commitment set by the organization(s). You can also underwrite the cost of a "Volunteer of The Year" award to be given to the individual selected by the organization. Include your store's name in the award title.

An Annual Donation

If your budget permits, consider making an annual cash contribution to a charity in the name of your customers. Send an end-of-the-year letter thanking them for their support and that, in appreciation, you are making a contribution in their name to (name of organization).

Another version would be to thank your customers and ask them to name the organization to which the contribution should be sent. Tally up the responses, and figure the percentage which should be sent to each nominated organization.

Sponsor Scholarships

The establishment of a scholarship program for local high school graduates is another possible community project to undertake. You could make an initial contribution and add to it each year, or invite your customers to donate. You could even ask your suppliers to contribute. You could also earmark the proceeds of one or more shopping days to the program.

The awarding of the scholarships should be administered by the local school system, but you should make the presentation.

Encourage high school students to apply in your advertisements, in-store and window signage, bill stuffers and other promotional materials. You might also distribute circulars at the local high schools for placement on bulletin boards.

Sponsor a Cook-Off

Cook-offs are fun and a good way to raise money for charity. While such promotions are ideal for retailers who sell food products, cooking or barbecuing equipment, any sponsor will get good exposure for its store.

Logistically, a barbecuing competition may be the easiest to conduct. You could hold it in your parking lot or some other appropriate area in the city. The store would underwrite the costs, which would be nominal. Basically it would cover prizes, and promotional expenses.

Tie in with a charitable organization. The competitor entry fees, as well as spectator admission fees, would go to the charity. Get local newspaper food writers and a few restaurant chefs as judges. Following the judging, the spectators get to sample the food. You might even run two competitions at the same time: one for the amateur chefs, the other for the professionals.

For better promotional visibility, supply all participating chefs with hats and aprons with your store name or logo prominently displayed. Work both the store name and the charity into the cookoff name. Provide the winning recipes to the local food writers, and invite media coverage of the event. It is a natural for television.

Sponsor Competitors in Walk-A-Thons, Bike-A-Thons

The way money is raised in charity walk-a-thons and bike-a-thons is through pledges competitors collect. Each person making a pledge promises to donate X-dollars for every mile the competitor completes. Contact the charity and offer to launch the pledge compaign by backing a significant number of competitors. What a "significant number" is will depend upon your area and the number of expected competitors. It might be 50 or 100, or possibly only 25. Give each of the competitors whom you are backing a store T-shirt or hat to wear during the event. Invite all of the competitors you are sponsoring to the store a few days prior to the event for a "send-off" party. Invite the media to cover. The charity will be happy to cooperate since this will help hype the event.

Pledge Donations Based on Sports Feats

Consider pledging X-dollars to a local charity for every home run hit, game won, touchdown scored, etc. by a local team. Keep a running scoreboard in the window, or in the store, on the donations made to date. Try to get the teams to flash on their scoreboards the running total of money donated to date. If you advertise at the stadium or arena, this should not be difficult to arrange. If you do not advertise, ask the charitable organization to try to arrange it. They may have more clout. Look into what it would cost for advertising time on game coverage when these feats occur. When a home run is hit, the announcement might be, "Another (name of team) home run means Joe's Sporting Goods is donating $50 to the Ourtown Boys Club."

Library Books

A joint promotion with your customers to add books to one or more local libraries will create goodwill in the community. There are several ways this promotion can work. Get the library to provide a list of books it needs. Whenever a customer donates a book, your store can match it by donating another book on the list. Or collect contributions for the book fund, and match dollar-for-dollar what your customers contribute. Perhaps you can pledge to give one dollar to a local library book fund on all purchases over a certain amount (perhaps $25). If there are several libraries in the area, let the customer select the one to which the donation should be made.

MAKING A PERSONAL COMMITMENT TO THE COMMUNITY

In addition to your store's commitment to charitable and non-profit organizations, you, personally, should become involved with one or more groups. Active participation will enable you to get your name better known in the community as a civic leader. This will enhance your overall image, and can be a positive factor in attracting customers to your store.

Which organization(s) to support is a decision you have to make on your own. Undoubtedly this decision will be influenced by your personal feelings, beliefs and experiences.

From a business standpoint, you should become involved with at least one organization in which business, community and political leaders are active. This will provide you with the opportunity to develop relationships which may be helpful in the future.

It is also important to become active in organizations which represent the business community in your city and immediate area. This includes chambers of commerce, retailers' associations, block associations and business and tourism promotion groups. These groups not only work toward developing a better community, but most important a *better business community*.

SPONSORING HIGH VISIBILITY COMMUNITY EVENTS

There are all types of events which you might consider sponsoring or even co-sponsoring with other local businesses. While your store will get the major recognition and exposure as the sole sponsor of an event, it can be a very costly investment. Co-sponsorship, even though it is less costly, will still enable you to get good exposure if you aggressively promote your participation in the event.

From a standpoint of logistics, it would be best to sponsor already existing events which are probably well-organized with the mechanics for conducting them already in place.

The Easter Egg Roll

A tradition in most cities, the Easter Egg Roll brings out young children and their families. It is a good target audience for most retailers. The value of sponsorship is getting your name across to the community. Try to work your name into the title of the egg roll and arrange signage at the event (both the starting and finishing lines). Since the egg roll gets good coverage in the media, your name will get good visibility, too. You could just sponsor the prizes, or in addition you might award products not only to the children but also to the winners' parents. You could also sponsor an annual egg hunt, with eggs hidden all over the location. Several of the hidden eggs bearing your store's name would be the winning eggs, with the finders receiving prizes. As part of your sponsorship, require that all entries be dropped off at, or mailed to, your store. This will create additional visibility for your name, and perhaps even some new customers.

Local Band Concerts

Popular in many cities, especially in the summer, outdoor band concerts are usually held in a park, or some other public place. The cost of sponsorship will depend upon whether amateur or professional musicians are playing. If you underwrite the concerts, get the store name in either the name of the series, or the name of the band.

Since band concerts are community events, try to get the local utility companies to promote them in their bill stuffers. Ask the media to list them in "events" columns. And, of course, promote them through your store windows and in-store signage. You might even have the band, or several of its members, playing outside the store to promote the concerts.

An Annual Baby Parade

Some cities have them, others don't. Parents decorate their children's carriages, sometimes build small floats, and dress up the children for the event. It is an ideal event to sponsor if you sell baby or toddler wear, food products, maternity clothing, or any products aimed at young marrieds.

The parade is usually held during the summer months, very often on the boardwalk at seashore cities, in a local park, or in a shopping area. Baby parades usually draw big crowds and, therefore, good media coverage. Prizes are usually given by age division (under six months, six months to a year, one year to 18 months, etc.). Cut-off age should probably be about three years old. Prizes can be for best decorated carriage, most original float, best costume, prettiest smile, etc. The parade might be organized by, or co-sponsored with, a children's hospital, a chamber of commerce, or an area retailers' association. It could be also co-sponsored by a group of noncompeting retailers anxious to reach the baby and toddler markets, as well as their parents.

Senior Citizen Month Event

May is "Senior Citizens Month" and there are many opportunities for retailers to get involved in programs paying tribute to them. Seniors are loyal
to retailers who take an interest. Moreover, their children also often show
their appreciation by patronizing retailers who conduct programs for their
parents.

Consider sponsoring or co-sponsoring a one-day citywide fair during
the month. Hold it at a park, armory, or other location. Ask local high
schools and colleges to provide talent to entertain. Seek out talented seniors, too. Encourage each senior citizen center to display paintings and
other works by talented seniors. You might even have a senior citizen art
show in conjunction with the fair. You can expect good media coverage.

You might also sponsor an awards program, honoring the city's "Senior
Citizen of The Year," as well as the "Outstanding Senior Citizen" at each
center. Let the seniors at each center select among themselves the honoree
for the award which should include the store's name "(Name of store) Senior
Citizen of The Year Award". To add credibility, have the mayor present the
awards at a City Hall ceremony. The mayor's office will arrange press coverage.

A Halloween or Ragamuffin Parade

In cities where annual Halloween or Ragamuffin parades are held, large
crowds of spectators usually turn out to watch and cheer on the marchers.
You might want to consider sponsorship of such a parade, or some type of
participation.

If you are convinced that the exposure you will receive is well worth
the cost, and you have the budget, by all means sponsor the event. If you
do, be certain that your name is part of the parade title (just like Macy's
Thanksgiving Day Parade). Also make sure that banners along the parade
route carry the name.

One alternative to sponsorship is to underwrite the awards for the best
floats, costumes, etc. Or you might want to sponsor one or more floats in
the parade, having your employees, children of customers, or other residents manning it.

An Amateur Play/Theater Group

You might consider underwriting a production by a well-respected local high school, college, or amateur theater company. Your sponsorship might enable the company to drop admission charges for its performances, or enable the company to take its production to hospitals, nursing homes, and other shut-ins. An ideal production to underwrite is one which has been written by a local playwright, an all-time classic, or a popular musical. It could also be a special production in connection with a local festival or celebration.

If you do participate, be certain that you get recognition with signage outside the theater and in the lobby. Also, an ad in the program, on the reverse side of the tickets, and editorial comment in the program should acknowledge your participation. Also request a few reserved seats to each performance. Hold a drawing for those tickets among your customers.

Another way to participate, if you have the appropriate products, is to provide the stage settings, cast costumes, hair stylings, or make-up. You will get credits in the program. In addition, if what you provide for the set or cast is spectacular, some in the audience might be motivated to visit your shop. In order to promote the show and your contributions, you might feature huge photos or the props themselves in your windows.

Museum Exhibit

Museums are always looking for sponsors to help underwrite special exhibitions. Some can be very expensive, while others may be affordable. Contact the local museum and discuss its needs as well as yours. It may be possible to make a match based on what you sell and some exhibitions it would like to stage. This might be appealing to antique dealers, furniture stores, or even general merchandise stores. For the latter, for example, an exhibition of paintings of the Maine coast might be appealing if it sells products from Maine. An exhibition of oils of ships might interest a boat dealer, or sporting goods store. If you underwrite or co-sponsor such an exhibition, be certain to negotiate a special preview showing for your customers. Also arrange for discount tickets for them if there will be an admission charge. Be certain that your store is prominently mentioned in the program, as well as on museum signage and any advertising for the show. If a poster will be issued, try to get the store's name included on it. And, try to get a quantity of the posters to use as door prizes at the store.

SUPPORTING LOCAL CONTESTS AND COMPETITIONS

Marching Band, Cheerleader, and Drill Team Competitions

There are several types of high school, junior college and/or college competitions that might provide good sponsor opportunities. Money will be needed to cover stadium or arena rental, as well as trophies. However, if the stadium or arena can be obtained rent-free, or admission fees will cover the rental, the expenses involved can be minimal.

A marching band competition among area high schools can be a very popular event. It should not only bring out the student bodies, but also parents and alumni. Sponsorship would be ideal for the retailer targeting this age group. It should be organized through contact with the local school board or administration. Profits from the sale of tickets should be split among the participating schools. If there are several colleges, or junior colleges in the area, you might also consider a competition among them.

A high school or college cheerleader competition will also be a popular event to sponsor. You really do not need too much space, and it could be held in a high school gym. This event will attract media coverage.

Schools with ROTC often have drill teams. If there are a few in your area, you might consider sponsoring a competition among them. A gym or an armory is an ideal place to hold this event. If such a competition does not already exist, contact the high school and college ROTC units in the area. Tell them you would be willing to sponsor a drill team competition if they organized it and arranged for the site.

Competition Among Volunteer Fire Departments

If there are volunteer fire departments in your area, and they have an annual competition, you might want to participate. You could, perhaps, sponsor the entire event, or you could underwrite the awards, or one award. Perhaps you could provide merchandise as prizes for any raffles held in connection with the event. At the very least, you could devote a store window to the event, displaying the trophies to be presented as well as photographs from last year's competition.

If such a competition does not already exist, you might contact the various departments and offer to help organize it.

Paper Airplane, Model Boat, Boomerang-Throwing Contests

There are many other competitions which can be fun to hold and sponsor. They will attract spectators, and the media. Most important, they are easy to conduct.

In a paper airplane flying contest, competitors make a simple paper plane and then toss it into the air. The plane which flies the furthest wins the prize. Another form of the contest is to lay out the field with several different targets, each offering a specific prize. The first plane to land in the center of the target wins that prize. This contest might be co-sponsored with a local engineering college, a school of aeronautics or the operators of a local airport.

Model boat contests can take on one of two forms: competitors exhibit the model boats they have made, and they are then judged on their craftsmanship; or the boats race, or sail in a pond or lake. This latter form of competition is more interesting, will draw spectators, and is more appealing to the media. It could be arranged through a local model boat club, with the local city parks department, or even an office or industrial park which has a pond.

Boomerang-throwing contests and demonstrations have been held in many cities. Spectators enjoy watching the competition, and then have fun trying their hand at the Australian sport. It is an ideal sponsor opportunity for a sporting goods store (especially since many sell boomerangs), or a retailer who sells many Australian products. It is a very appealing competition for media to cover, especially television.

The Largest Tomato, Pumpkin, Cucumber

It may be as "old as the hills" but it works! Whenever there is a competition among local gardeners for the largest tomato, pumpkin, cucumber, or other vegetable, there is a lot of interest and entries. This is an ideal contest to sponsor if you sell produce or any type of food, gardening equipment, or seeds. It can be co-sponsored with the local state department of agriculture, or a garden or 4-H club. The competition can be run several times a year: tomato contest in the early summer, the pumpkin contest around Halloween, etc. If you sponsor the event, be certain that you will be able to display the winning vegetable at your store for at least a week.

Another angle might be to agree to donate to a local charity a premium price for each pound the winning vegetable weighs. Perhaps $10 per pound for the pumpkin and $100 a pound for the tomato.

Beauty Pageants and Competitions for Titles

There are usually many different pageants and competitions for titles held in a city. They may range from the local preliminaries of the "Miss America" contest to the "Queen of The Prom" contest at a high school, from "Businessman of The Year" to "Housewife of The Year."

Sponsorship of the local preliminaries for national and international beauty contests usually requires the payment of a franchise fee. However, you might be able to get involved by providing prizes and merchandise. If you sell women's clothing, provide the wardrobe for the local winner. If she gets to the national finals, the exposure for your store will greatly increase. Other merchandise award possibilities include luggage, cosmetics, bathing suits, and shoes. A beauty salon might get involved by setting the hair of the contestants.

Some of the local competitions fall into the category of beauty contests, while others honor accomplishments in business, volunteer work, etc. Sometimes the winners are selected at local pageants, and other times by business or civic organizations. There are opportunities for retailers to sponsor some of the awards. It might mean a cash contribution, providing merchandise to the winners, or providing the trophies or certificates. In some cases, a sponsoring merchant might want to have the winner appear at the store as part of a promotion. In all cases, if you are a sponsor, or are involved in the promotion, you should devote both window and in-store displays and/or signage to your role.

Among the contests to consider are:

"Most Beautiful Baby"

"Grandmother of The Year"

"Grandfather of The Year"

"Career Woman of The Year"

"Housewife of The Year"

"Teen-agers of The Year"

"Businessman of The Year"

"Businesswoman of The Year"

"Secretary of The Year"

"Executive of The Year"

"Student of The Year"

FINDING OTHER CIVIC INVOLVEMENT PROJECTS TO SUPPORT

There are a multitude of other ways to get involved in civic activities.

Community Awards

In many cities opportunities exist to sponsor awards honoring public servants as well as citizens who perform heroic deeds. If your city already has a program in place, you might get involved by offering a gift certificate to your store as one of the prizes. Or underwrite a more attractive award (i.e., a trophy instead of a certificate of appreciation). If your city does not have a program in place, you can take the initiative and sponsor it by underwriting costs for trophies, certificates of appreciation, or gift certificates.

Another way might be to sponsor a permanent "Honor Roll" in a central location on which the names of the honored are listed.

Among the awards to consider are:

"Police Officer of The Month (Year)"

"Firefighter of The Month (Year)"

"Civil Servant of The Month (Year)"

"Teacher of The Month (Year)"

Heroism awards for civilians who distinguish themselves by coming to the aid of fellow citizens, or law enforcement officials.

While you might participate as a sponsor of these awards, the actual selection of the winners should be by an official committee (i.e., the police selecting the officer of the month, etc.).

Donate A Horse To Your Police Department

If your police department has a mounted unit, see if your store could donate a horse to it. You would want the horse to carry the store's name. Ask the police to arrange a photo opportunity when you turn over the horse to them. Invite media coverage. Each year, hold a "birthday party" outside of the store for the horse. Invite customers to attend. This, too, will make an excellent media photo opportunity.

Promoting Voting

During voter registration and before elections, you might sponsor or help promote "get out the vote" campaigns. You could do this through your advertising, window displays and in-store signage, stuffers with your monthly bill mailings, and participation in citywide campaigns. One method might be to conduct a drawing for prizes among everyone of voting age who signs a pledge at the store that he or she will vote. If there is a citywide drawing for prizes among those who register for the first time, consider donating gift certificates or merchandise from your store. If there is not such a drawing, consider organizing one. The publicity you will generate in the media will be outstanding.

An Essay Contest Among High School Students

In cooperation with the local school system, you might underwrite the prizes for an essay contest among high school students. You might let the school system select the subject, or you might suggest one related to the economic future of the community, perhaps "The Role of The Small Retailer In Today's Economic Environment," or "The Future Of Our Downtown Area."

IF A DISASTER SHOULD STRIKE . . .

If a disaster should occur in the community, you should immediately react by offering whatever assistance you can. This could include donating your facilities if they are needed, as well as supplies and products.

In addition, you might offer discounts to people who must replace what they lost, and even extend credit to them.

Anything you do in such a time of need will be appreciated and recognized by the community.

CHAPTER 13

Getting Publicity Exposure in the Local Media

There are two ways to get your store's name and information about it in newspapers and magazines, or on radio and television. You can do it by buying advertising time and space (see Chapter 15), or through publicity. Media *does not charge for publicity* but you must have a good, unique story or picture opportunity in order to interest them in giving you free space or time.

There are also opportunities to gain promotional exposure in media by providing products for various uses including contests they might sponsor.

While daily newspapers and radio and television have the greatest impact, and reach the largest number of people in a city or metropolitan area, there are other media opportunities you should not overlook. This includes weekly newspapers, cable television, ethnic and foreign language media, high school and college newspapers, union publications, company house organs, college radio stations, local magazines, tourist publications, and the publications of various business, civic, religious, patriotic and non-profit organizations.

You may find that you have a great number of customers and potential customers reading some of these smaller circulated publications. That

is why it is very important to determine the reading, listening and viewing habits of your audience (see Chapter Two).

While a professional public relations person is the ideal candidate to conduct your publicity program, it is possible to achieve significant results with a limited effort handled by a less experienced individual. The smaller retailer usually does not need a full-time person.

This chapter is designed to show the "less experienced" individual how to get that publicity exposure. It discusses the various types of media, who to contact at each, and ideas to propose to them. (Chapter Fourteen contains examples of material to send to media.) As you will see, many of the ideas relate to promotions, sales, special events and other programs described in previous chapters. In many cases, you will find that the same idea can be offered to more than one source, sometimes using the same angle. Other times, you must offer different approaches to different media.

ORGANIZING YOUR PUBLICITY PROGRAM

There are several different ways to organize your publicity program. They range from doing it yourself to hiring an agency.

Do It Yourself

It will take some of your time, but it is possible to conduct your own publicity program. It may not be as thorough as one conducted by professionals, but it will get you exposure in media. The key to conducting your own program is to follow carefully the instructions in this chapter.

Decide which media are the most important to you. Base your decision on the results of your research as to what your customers and potential customers read, listen to, and view. *Concentrate your efforts on this media.* Contact each and get the names of the key people, based on the titles discussed in this chapter. *This is your media list.* Familiarize yourself with the "pitch letters," media advisories, and fact sheets in Chapter Fourteen. You will find the formats for each simple to follow. *Much of your contact work with media will be through these three formats, and follow-up telephone calls.*

If you feel sure of your writing skills, you can also prepare press releases to send to media. There are sample releases in Chapter Fourteen for all types of events and announcements. Some can be edited and used by your store. You should also get from these sample releases a feeling of what information a release should contain. *Unless you or an employee has writing skills, you should probably try to avoid writing press releases, and stick with pitch letters and media advisories.* In hiring people for the store, you might try to find someone interested in a sales position who also has a flair for writing. The person could, perhaps, spend one day a week, or two hours a day, handling your publicity, and the rest of the time on the selling floor.

A point to remember is that as an amateur, you can sometimes accomplish things which a professional public relations person may not be able to do. For example, when contacting an editor, or broadcaster, state initially that you own the store and are not a public relations person. You were wondering how you might be able to get a business page story about the store, or how you could arrange to be a guest on the station's talk show. You will find that the editors and broadcasters will often be sympathetic and reach out to help "amateurs." Also, do not hesitate to make a blind call and say that you think you have a story but you are not sure to whom it should be sent. Again, you will find that you will probably be directed to the right party. After you get a story in print, or on the air, be certain to send a thank-you note to the person at the paper or station who arranged it. They appreciate receiving thank-you notes.

It is important not to flood media with so-called "non-stories" — promotions and special events which are not out of the ordinary. For example, if you are holding a "Christmas in August" promotion, invite media coverage of Santa's arrival. If you are holding a half-price sale, forget about contacting the media. There will not be any interest, and you will wear out your welcome by sending material about non-newsworthy events. So be discreet with what you send, and don't flood media with material unless it is something unique and newsworthy. You will find ideas for and examples of potential newsworthy stories throughout this chapter.

Internship Programs

A method for obtaining free public relations services is through internship programs at local colleges. Check to see if any such programs are available in your area. There are two types of internship programs: a term project for one or more students which is closely monitored by the professor, or a project in which the student works directly for you and under your guidance and direction. It is important to remember that you are not getting an experienced professional, and many of the interns may be undergraduates. However, the type of material and information in this chapter will give the intern the guidance he or she needs to follow to get results for your store.

Interns are usually not paid. However, it is often customary to give them a small stipend to cover meals and carfare.

One-Person Agencies/Free-Lance Help

There are usually one-person public relations firms and free-lance help available in most major cities. You will find some very talented people among them. Some are listed in the Yellow Pages under "Public Relations Counselors" or "Publicity Services." An advantage in using one-person agencies and free-lance help is cost. Because of lower overhead, these single practitioners can afford to charge smaller fees than larger agencies. Use the same standards in selecting them as suggested for full-size agencies, including recommendations from satisfied clients. Be sure to look also at the work they have done for others.

One area to watch carefully is the amount of time they can devote to your business. Make certain that they are not handling so much business that they won't have the time to do a professional job for you. Get a firm commitment as to the number of hours they will spend on your business. A sure sign of a problem is when they miss deadlines, and you have trouble arranging meetings with them.

Hire a Public Relations Agency

If you have the money, you might want to hire a local public relations agency to develop and conduct your program. Agencies usually charge a monthly fee, and also bill you extra for such expenses as postage, reproduction of press releases, photography, etc. Fees will vary from city to city, and are usually based upon the time needed to conduct the agreed-upon program. As already indicated, you probably do not need a full-time person on your account.

It is always best to select an agency which comes highly recommended. Ask local businessmen, business associations, and even the business editor at the local newspaper for suggestions based on their experience. Agencies are usually listed in the Yellow Pages under the headings of "Public Relations Counselors" or "Publicity Services." Some advertising agencies also have public relations departments which will handle your work. You can also usually hire an agency on a project basis to handle an important special event or promotion. Again the fee will vary from agency to agency and city to city.

Before hiring an agency, be certain that you become familiar with the person(s) who will work on your account. You should be confident that you will be able to get along with him or her, and that the experience level is sufficient to do an effective job for you. While knowledge of, or experience in, retail is not necessary, the person(s) assigned to your account should have experience in the consumer products or services area, and be promotion-oriented. In addition to possessing a writing ability, he or she should generate ideas, and know the way around the local media. Ask the agency to show you samples of its work, and its current client list. Contact some of the firms on that list for reference purposes.

HOW TO WORK WITH THE MEDIA

On the pages that follow is information about the types of media you will probably find in your area, the key titles you will probably want to contact, and the types of stories in which each will probably be interested.

Note that titles and responsibilities may vary from newspaper to newspaper, radio station to radio station, television channel to television channel, etc. So when calling to get the names of people to contact, you may have to describe the function of the person you seek.

Radio

As with all media, focus in on the radio stations to which your customers and potential customers listen, as well as any others which might offer large listening audiences and exposure opportunities.

The key people to get to know at radio stations are the program director, promotion director, news director, individual show producers, and the program hosts including disc jockeys.

The Program Director is the person responsible for everything that goes out over the air. In big city stations, the program director may not be involved in any of the activities in which you will be interested. In smaller cities, however, and sometimes at smaller stations in bigger cities, the program director may book guests for shows, develop on-air promotions, and handle other assignments.

The Promotion Director is in charge of the great number of on-air promotions that radio stations do, as well as others aimed at increasing numbers of listeners. Many are in the form of contests, and prizes are always needed as well as contest ideas.

When you have a story worthy of coverage, let the News Director know about it. He or she is in charge of assignments and is usually the person who decides what gets on the air.

In larger markets, most live radio programs, including disc jockeys, have individual show producers. He or she usually books guests, screens material and ideas you might send, and generally handles all the arrangements for the host.

In many smaller markets, and even at some larger market stations, the program hosts and disc jockeys are taking on many of the responsibilities formerly held by producers. So you may find you will be contacting these hosts and disc jockeys directly.

Techniques for Contacting Radio Station Personnel

Unless you are familiar with any of the individuals, or have a hot news story, it is always best to mail (or FAX) a letter explaining your idea. Then follow up with a telephone call a few days later. Samples of these letters can be found in Chapter Fourteen.

Avoid saying in your follow-up call, "I just wanted to check and see if you received my letter." Media people turn every color of the rainbow when they hear that! Instead, try to offer a few more selling points about the story or idea you sent along. You are a salesman in your business, so use your salesmanship when talking to the media, too.

If it is a news story, send a covering letter and a media advisory unless, of course, it is a story which is happening at that very moment. Then it should be telephoned in immediately. Examples of such stories might be the line of 2000 people waiting to get into the store for a sale, surprise shopping visit by an internationally known celebrity who happens to be in the area (providing, of course, the celebrity approves), etc.

If it is an idea for a guest appearance, send a covering letter, the biography of the person, and details on some of the subjects he or she will be prepared to discuss.

Types of Exposure You Can Get on Local Radio Stations

Radio may offer you the greatest flexibility of all the media when it comes to getting exposure for your store. Within a city, there are so many different formats, different personalities with different interests, and different programs that just about any retailer can get some free exposure if he or she makes contact with the stations.

Stations and individual programs often run listener contests and need prizes to give to the winners. Since the prizes are promoted on-air (and sometimes in other advertising), these contests offer you an excellent opportunity to get good exposure for your store and product line. Prizes you might offer would include specific products, a shopping spree with a dollar value, gift certificates or a gift a month for a three- or six-month period. If you are an advertiser on the station, you might be able to require that entries be picked up, or deposited at your store. This would help to build traffic.

While stations might give preference to advertisers, do not let the fact that you are not an advertiser deter you from offering to provide prizes. Instead, offer to help the station promote the contest by providing window space, in-store signage, information with customer bills and on other promotional materials. To get involved in these promotions, send a letter to the promotion directors at the stations indicating your interest. If you advertise, also let the salesman who calls on you be aware of your interest in providing prizes. See Chapter Fourteen for a sample letter.

Some talk shows, as well as the pre- and post-game shows of sporting events, give gifts to guests who are interviewed. The value of these gifts can range from $50 to $250, depending upon the show and the market. By providing the gifts, your store will receive on-air mention. If you get involved in such a promotion, make certain that you get the right to approve the promotional announcement mentioning your store. You might contact the manufacturer of the product and see if it will share expenses by providing the gift at no cost, or at a reduced cost.

In some cases, you will also have to pay a small promotional fee to the show's producers. You may be able to negotiate around the fee, especially if the gift is valued at the high end of the price range. If the gifts are to be given to celebrities, try to arrange for photographs to be taken of some, if not all of the presentations. To arrange this tie-in, contact the show's producer. If he or she is not handling the arrangements for gifts, you will be put in contact with the right party.

Radio offers many opportunities for guest appearances by people who have something interesting to discuss. As a retailer, you fit into that category since you are in a position to discuss trends and other subjects in which listeners will be interested. While stations with "talk radio" formats will offer the greatest opportunity, virtually every station has some programs on which you can get some free air time. The types of programs on which you might appear include:

- General interview shows. The host has a guest and conducts the interview.
- Interview/call-in shows. After a brief interview, the telephones are open for listeners to call in their questions.
- Specialized programming (business, sports, education, political, etc.).
- Panel shows in which an expert is interviewed by more than one reporter. While these shows usually deal with political figures, there is also an opportunity for business guests to discuss significant topics.

What are some of the subjects you, a retailer, can discuss? First, trends in retailing, and specifically in your product areas. These include (based on your product lines):

- What's new in fall (spring/winter/summer) fashions.
- What new toys can we expect this Christmas.
- What new cooking appliances are being introduced.
- What's the latest in gourmet foods.
- What are the latest popular colors in home decorating.
- What's the store of tomorrow going to be like. (You can make all types of predictions of what the retail look will be in the year 2000. It will generate a lot of interest and perhaps even controversy. You do not have to be afraid of what you predict since no one will remember what you said come the year 2000.)
- What gifts men are buying for women.
- What gifts women are buying for men.
- Is it gold or silver? Trends in jewelry.
- How the small retailer can take on the giants.

You can also talk in depth about consumerism and product safety. With broad interest in both subjects among consumers, it is to your advantage to be a consumer advocate and spokesperson on as many shows as possible. Areas of discussion might include:

- The importance of product safety in the marketplace.
- What to look for in reading labels, and product instructions.
- Importance of using products only as directed.
- How to get additional information from a manufacturer.

- What to do in an emergency.
- What a store owner's responsibilities are to his or her customers.
- What the rights of a customer are.
- What to look for in a warranty.
- What the law is regarding refunds and exchanges. (If your store's policies are much more liberal, make a point of it.)
- How to get satisfaction if the retailer or the manufacturer is not responsive to your complaints.

Other subjects you might discuss include:

- How to break into retail.
- Careers in retail.
- Your store's growth and history.
- Promotional programs which will benefit local charities and non-profit organizations.
- Promotional programs involving local sports teams and/or players.

When appearing as a guest on radio talk shows, you should not mention your store's name in every other sentence. If you do, you will come across as too commercial and will lose credibility among the listeners. Chances are you also will never be invited back on the show by the host. Instead, speak as an industry spokesperson and as an expert in the field of retailing. You will gain credibility and the respect of the audience and this will help create a positive image for your store. Of course it is acceptable to work in the store name from time to time but be discreet on how you do it. In discussing industry trends, you might reinforce your theories with examples from the store. During a discussion on consumerism, you might point out that "It has been our experience that customers . . . , etc." Your host will also mention your affiliation during the course of the broadcast.

To get on talk shows, contact the producer of each show and offer one or more timely topics you are prepared to discuss. Also send general letters to the producers explaining your interest and availability to appear anytime they need an expert in the area of retailing. Examples of the types of letters to send can be found in Chapter Fourteen.

Some disc jockeys develop a core of regular call-in guests. Who they are, and what they talk about usually depends upon the disc jockey. This is particularly true during morning drive-time (a term used to describe the hours people are driving to work). Listen to the various disc jockeys to see if there are any you can find with whom you might relate. You might make your first move by looking for a unique, fun product to send as a gift. For example, if you sell socks, you might send a dozen pairs of green ones for St. Patrick's Day. Then follow it up with other gifts. If you sell food, you might make it a habit of sending coffee and doughnuts each day, with special treats on special occasions. Or perhaps sandwiches and other refreshments. The all-night shows are usually the most generous in acknowledging food.

Even if you do not sell a particular product, you can still send it along as a promotional gimmick. For example, on Valentine's Day, send 1000 chocolate kisses "from the saleswomen" at the store, and have each one sign the accompanying card. Send a special cake on the disc jockey's birthday, and point out it was homebaked for him or her. Have some unique decorations on it.

Another gimmick is to send "firsts" to disc jockeys: the first box of Bosc pears to arrive in the city; the first set of this year's baseball cards; the first bag of jelly beans; the first roll of Christmas wrapping paper (send it in October). You can make your own "firsts" as you go along, and the crazier the better. The disc jockeys will like it because most have a sense of humor, and it gives them something to talk about. You can have a lot of fun sending these gifts and chances are good that the disc jockey will mention the store's name on the air. If you keep sending stuff on an ongoing basis, the relationship will develop and might result in on-air appearances, and a lot of on-air exposure for the store's name.

Send the gifts so that they arrive just before he or she goes on the air. If you can arrange for someone to bring it into the studio, you might even send the gifts while the show is on the air. It might get an even bigger play that way. In working with disc jockeys, you may be dealing with a producer or a production assistant as well.

Some stations will, from time to time, do remote broadcasts from a store. Usually they are more receptive to do remotes from advertisers' stores; however, there may be exceptions to the rule. If you are in an outstanding central location, a station might be persuaded to have one of its programs come from your store window. It might also agree to a remote broadcast if you would agree to run a week-long salute to the station, with window and in-store displays about its on-air personalities and shows.

A significant milestone anniversary (50th, 100th, etc.) might also be the occasion for a remote, as would be such special events as the arrival of Santa Claus, the in-store appearance of a famous entertainment or sports personality, etc.

A special "charity day" at the store during which part of the proceeds would go to a particular organization might be another occasion. Work with the organization in developing the promotion since it might have better contacts with the station, and might be in a better position to arrange the remote broadcast.

There may be some costs you will have to absorb in connection with remote broadcasts. To arrange remotes, contact the show's producer. You may also have to contact the program director.

You might want to arrange, for a fee, to have a disc jockey or other on-air personality appear at the store to sign autographs, pose for pictures with customers, etc. When on-air personalities make such off-the-air appearances, they often promote them in advance on the air. This can be an effective way to get on-air exposure and build traffic for the store at relatively modest cost. Such personal appearances should be scheduled directly through the personality.

There is a lot of competition to get time on local radio newscasts. Even "all news" stations are very selective in what gets on the air. While you will occasionally have a good news story, your best bet for getting air time will be with something unique or with a humorous slant. (News story ideas appear throughout the book, especially in Chapters Five, Six, Seven, Eight, Nine, and Twelve.) Some, as you will see, can be sent to the news director with a covering letter. This might include an upcoming special event, personal appearance by a celebrity, or a milestone anniversary. Other stories are more immediate, and should be called in to the news director. This might include a huge turn out for a sale (crowds around the block), comments you want to make in response to legislation introduced that day which will impact on your business or consumers.

You should also send the news director at each station a telephone index card with your name, store, title, and areas of expertise which you would be willing to discuss on air. Very often news directors have fast-breaking stories on which they want comments from different people in the field. Let them know you are available. Also provide them with your home telephone number so that they can reach you in an emergency after regular business hours.

Television

While local television offers fewer opportunities to you for publicity than radio and newspapers, it is not impossible to get this valuable exposure for your store. It is just a matter of developing appealing ideas, and calling them to the attention of your local channels.

The first step is to know who the key people are at each television channel and how they can help you: Promotion Director, News Director, News Assignment Editor, individual producers, and talent coordinators. The titles and responsibilities can vary from channel to channel.

Television channels are not as contest-oriented as radio stations but whatever promotions they conduct fall within the bailiwick of the Promotion Director.

The News Director is responsible for the big picture: the channel's news programs and overall coverage. At smaller channels, the News Director may also be involved in deciding which individual stories will be covered. If the News Director is calling those shots, he or she will be your principal contact for getting news coverage.

At larger channels, there is usually a News Assignment Editor who presides over a "news assignment desk." If your local channels are organized this way, your primary contact for getting news coverage will be the News Assignment Editor or desk.

Each locally produced show has its own individual producer, as do many of the news segments (medical and health, business, sports, weather). The news segment producers will be important to you if you have news or feature stories/ideas which fit within their particular areas of interest. The producers of the other local shows are often the people to contact regarding guest appearances and special segments.

Finally, at larger channels, the shows which often use guests have a "talent coordinator." This person is responsible for arranging for guests to appear on the programs.

Techniques For Contacting Television Channel Personnel

Unless you have a fast-breaking news story, or you have a good working relationship with a producer or news person, it is best to mail (or FAX) a letter with your idea. When you send a letter requesting coverage of a special event, always include a media advisory containing full information about that event. Examples of both the letter and media advisory can be found in Chapter Fourteen.

If it is a hot news story, don't hesitate to call it in, and the earlier in the day you call it in, the better your chances of getting it covered.

When you mail, or FAX an idea, be sure to follow up with a telephone call a few days later. During your follow-up call be prepared to use a little salesmanship to reinforce your original letter. Perhaps you can offer additional angles in order to make your idea an even more interesting and appealing story.

As with radio, when you are trying to arrange for a guest to appear on a program, be certain to include the person's biography and details of what he or she can discuss.

Types of Exposure You Can Get on Local Television Channels

As already pointed out, the opportunities for local television coverage are greatly limited. Most of the channels carry network or syndicated programming and have only a small number of locally produced shows. Your greatest opportunity for exposure may be on the various news shows, and even this is limited.

It is important to remember that television is a visual medium, and that the staff at local channels will not only be evaluating your ideas for creativity and interest but also from a visual standpoint. So always think "visual" when developing an idea and proposing it to a channel. Your "pitch letter" should include how the story can be illustrated. (See the sample letters in Chapter Fourteen.)

Here are some ideas about how you may be able to get local television coverage for your store.

A growing number of channels have locally produced magazine shows and/or live audience programs which use guests. These can offer you an excellent opportunity for exposure in a variety of ways.

- As an expert in your field, you can go on and talk about product trends. To make it more visual, show and demonstrate the products.

- If you sell clothing, offer to bring models to the studio to show the latest fashions. This can be done for each season, just as the new lines come in. Other opportunities would be to show jewelry (perhaps with the designer commenting on the work), hats, bathing suits, and shoes.

- If you sell toys, offer to show and demonstrate them as soon as you get the new Christmas line. A unique approach to offer the producer is to have children doing the actual demonstration.

- Bring on a one-of-its-kind product, or one that has a high price tag: a one-million dollar necklace; a handmade dress which might have taken two years to finish; a rare painting. The products you bring on should be for sale, or on display at your store.

- Perhaps you can put together a historic collection of products. If you sell clothing, show the different fashions over the last 50 years. You may be able to borrow the old fashions from a museum, or you could show, through illustrations, how fashion has evolved. Of course, the finale is to show today's actual fashions on live models. Similar historic collections can be put together on shoes, bathing suits, baseball uniforms (if you sell sporting goods), hats, furniture, appliances, typewriters, writing instruments, and just about any product line you carry. Beauty salons can even show hair styles through the years.

- If you got into retail via a unique route, it could make an interesting interview: the oversized person who couldn't find his or her size ends up opening a shop specializing in extra-large clothing. The dentist who receives so many compliments about his ties that he opens a tie store. The college student who takes a summer job at a store and five years later ends up as its owner.

- If you are the fourth or fifth generation of a family of retailers, you might be able to talk about the differences between retail today and during the days of your ancestors. It would be helpful if you had photographs, sketches, or memorabilia from your family's past retail ventures to show during the interview.

- Offer pie-in-the-sky predictions of what retail will be like 25 or 50 years from now. The sky can really be the limit on this one so use your imagination.

- Offer a recap of the changes that have taken place at retail in only the last 25 years, including the size and types of stores, the influence of bank credit cards, and the disappearance of major retail names.

- If you are knowledgeable and have strong feelings about such topics as government regulations regarding retailing, consumerism, product safety, or other issues, offer to discuss them, or appear on a panel discussing them.

- To place guests on shows, contact the talent coordinator (if there is one), or the producer. For fashion shows and other more visual presentations, contact the show's producer.

When you have an interesting promotion or special event, a local channel's magazine show might want to tape the activities at the store. They can then edit it and run it as one of the show's segments. Another possibility is for a local show to do a live segment from the store during one of your promotions or special events. Among candidates for remote segment coverage would be a "Christmas in August" promotion including an interview with Santa Claus; a New Year's promotion if you celebrated "New Year's Eve" each night of the event (see Chapter Five); an in-store memorabilia exhibit (see Chapter Six). To arrange these remotes from your store, contact the producer of the show.

If you have the appropriate products, offer to provide furnishings for the sets of local programs. The products could range from furniture and carpeting to flowers and drapes. In return for providing the furnishings, insist upon on-screen credits. The product that will probably get the most exposure will be flowers. If you change the arrangements on a regular basis, the host and guests are bound to comment about them. Other products that would probably generate conversation would be art, especially sculptures, unique lamp shades, an odd-shaped coffee table or desk. If you are in the food business, you might consider providing refreshments for the cast, guests and studio audience. You should get on-screen credits. The person to talk to in order to arrange these tie-ins would be the show's producer.

Some locally produced shows give gifts to guests who appear on the program. You might consider offering to provide the gifts, or gift certificates if the channel will give you both on-screen and voice credits. It is a good way to gain television exposure at a relatively inexpensive cost.

As with radio, pre- and post-game programs of sporting events usually give gifts to their guests. Contact the program director at the station to determine who is the proper person to speak to about providing these gifts. Very often, the teams control these programs directly or through an independent production company. In addition to providing the gifts, you may be asked to pay a small promotional fee.

If local channels run promotional contests, offer to provide prizes for on-screen credits. Be sure that you get the right to approve the promotional announcement mentioning your store. Contact the product's manufacturer to see if it will share expenses. Try to get it to provide the product at no cost, or at reduced cost.

To arrange the gifts for guests, other than on sporting events programming, speak to the show producer. To arrange prizes for promotional contests, talk to the channel's promotion director.

Many program hosts like to show new and unusual products and fun gimmicks during their monologues. If you carry such products, and they are relatively inexpensive, send one to the host. Your covering letter should be light and funny, and offer directions on how the product works. Examples of such products might be moving toys, talking mirrors, unique T-shirts, tricks, etc. Seasonal gifts to send might include a pumpkin carved for

Halloween with a pipe in its mouth (ideal for a gift from a tobacco store); a pair of boxer shorts with hearts for Valentine's Day (from a haberdasher); a personalized sun visor for summer (from a sporting goods store), etc.

If it is a more expensive product, first contact the producer and describe the product. If you have a picture of it, send it along. Then follow up with a telephone call and send the product only if the producer expresses interest in using it on the show.

News stories are difficult to get on television. However, it is *not* impossible to do. News directors and the assignment desks are always looking for good human interest stories as well as those with good visual appeal. Many of the ideas outlined in chapters on promotions, special events, community involvement and sports are tailored for television because of their visual appeal. Several different types of stories will appeal to television news:

- Fast-breaking stories which pop up without any advance notice. These will probably be very rare in a retail environment. They might include a three-block long line that formed for a sale, or to get a celebrity's autograph; a customer who proposes marriage to his girl friend while in the store; the unexpected delivery of a highly desired product which has been in back order for a long time (for example, when Cabbage Patch dolls were impossible to get some years back); A 10-year old walks into the store unannounced with his piggy bank and wants to make a down payment for a gift for his mother. These types of stories might prompt a channel to send a crew quickly to the store. To get this coverage, you should immediately telephone the news assignment desk and explain the story.

- Another form of fast-breaking news is when you have strong comments to make concerning pending legislation or remarks rebutting what a legislator or government official said. Call the news assignment desk, identify yourself, and explain your position and how the legislation or comments by the government official will impact on your business. They might send a crew to the store to tape your comments. This type of opportunity will probably only be available within 24 hours after the original story breaks.

Other news coverage you seek will probably be for upcoming promotions or special events. Your approach to the station should be through a covering letter and media advisory explaining the event. Remember to stress the visual opportunities. This material should also be sent to the news assignment desk. And don't forget to follow up with a telephone call a few days later. (See Chapter Fourteen for sample letters and media advisories.)

Local television show hosts will often make in-store appearances for a fee. He or she will sign autographs, pose for pictures with customers, tell of television experiences, etc. Most important, the host will usually announce such an appearance in advance on the show. This, of course, will attract viewers to the store on the day of the host's appearance. To make arrangements, contact the host directly, or his or her agent.

Daily Newspapers

Working with print media is different from radio and television in that you will be more directly involved with the "front line" troops — the reporters and writers who cover your areas of interest — and not intermediaries. On many occasions, when you have a story idea, you will be contacting a reporter or writer directly rather than an editor.

Editorial responsibilities also vary more widely from newspaper to newspaper than in any of the other media with which you will be dealing. That's why we strongly recommend that you contact your local daily newspapers and try to identify who your prime contacts should be.

- Who to contact when you have a news story.
- Who to contact when you have a good photo idea.
- Who to contact when you have a business page story.
- Who to contact when you have an idea for a feature story.
- If the paper has sections covering different parts of the city, who is the contact on the sections in which you would like to get coverage.

You might call the newspaper's public relations department, if it has one, or its promotion department. If that is of no help, call the city editor, business editor, photo editor and feature editor. Explain that you are not a public relations person but would like to get publicity for your store and want to know the correct contact when you have a story idea. Indicate the type of store you own and the types of newsworthy promotions and special events you hold.

There are many people with whom you will be dealing.

The City Editor and assistants (they man the city desk) are usually responsible for deciding which local news stories will be covered each day.

At some newspapers, this responsibility may be handled by the metropolitan editor, or the news editor. But the City Editor is probably the most commonly used title for this responsibility.

The Photography Editor may have responsibility for assigning photographers to stories, especially major picture page features and photo essays.

What had been the women's section of daily newspapers is now pretty much known as the Lifestyle Section and has been expanded to cover anything to do with lifestyles. It will run stories about men as well as women. While the Lifestyle Editor calls the shots, there are usually reporters covering specific beats (food, cooking, fashion, home, etc.). When you have a story idea which falls within the area of a "beat" reporter, contact him or her directly. If you don't know your contact, or there isn't a beat reporter assigned to the subject, contact the Lifestyle Editor.

Feature Editor responsibility can vary from newspaper to newspaper. He or she may have responsibility for feature stories in the daily editions, Sunday editions, or the special sections. How the Feature Editor can help you is something you are going to have to determine locally.

By reading your newspapers, you will be able to identify which local columnists would cover stories related to your business. Whenever you have a story for one, contact him or her directly.

The person who holds the title of Business Editor usually decides what stories will be covered on the business pages. Sometimes there are "beat" reporters assigned to specific business areas (advertising, banking, retailing, etc.). In those cases, you might be dealing directly with the reporter whenever you have a business story idea.

Newspapers often sponsor various promotions aimed at increasing circulation. Sometimes they are in the form of contests, and prizes are needed. It is the Promotion Manager who puts the contest together and the person you should contact if you want to offer prizes.

Techniques for Contacting Daily Newspaper Personnel

Mail or FAX material unless it is a late-breaking news story. If it is, call the appropriate editor and tell him or her directly. As with radio and television, when you send a story idea to a newspaper by mail or FAX, be sure to follow up with a telephone call a few days later. Try to give additional facts about the story during that follow-up phone call. If it is an informative story, explain how it will be of benefit to the paper's readers.

Do not make follow-up telephone calls when you send routine press releases.

When you are trying to arrange coverage of an event, always send a media advisory along with your letter. The media advisory should, in outline form, quickly explain all the facts about the event. (Samples of media advisories can be found in Chapter Fourteen.)

For a feature story idea, send a fact sheet, outlining the idea, with your letter. Try to keep the fact sheet to a single page, but no more than two. (Sample fact sheets can also be found in Chapter Fourteen.)

If you would like some advance publicity for an upcoming promotion or special event, send a press release. (See Chapter Fourteen for sample press releases.)

If you are trying to arrange an interview for yourself or someone else (i.e., a supplier president coming to town), send a biography with the "pitch letter."

You may find that some writers and editors may encourage you to call them when you have an idea. When you make an initial contact with an editor or writer, ask about his or her preference for contact by mail or telephone.

It is also important to recognize that when you call an editor with a fast-breaking story, you might be asked to FAX further information. If you don't have a FAX, be aware of where you can find the nearest one to use.

Once you have established who your contacts will be, send each of them a card for their telephone files. It should contain your name and title, store name and telephone number, home telephone number, and the subjects about which you can provide information.

If you have an aggressive program of special events and promotions, you might sometimes be able to get news coverage. A community event you sponsor such as a baby parade, the kick-off of a drive you are sponsoring to recruit more volunteers for non-profit organizations, or the paper airplane-throwing contest you are underwriting might merit a story. Special events at the store including celebrity appearances, the talking robot, and the opening of an in-store memorabilia exhibit could be of interest. Fast-breaking stories might include the mob scene being generated by a sale, comments on proposed city zoning laws which might have impact on your store, and the one millionth customer since the store opened 25 years ago.

The fast-breaking stories, of course, should be telephoned to the city editor. Information about the events to take place should be sent by mail or FAX. A letter and media advisory should contain full information about the event.

Many of the story ideas you generate will be appropriate for the business pages. Since the type of business page coverage varies from newspaper to newspaper, it is impossible to predict the exact stories which your newspapers will cover but they might include the following:

- Promotions and special events draw customers to store.
- Twenty-fifth anniversary year a record one for store.
- Profile of owner.
- Picture bright for retailing according to local owner.
- Trends in retailing, and particularly in your area of products.
- Personnel appointments (manager level).
- Customer should be "king" according to local retailer.
- How the small retailer can take on the giants.

Story ideas like those above should be sent to the business editor or any other contact you have established in the business section.

Feature stories include those appropriate for the lifestyle pages, other sections of the newspaper, and columnists. Such stories would be about new spring (summer, fall, winter) fashions; Santa's coming to town with a new bag of toys; trade-in sale which brings all types of relics to store; what men are buying this Valentine's Day; what to look for when reading labels, warranties, and instructional booklets; how to get satisfaction from a store or manufacturer who isn't responding to your complaints, from a retailer's viewpoint. These types of ideas should go to the appropriate section editor, or columnist. They represent just a few of the feature ideas you can try to place with your local newspapers. Some of the ideas covered in radio and television could also be used for daily newspapers.

Very often you will find that while you don't have a strong story to tell, you do have a potentially good photo opportunity. Most of the holiday and seasonal promotions in Chapter Five will fall into this category, as will some of the sales and special event ideas. For example, a "Christmas in August" sale might suggest to the paper a picture of Santa wiping his brow next to a thermometer showing the August temperature. A "New Year's Eve Party Sale," which runs the entire first week of January, might suggest a picture of two of your salespeople (a man and a woman) dressed in formal wear, with a calendar showing it is January 3, and a sign in the background saying, "The Party Never Ends." The opportunities are endless — for an April Fool's Day event, suggest a picture of one of your sales people holding a fake newspaper headline reading, "U. S. Government Finishes With Surplus; $1000 Dividend To Be Sent To All Taxpayers."

Photography ideas should be sent to either the City Editor or Photo Editor, depending upon the organization of your local newspaper.

Most newspapers publish special thematic sections during the year. They might include a Christmas gift section, new automobile models section, health section, summer travel section, etc.

While most of the sections are published to draw additional advertising, they run editorial material, too. Though advertisers usually appear to get preference when it comes to the editorial support, it doesn't mean a non-advertiser cannot get a story in the section. You just have to come up with a strong angle or unique story idea. There is usually a special sections editor at each newspaper who handles these projects.

In addition, many large daily metropolitan newspapers print special sections for the different suburbs or areas of the city. If you have customers from any of the covered areas, or if your store is located in one of the special areas, you must try to get publicity in those section(s). Find out who is editor and make contact. Ask about the type of stories that would be of interest and invite him or her over to the store next time you are having a special event or sale. Send the special area section editor copies of all press releases, including those you may have already sent to the city desk. Make sure he or she knows what you had previously submitted to the city desk. Then, if the main section doesn't carry the story, at least you will have a shot at getting it in the area section. Always send media advisories of upcoming events, even if you also sent them to the city desk. The section editor might cover it from a different angle than the main section, or cover it while the main section ignores the event.

Weekly Newspapers

Weekly newspapers usually cover a specific section of a city or a suburb and are primarily interested in news about the people, businesses, and events taking place within their area. Some publishers own and operate several different weekly newspapers within a metropolitan area.

Some weekly newspapers are sold, while others are distributed free of charge. The staffs usually vary in size and responsibilities from paper to paper, as do the editorial policies and standards.

It is important that you read the various weekly newspapers in your city and determine which offer you the best opportunity for publicity exposure. When doing so, be sure to take into consideration the results of any research you have done to pinpoint where your customers and potential customers live.

The key person to contact at the weekly is the editor. Call and ask:

- What type of material he or she would be interested in getting from your store.
- To whom it should be sent.
- When you have a story idea, whom should you call at the paper.
- Anyone else at the weekly you should contact.

Techniques For Contacting Weekly Newspapers' Editors/Writers

You will find contact with weekly newspaper staffs is more informal than with daily newspaper editors and writers. You can usually reach them on the telephone on a regular basis. However, be aware of the weekly deadline day and avoid calling then. For the most part, everything you send to the weekly will be by mail. The earlier in the new week (the day after the last edition went to press) the better the chances for it to be published.

Because of small staffs, many weeklies limit greatly the number of events they cover. Generally you have a better chance for getting a story in a weekly if you write it and send it to the editor; the same works with photographs. If you can supply them, you have a better chance of getting visual coverage. If you can supply photographs, call and speak to the editor before sending them in, for the editor might suggest that you hand carry them down to the paper.

Types of Stories to Send to Weekly Newspapers

The types of stories in which weekly newspapers probably will be most interested include:

- News about your store if it is located within its circulation area.
- Advance stories on special events and promotions.
- After-the-fact stories on special events, promotions.
- Advance stories on special sales.
- Community outreach programs sponsored by the store.

- Profile of the owner, manager, or exceptional sales person, if the individual also lives within the circulation area.
- New fashions, and seasonal lines available at store.
- Unique new products introduced.
- Start of frequent buyer's club.
- Renovation of store.
- Any steps being taken to make it easier for shoppers (longer hours, clearer pricing information, new policy on refunds and exchanges, etc.).

News about customers who might live within the area.

- Winning one of store's contests.
- Modeling at store's fashion show.
- Appointment to store's advisory committee.
- Picture with Santa Claus, robot, costumed character, magician, celebrity at the store.
- Cashing in frequent buyer's club points for expensive gift.
- Named customer of the month.

If you have unique expertise in an area which will be of interest to the newspaper's readers, you might offer to do a weekly or biweekly column. While it will take some of your time to write, the column will help get you and your store better known among the weekly's readers, and hopefully build additional traffic. Examples of the subject matter might include fashions, home improvements and how to do them, home decorating, hobbies, stamp and coin collecting, etc. The subject should relate to the type of products you sell, but the column should never be a blatant advertisement for your store. Rather, it should be non-commercial and not mention any brand names. You and your store will gain credibility since the column will project your expertise in the field. Another column approach would use the same subject themes but the format might be to answer reader questions. The editor would be the person to talk to about doing a column. You should prepare a few sample columns to show at your meeting in which you would stress the advantage to the newspaper: a consumer-oriented column of interest to readers, at no cost to the paper.

Weekly newspapers sometimes run contests to build circulation, and also advertiser awareness among its readers. Offer to contribute the prizes in return for promotional exposure in the paper.

Ethnic Newspapers

Newspapers published for local ethnic groups are important outlets for you to use to gain exposure for your store. Concentrate on those publications appealing to significant numbers of current, as well as potential customers.

Contact the editor of each publication to find out what stories it would be interested in running, to whom they should be sent, and who you should be contacting when you have an idea.

There is one very important point to remember when dealing with ethnic publications. They will usually be interested only in news and features which involve the ethnic group they cover. This limits what you can get in the publication. Those stories which will have appeal will be personality stories about the owner or manager if he or she is a member of the appropriate ethnic group; customers of the ethnic group who win store contests, serve on its advisory committee, are named "Customer of The Month," or model at the store's fashion show; a salesperson who is honored for distinguished service; a special in-store exhibit honoring the ethnic group, or one of its distinguished leaders (Dr. Martin Luther King, etc.); an in-store special event which will have wide appeal to the ethnic group; or pictures with the robot, Santa Claus, a celebrity appearing at the store, etc.

Some of the story ideas mentioned earlier in this chapter can be used for various ethnic publications as long as they involve a member of the respective group.

Foreign Language Newspapers

If there are significant numbers of foreign language-speaking residents in your community, chances are there will be newspapers published for them. These publications may offer good publicity opportunities to a retailer. You should be interested in those newspapers read by your target audience.

Contact the editor and find out what type of stories the publication would run, to whom they should be sent, and whether they must be translated into the published language.

Foreign language newspapers, like ethnic publications, will only be interested in stories which have a relationship to their readers. The list of stories would be similar to those included under "Ethnic Newspapers"; however, there are additional topics and angles in which foreign language newspapers would be interested:

- Foreign language assistance offered to customers at the store.
- Products sold at the store which are manufactured in the country from which its readers originated.
- Shopping visit to the store by a large tour group from the country.
- Service offered by the store to handle the shipping of purchases to the country.
- Any promotions or special events honoring the country, or one of its citizens.
- Interview with the store owner or manager upon his or her return from a visit to the country in which a comparison is made of retailing in both countries.

Cable Television Systems

Cable offers limited publicity opportunities to the retailer since network programming occupies most of cable systems' channels. However, there are exceptions. Some all-news regional networks have been developed. In some cases, the network covers a single city, a metropolitan area, or, in the case of New England, an entire section of the country. There are also local educational channels in some areas. Public access channels are noncommercial and set aside by cable systems for use by the public on a first-come, first-served basis. Some systems have leased channels for which programmers pay a nominal fee for use and are thereby permitted to sell commercial time in their programming. Contact the cable system(s) in your area to get more information about its public access and leased access channels and how to go about getting time on them. Also, ask if there are any opportunities for cable exposure other than advertising.

Types Of Material You Might Be Able To Get On Cable

Each of the four types of programming mentioned above offers you some opportunity to get publicity on cable for your store.

The regional news networks are like "all news" radio stations. The type of material in which they have interest is similar to what you can place on local television channel news shows. Your chance for getting on might be a little better because, unlike the local television news shows, these cable news programs usually do not cover any national news, only local news. The procedures for contacting cable's regional news networks are the same as for "Television," discussed earlier in this chapter. So are the ideas. The regional news networks will be interested in fast-breaking news and special events and promotions which offer good visual coverage opportunities. Your contact will probably be the News Director, or it might be a reporter assigned to the "beat" where you are located. Call the News Director, introduce yourself and ask who you should be calling or writing to when you have a story or idea.

Some systems might have a channel assigned to a school system or college for educational programming. Though you will not receive heavy promotional publicity for your store, you might consider getting on one of the programs to discuss related educational subjects which could include career opportunities in retailing, how to get your first job in retailing, and/or the principles of merchandising for the small retailer. Another possibility is to teach a retailing course on the channel. It would be a chance to demonstrate your expertise in the field, and get some exposure for your store. You would be identified as the owner of the store at the start and end of each show, so that viewers would be aware of your retail affiliation. The knowledge you impart to the viewers would have a positive effect on the store's image. This positive image would help not only to attract new customers but also to assist in recruiting store personnel.

Public access channels offer you two opportunities to consider: scheduling your own weekly program to discuss subjects in your areas of expertise and/or answer viewer call-ins; or appearing on other public access programs as a guest, also discussing topics in which you are considered an expert. Programs on public access channels cannot be blatantly commercial and must be designed to offer assistance to viewers. If you are interested in the possibility of developing your own program on your local system's public access channel, you should contact the system for further information. There are usually some minimal studio and production costs involved.

If they are available on your system, leased access channels would enable you to conduct a more commercially-oriented show than you could do on public access. There is normally a nominal fee involved, and you can run advertising on your show. If you sell audio equipment, you might develop a program positioning yourself as "Mr. Audio" and offer technical advice along with information on how to do simple repairs and maintenance work. If you sell clothing, you might feature current fashions, past fashions, care of clothing, and invite guest designers, design teachers, a seamstress, call-ins to answer fashion questions, etc. Another opportunity would be to appear as a guest on other people's leased access programs. If leased access is available on your system(s), contact it for additional information.

Local Magazine

Many cities now have local magazines. Some cover the local business scene, while others cover a variety of subjects about the city and activities taking place within it.

Circulation is usually upscale, with the "movers and shakers" of the community among the readers. It is a good audience to reach.

The editorial contents vary from magazine to magazine so you are going to have to determine how you can best fit into the picture at each one. Contact the respective editors to determine how you can work closer with them, and the type of material they would like to receive from your store. If the magazine has a shopping column, pick out products you have which might be attractive to readers. Send a description, along with Polaroid™ pictures to the column's editor. If he or she likes the product, the magazine will probably borrow it for photography. Another way to handle this is to contact the editor and tell him or her about your product line and issue an invitation to visit the store. During Christmas gift season the magazine may run a more extensive gift section. Getting into it should be a very important objective. Since the editors may be working months in advance on it, contact them in May to find out when the deadline will be for submitting product ideas.

Some run profile stories on successful and/or unique businesses and their owners. Try selling them on doing a story on your store, or yourself. Perhaps develop the angle around unique promotions and special events, or the array of merchandise, or your frequent buyer's program, etc.

If any of the magazines have calendars of upcoming sales or events, be sure that they receive information about the ones you plan. Since they may be working on issues a month or so in advance, make certain you are aware of their deadlines. You may have to send them information weeks before you send it to the rest of the media.

If a local business magazine has a reporter covering retail, be certain you get to know who it is, issue an invitation to visit the store, and make him or her aware that you are very interested in cooperating. Encourage contact with you anytime he or she needs background information about retailing, a quote on any aspect of it, or comments about the business climate in general.

These publications may also run reader promotion contests and will need prizes for the winners. You might consider contacting the promotion directors or managers to let them know you are interested in cooperating next time they run a contest. As with other media, cooperate only if you will be getting good exposure in the contest's advertising and promotional materials.

Tourist Publications

These are usually available at hotels, airports and other tourist destinations in the city. They usually contain listings of stores, entertainment, tourist facilities, museums and other tourist destinations. They also tend to list only those stores which advertise in the publication.

However, even if you do not advertise, you should send them material about your special sales, exhibits, promotions, new and unique products, as well as a description of the store and its product lines.

High School Newspapers

If your merchandise appeals to high school students, try to get some publicity in the local high school newspapers. It is not the easiest thing to do. Your stories should be informative, and aimed at helping the students.

First develop an idea, and then contact the editor by mail to ask him or her to consider assigning a reporter to write it. You might announce an internship program for high school seniors. Or the reporter could interview a student from the school who is doing an outstanding job for you on a part-time basis. (Perhaps he or she became your first part-time employee to be named "Employee Of The Month.") You could be interviewed on the subject of "Careers In Retailing" or "How To Break Into Retailing." You might announce the sponsorship of a student award, a scholarship or perhaps a contest for students (art, essay, etc.). Perhaps you could announce a special discount or sale for students from the specific school. It might be for all students, or just the ones with perfect attendance, or all-A's. How about offering products for a student auction, raffle, or any other school contest? Or maybe you might announce underwriting of a student activity, theater production, or senior class night.

College Newspapers

Like high school papers, college newspapers are tough to crack. However, if college students are among your target audience, you have to try to reach them through this medium.

Most of the ideas suggested for the high school newspapers may also be used for college publications. (The only exception would be to eliminate the "perfect attendance" or "all-A-s" requirement for a special discount.)

Additional ideas for the college newspaper might include announcing a special College Night at the store one evening a month, with refreshments and special discounts, or an announcement about underwriting a lecture series on retailing. You could also offer to underwrite the newspaper's annual writing awards program. If it doesn't have one, offer to underwrite its start-up.

Your first contact with the college newspaper should be with its editor.

College Radio Station

If any of the local colleges has its own student-run radio station, and college students are among your target audience, be sure to contact the station program manager and see how you can cooperate. Be interviewed on a program, discussing retail as a career, how to break in, the small retailer vs. the giant, etc. Suggest remotes from the store, especially if you have an interesting special event, a celebrity signing autographs, or even a College Night. Provide information on fads, new products and other items the on-air personality may talk about, as well as news about special promotions and special sales for college students only. Make sure the station knows about the store's positive relationship with the college. (See ideas under "High School" and "College Newspapers." If the station sponsors listener contests, offer gift certificates to your store as prizes.

Union Newspapers and Magazines

If you have many union members as customers, and/or would like to attract them, don't overlook getting publicity in the various union newspapers and magazines.

Your only chance for getting exposure in these publications will be if you have a strong "union" slant to your story.

Consider a special sale set up for union members only. Do a profile on the store if it is unionized, and if you have a good relationship with the union and your employees. Share news about your employees who are the spouses or children of union members. Always welcome by the publication will be stories about products available at your store made by members of the particular union. (The angle here is that the union members who made it should encourage people to purchase it at your store since the more you sell, the more they have to make and the safer their jobs are.) Feature pictures of union members with Santa Claus, the robot, or other personalities who appear at your store. Emphasize stories on union members who win prizes in any contests you sponsor.

Contact the editors of the various union publications to determine what types of stories you should send along.

Company House Organs

Just like union publications, anything you want to get published in local area company house organs will have to have a relationship to that company or its employees.

The types of stories they will consider running are similar to those wanted by union publications. They will be interested in special sales for company employees only, and in stories about company-manufactured products sold at your store. The house organ editor might even come down and interview customers on their reactions to the products, why they are purchasing them, etc. Always of interest is news about the children and spouses of company employees who work at your store, their accomplishments, pictures with Santa, celebrities, etc. A profile on your store is a possibility if it sells a great many products manufactured by the company. Such a story would include how you do it, techniques of marketing those products, how you train your sales force, etc. The publication might also feature a story about an employee who wins one of your contests or pictures of employees with special event personalities at the store (Santa, the robot, cartoon character, etc.).

Miscellaneous Publications

Within any city can be found a large number of different organizations which print anything from two-page typed newsletters to more sophisticated publications. They may include fraternal, religious, business, civic, veterans, patriotic, senior citizens, and non-profit organizations.

While you will not be able to get much coverage in these publications, you can get some when your information relates directly to its members or the organization itself. They might feature news about members who work for you, or news about members who may have won a contest at your store. Particularly attractive to them will be sales, discounts, or special events which focus on an area of interest to its members. For example, veterans and patriotic groups will be interested in your Armed Forces Day and Veterans Day promotions; senior citizens would be interested in any senior citizen month events.

CHAPTER 14

Samples of Materials to Send to Media to Get Publicity

This entire chapter contains samples of material to send to media in order to generate publicity for your store.

The material includes:

Pitch Letters

As the name implies, they "pitch" a story idea, or a guest appearance. The letter should be as brief as possible and never more than two pages. You want to convince an editor or producer that you have a good story. Give a quick summary of the idea, what an interview subject can discuss, why it is unique. It is often sent along with a fact sheet or a media advisory.

Media Advisories

Sometimes called assignment memos, they contain all the important information the decision-makers at media would need in order to decide whether or not to send someone to cover the event. They tell what the event is, where

it will be held, when, and who the participants will be. They also directly or indirectly provide various story and picture possibilities.

Fact Sheets

Outlines of important facts which can be used by media to prepare a story, to prepare for an interview, or to use as talking points on radio or television.

Press Releases

Stories which are sent to media for possible use. For your purpose, press releases will contain information about coming promotions, special events, sales, and other activities. You might also send some press releases regarding accomplishments which reflect favorably on the image of the store. Press releases are often rewritten before being used, and sometimes lead to a more comprehensive staff-written story about the store. It is important to understand that not all press releases you send will be used. So don't get discouraged.

General Letters

Also provided are samples of several general letters you should consider sending to media. They indicate availability to become a regular source for news, and express an interest in providing prizes for media contests and gifts to guests on radio and television programs.

While you may be able to use some of the sample materials as they have been written, chances are you will have to rewrite most so that they actually reflect the facts and story you are proposing.

By following the formats of the samples, the preparation of the actual materials will be relatively easy.

In order to provide you with an idea of what a "family" of materials for a specific event will look like, the first four samples will be of a pitch letter, media advisory, fact sheet, and press release for a "Witches Brew Recipe Contest."

Pitch Letter to Local Media to Cover In-Store Event

Dear :

The annual "Witches Brew Recipe Contest" finals will be held at Smith's Kitchen Products Store, Saturday, October 27 at 10 AM. We hope you will be able to cover.

Seven recipes have been selected for the finals, to be judged by two witches and one warlock, along with Mary Ames of Ames Cooking School.

Samples of the seven finalists' brews will be available to everyone who attends the "taste-off."

The person who submits the winning recipe will receive a one-week, all-expense-paid trip for two to Salem, MA. The runners-up will receive a one year's supply of brooms. All seven will also receive $100 worth of kitchenware from Smith's.

Smith's Kitchen Products Store will have Halloween decorations in its windows and throughout the store, including a 250-pound pumpkin thought to be the largest grown in the area.

Along with this letter, you will find a media advisory with additional facts on the event.

If you need additional information, please call 345-7896.

Hope your publication (station, channel) will cover the event.

Sincerely,

NOTE: Pitch letters should always be sent on store letterhead.

Media Advisory to Send to Radio, Television, Newspapers to Encourage Coverage of the Event

MEDIA ADVISORY

WITCHES BREW RECIPE CONTEST FINALS SET FOR OCTOBER 27

The fourth annual "Witches Brew Recipe Contest" finals will be held Saturday, October 27 at 10 AM at Smith's Kitchen Products Store.

The Event:	Seven finalists have been selected and their recipes will be judged during a "taste-off"
The Judges:	Two witches, one warlock, and Mary Ames, of the Ames Cooking School
The time:	10 AM
The Date:	Saturday, October 27
The Place:	Smith's Kitchen Products Store
	1234 Main Street (corner of Oak Avenue)

Photo Opportunities

- Witches and Warlock judges will be in costumes
- Finalists' brews will be available for sampling by all customers
- Store and windows will be decorated for Halloween
- On display at the store will be a 250-pound pumpkin said to be the largest grown in the area
- Presentation of prizes: Winner gets one-week, all-expense-paid trip for two to Salem, MA. Presentation will be made by a "certified witch"
- Runners-up get a one year's supply of brooms
- All seven finalists will also receive $100 worth of kitchenware from Smith's

For further information, contact Arnold Smith, 345-7896.

NOTE: Media advisories should always be sent on store letterheads.

FACT SHEET

FOURTH ANNUAL WITCHES BREW RECIPE CONTEST FINALS

- For the fourth consecutive year, Smith's Kitchen Products Store is sponsoring a "Witches Brew Recipe Contest" in conjunction with Halloween.

- The finals will be held at Smith's Saturday, October 27 starting at 10 AM.

- From September 1–October 12, area residents had been invited to enter the contest by submitting their original recipes for a "witches brew." There were no restrictions as to who might enter the contest.

- On the closing date, 1276 entries had been received. That was 129 more than last year, and 764 more than the first year of the contest.

- Preliminary testing and judging of the recipes was done by Mary Ames and her staff at the Ames Cooking School.

- Seven finalists were selected. They are: Sarah Kling, 444 East Oak Street; Arthur Goldler, 309 Stir Drive, Oakdale; Susan Major, 1 West 101st Street, Kingswood; Dorian Scali, 9 East Jefferson Avenue; Bea Wiser, 2203 Central Avenue; Janice Lightlee, 410 West Avenue; and Robert Leonard, 16 Rush Street, Oakdale.

- The finalists will prepare their brews the morning of October 27 at Smith's. Judging will begin at 10 AM.

- The judges will be Mary Ames, two witches, and one warlock. The witches are Dame Ellen Mae, and Flying Florence. The warlock goes under the name of Exzee. All three claim they were born in Transylvania.

- The winner will receive a one-week, all-expense-paid trip for two to Salem, MA. The six runners-up will receive one year's supply of brooms. All seven will also receive $100 worth of kitchenware from Smith's.

- Following the judging, the brews concocted by all seven will be available for sampling. The seven recipes will also be distributed.

- The public is invited.

- Smith's Kitchen Products Store sells a complete line of kitchenware and food products. It also owns the Ames Cooking School and provides free cooking lessons to customers who purchase a minimum of $500 worth of products a year.

NOTE: Fact sheets should always be on 8-1/2 x 11 white stationery or paper, contain the store's name and address, date, and the name of a contact person for further information.

SMITH'S KITCHEN PRODUCTS STORE
1234 MAIN STREET
THISTOWN, USA 23456

FOR IMMEDIATE RELEASE   Contact: Ed Greene
                                                         789-5432

TWO WITCHES AND ONE WARLOCK TO JUDGE ANNUAL WITCHES
BREW RECIPE CONTEST FINALS ON OCTOBER 27; PUBLIC WELCOME

The fourth annual "Witches Brew Recipe Contest" finals will be held Saturday, October 27 at Smith's Kitchen Products Store, 1234 Main Street. The judging will begin at 10 AM, and the public is invited to sample the brews.

Two witches, Dame Ellen Mae and Flying Florence, and one warlock, Exzee, will join Mary Ames of the Ames Cooking School in judging the concoctions of the seven finalists. The public is invited to attend and will be able to sample all seven brews.

The entrant whose brew is judged the best will win a one-week, all-expense-paid trip for two to Salem, MA. Runners-up will receive a one year's supply of brooms. All seven will also receive $100 worth of kitchenware from Smith's.

The seven finalists are Sarah Kling, 444 East Oak Street; Arthur Goldler, 309 Stir Drive, Oakdale; Susan Major, 1 West 101st Street, Kingswood; Dorian Scali, 9 East Jefferson Avenue; Bea Wiser, 2203 Central Avenue; Janice Lightlee, 410 West Avenue: and Robert Leonard, 16 Rush Street, Oakdale.

NOTE: Press releases should be on 8-1/2 x 11 white letterhead or white paper, and follow the format above.

NOTE: This format for a press release includes the following:

- Always use your company name and address at the top of the first page.
- Always indicate a release date, or "For Immediate Release." Release dates are rarely used by retailers.
- Always list a contact, along with a telephone number where the person can be reached. That's the person media will call if there are any

questions. That person must be knowledgeable, and have your authorization to speak to any callers.

- The headline should tell, in a few words, what the story is all about. The headline on your release *is not* the headline which will appear in print. Rather, its purpose is to get the media person's attention and interest.

- The first paragraph is the "lead" and should tell the story as quickly as possible. It usually provides the basic facts: Who, What, When, Where, Why.

- The rest of the story is the "body text" and this is where you present in greater detail the facts to back up the information in the lead.

Pitch Letter to Send to Radio or Television Producer to Arrange Interview with Store Owner

Dear :

"Too many Americans spend too much money for unnecessary automobile repairs . . . "

That's not a statement by Ralph Nader.

It is by John Burns, owner of Burns Automotive Sales and Repairs on 2343 Central Avenue.

The 35-year-old Burns, whose dealership sells more than 200 cars annually and services and repairs more than 3000 a year, estimates that more than 20 percent of automotive repairs are unnecessary, or can be easily done by the car owner.

We thought that you might like to have John appear on your program to discuss the subject of unnecessary automotive repairs. Coming from someone in the business, it is bound to attract significant listener (for television use "viewer") interest.

Specific subjects John will be prepared to discuss include:

- How to determine if a repair is really necessary
- How to find out if you are being ripped off on the pricing for replacement parts
- Ten simple adjustments and repairs anyone can do and save $250 in the process.

Along with this letter, I am sending John's biography, and a complete list of subjects he can discuss.

If you need additional information, please call me at 666-7777.

Sincerely,

NOTE: This format can be used for letters to arrange newspaper or radio or television interviews on a variety of subjects in the consumerism field. Start off with a dramatic opening line which the recipient would not expect to be coming from a retailer. Identify yourself and your business, then offer the highlights of what you can discuss.

Be sure to follow up with a telephone call to the person to whom you sent the letter if he or she doesn't call you in a few days.

Pitch Letter to Send to Radio or Television Producer or Newspaper Business Editor to Arrange Interview with Owner

Dear :

They must be doing something right at 475 Madison Street.

That's where Jones Hardware store is completing its third expansion in the past five years. They have also added ten additional employees, and tripled sales during the same period.

Jones is also celebrating its 45th anniversary this year.

We thought you might be interested in having John Jones, the fourth generation of the family in the business, as a guest on your show. (For newspapers substitute "in interviewing John Jones, the fourth generation of the family in the business, for a story.")

John can discuss:

- The formula for success developed by Jones Hardware
- Why the customer is always right
- New products revolutionizing the hardware business
- How retail has changed in Thistown over the past half century
- Interesting facts about Jones Hardware

John can also demonstrate a half-dozen new products which will make home repairs easier for everyone. (This last paragraph for radio and television only.) I am enclosing John Jones' biography, along with a fact sheet about the company and a more comprehensive list of subjects he can discuss.

Please call me at 777-8888 if you need additional information.

Sincerely,

NOTE: *Format to follow when trying to arrange interviews for a success story. Quickly establish the success angle, then reinforce it with the reasons for the success which you are prepared to discuss.*

Follow up with a telephone call if you do not hear from the editor or producer in a few days.

Pitch Letter to Television Producers to Demonstrate New Products

Dear :

Christmas may be 10 weeks away but Smith Toys has received its first shipment of Christmas toys.

There are a lot of exciting new toys being introduced this year:

- A singing country & western doll
- Night vision goggles similar to those used by the military
- A 100,000-piece jigsaw puzzle
- A remote controlled talking robot
- A remote controlled flying eagle

Arnold Smith, the owner of Smith Toys, would welcome the opportunity to appear on "This Day In Thistown" and demonstrate the newest of the new Christmas toys. To make this an even more interesting program, Mr. Smith could bring some local children with him to do the actual demonstrations.

(For newspaper lifestyle or feature editors, substitute this paragraph for the one above: "We would like you to see these toys and games in case you might want to prepare a Christmas toy preview feature. We could arrange this anytime at your convenience. We could also arrange to have some children available to test the toys so that you could obtain their reactions, or even photograph them.")

It should make an interesting, and informative segment (story) for your viewers (readers).

I am enclosing a fact sheet which describes these new toys and games in greater detail.

I will call you in 3-4 days to see if there is any interest on your part.

Many thanks for your consideration.

Sincerely,

NOTE: This format can be used to try to arrange any product previews including fashions, home entertainment equipment, computers, small appliances, etc. Establish the product line in your first paragraph and then describe the individual products. Attach a fact sheet about the products. This can also be revised and used to pitch radio and newspapers.

Pitch Letter to Television to Attempt to Arrange a Live Remote

Dear :

When was the last time you had a robot do the weather on the Five O'Clock News?

As a matter of fact, when did a robot *ever* do the weather at your station, or any other one in the area?

"Charley The Robot" is going to be at Olson's all day Friday, April 17 as part of our annual Spring promotion.

We thought it would be a pleasant change of pace for your viewers if Charley helped Bill Smith deliver his forecast that evening live from our store. Charley is quite a talker.

As part of our Spring promotion, we have two possible settings for the forecast: an April showers display of colorful umbrellas and rain slickers, or a May flowers display with a garden scene and live tulips.

We hope that you will be able to bring the weather center to our store on April 17.

Sincerely,

NOTE: *This format is for trying to arrange a live remote from a store. You must have something very unique in order to get a radio station or television channel to do a remote.*

Again, follow up with a telephone call within a week of sending the letter.

Pitch Letter to Newspaper
Lifestyle Editors

Dear :

Mary Jane Smith, one of our customers, recently told us that we helped solve a big problem for her last year. She wanted to wear one outfit to a New Year's Eve party at some friend's house while her husband wanted her to wear something else.

How did we help her solve her problem?

On New Year's Eve, she wore her husband's selection, and three nights later, she came to our New Year's Eve promotion in her favorite outfit.

For the 10th consecutive year, we are extending New Year's Eve for four additional nights. It is part of our annual New Year's promotion, which will run from January 2-5.

At 7:30 each evening we turn off the cash registers, break out the champagne and refreshments, pass out the noisemakers and party hats and begin our New Year's Eve gala. We turn on the video replays of the Times Square countdown and at 8 PM sharp, we recreate New Year's Eve.

It is all a lot of fun, and it gives people a chance to "recelebrate the New Year," make additional resolutions and, like Mary Jane, wear another special outfit.

Each year these post-New Year New Year's Eve parties have been getting bigger and bigger, dressier and dressier, and more fun.

This year, at the request of many customers, we are even adding a matinee performance on Saturday at 3 PM so that parents can bring their children and celebrate with them.

Because of its uniqueness, and growing popularity, we thought you might be interested in covering our party. There's the fashion angle, the party angle, and curiosity angle (Why get all dressed up to celebrate again two days after the real event?).

I will call you in a few days to see if you are interested in celebrating with us.

Sincerely,

NOTE: This format is for an in-store promotion. The idea is to present it as a unique event, with several news and visual angles. Try to have an attention-getting opening sentence or paragraph. This format can also be used for radio and television news.

Media Advisory to Send to Newspapers, Radio and Television to Encourage Them to Cover an Event

MEDIA ADVISORY

PRESIDENTS OF FIVE HOME APPLIANCE COMPANIES TO DEMONSTRATE THEIR PRODUCTS AT HELMS APPLIANCE STORE

The presidents of five major small appliance companies will demonstrate their most unique products at Helms Appliance Store Saturday, May 12 from noon to 5 PM.

The presidents and their products are:

- Tom Smith, Modern Make-It Corporation. A microprocessor-controlled ice cream maker.

- Michael Dossier, Slice And Cut, Inc. An automatic carrot and celery slicer.

- Marvin Eagle, Acme-Eagle Home Products. A remote-controlled miniature vacuum for reaching behind furniture.

- Suzanne Sendler, Bag-Der-Bag Company. A miniature bag sealing machine.

- Alexis Jones, Control-It Company. A portable controller which enables the user to control up to five appliances at one time.

The Event: Five Presidents Of Major Small Appliance Companies
Demonstrate Their Most Unique Products
The Place: Helms Appliance Store
234 Main Street
The Date: May 12, 1995
The Time: Noon To 5 PM
Contact: Robert Helms
234-5678

NOTE: The description of the event and products to be demonstrated are self-explanatory so it is not necessary to have a separate listing of visual opportunities.

Media Advisory to Send to Radio, Television and Newspapers on New Products Introduction

MEDIA ADVISORY

FIVE FOURTH-GRADERS TO TEST NEW CHRISTMAS TOYS AND REVEAL FINDINGS AT PRESS CONFERENCE

What do the potential end-users think of the new batch of Christmas toys introduced this year?

Five fourth-graders from P. S. 234 will test 12 of them on Tuesday, November 7, and then hold a press conference to announce their findings. They will select their favorites, and provide reactions to all of them.

The Event: Five Fourth-Graders Test 12 Of The New Christmas Toys, Select Their Favorites, Critique All At Press Conference
The Place: Green's Toy Store
9090 Grand Avenue
The Date: Tuesday November 7
The Time: Testing Of Toys —- 10:30-Noon (Media Invited)
Press Conference —- Noon
Contact: Charles Ryan
293-4857

NOTE: Can be used for almost any new seasonal products.

241

Media Advisory to Encourage Coverage of Special Promotion

MEDIA ADVISORY

SANTA CLAUS IS COMING TO TOWN NEXT WEEK FOR HIS ANNUAL CHRISTMAS IN AUGUST CELEBRATION

The annual "Christmas in August" celebration at Joyce's Department Store gets underway Tuesday, August 15 when Santa Claus arrives, the 40-foot Christmas tree is lit, and the Golden Age Club Chorus sings Christmas carols.

The Event: Annual "Christmas in August" celebration launched
The Place: Joyce's Department Store
            7687 Broadway
The Date: Tuesday, August 15
The Time: Noon: Santa arrives by helicopter
            12:30: Christmas Carols
            5:30: Lighting of 40-foot Christmas tree by Mayor Jones

Other Photo Opportunities

- Store will be completely decorated for Christmas
- Artificial snow will be in area where helicopter lands in the parking lot
- Exhibition of ice carvings in front of the store

Contact: Sinclair Stevens
            999-8888

NOTE: This is an example of how to seek coverage of a special promotion. The entire emphasis is on the event and the decor and scenery, with no mention of the sale. If emphasis was placed on the sale, chances of coverage would be nil.

MEDIA ADVISORY

100 YEAR OLD COAL-FIRED IRON, MODEL OF FIRST TOASTER ARE AMONG HISTORIC SMALL APPLIANCES AT LOCAL EXHIBIT

Twenty historic small appliances, including a model of the very first toaster, a 100-year old iron which was heated by coal, and a hand-operated malted maker will be on display and demonstrated at Small Appliances, Inc. March 3-10.

The Event: Historic Small Appliances Exhibit/Demonstration
The Place: Small Appliances, Inc.
            1600 Dean Street
The Dates: March 3-10
            Press Preview March 2
The Time: Press Preview 2 PM
            Regular Store Hours 9 AM-5 PM

Photo Opportunities

- Products will be demonstrated by people wearing costumes of the appropriate period
- Demonstrations will include the actual ironing of shirts with a coal-heated iron, malted milkshakes made by a hand-cranked machine, and toast as it was made 120 years ago.

Contact: Albert Thomas
            922-2229

Media Advisory on Special Leap Year Sale

MEDIA ADVISORY

TWENTY-FOUR LOCAL RESIDENTS BORN ON FEBRUARY 29 WILL CELEBRATE THEIR LEAP YEAR BIRTHDAY TOGETHER

Twenty-four local residents born on February 29 will be celebrating their quadrennial birthday together at Sleeper's Audio Store. It is believed to be the largest gathering of leap year birthday celebrants in the state. Everything will be done in fours: Four birthday cakes, four gifts for each attendee, and four wishes when they blow out the cakes.

The Event: Special Birthday Party For 24 Local Residents Born On February 29

The Place: Sleeper's Audio Store
9999 90th Street

The Date: February 29

The Time: 5-7 PM

Photo/Story Opportunities

- Largest gathering of leap year birthday celebrants
- Four cakes, one for each of the three years missed and the fourth for this year
- Comments from the 24 on when they usually celebrate their birthdays, if they feel they lose out on gifts and parties, whether they usually do something special every fourth year, what, if anything, do people say when they find out that they were born on February 29, etc.

Contact: Sharon Long
666-6666

NOTE: *Sometimes it is also necessary to include story ideas in a media advisory if it isn't apparent. In this case, while the photo opportunities were very obvious, the story ideas needed amplification. Again, there was no mention of a "Leap Year" sale being held in conjunction with the event.*

JONES HARDWARE CELEBRATES 45TH ANNIVERSARY WITH THIRD EXPANSION IN THE PAST FIVE YEARS; ADDS 10 EMPLOYEES, TRIPLES SALES

- Jones Hardware, 2345 Main Street, is celebrating its 45th anniversary this year. It was founded by Alvin Jones in 1949, and located at One Granger Street.

- Four generations of the Jones family have been connected with the business. Alvin, his son Tom, his grandson Bill, and his great-grandson John, the current president. Alvin passed away in 1965.

- The store's initial space consisted of 1000 square feet. Today, it occupies 60,000 square feet. During the past five years, the store expanded three times, adding 10,000 square feet. It just completed the final expansion of 5,000 square feet.

- It employs 35 men and women and has an annual payroll of over $900,000. Annual sales have tripled over the past five years.

- It carries more than 10,000 different products for use in the home, office, or shop.

- The store has a unique "The Customer Is Always Right" policy. All customer complaints and adjustments are resolved within 24 hours. A service representative will visit the home, office, or plant to exchange any unsatisfactory product. This eliminates the need for the customer to make a second trip to the store. If the original purchased product was defective, the customer also receives a 10 percent discount towards his or her next purchase.

- Since instituting this policy, sales have doubled and research has substantiated that it was because of "The Customer Is Always Right" program.

- A small shop area has been built in the rear of the store so that customers can test products before making a purchase. Every Tuesday and Thursday evening from 6-9 PM, instruction is offered free of charge to "do-it-yourselfers" or any other customer who has purchased a product, or has a problem on a project at home.

- Customers also receive a monthly newsletter with information about new products for "do-it-yourselfers."

- John Jones, its current president, is a graduate of Harvard University, and the Thistown Law School. He is treasurer of the Thistown Chamber of Commerce, and chairman of its retail business development committee.

NOTE: The format for a fact sheet is to provide very specific information about the subject in short paragraphs, and in some form of logical sequence. It should provide enough information for an editor or broadcaster to get an idea of the direction of a story, what type of additional information will be needed, and what questions to ask.)

FREQUENT BUYER'S ARE REWARDED WITH FREE MERCHANDISE AND SERVICES THROUGH GRETTA'S FREQUENT BUYER'S PROGRAM

- Two years ago Gretta's Variety Store, 2222 Olive Street, started a "Frequent Buyer's program" for its customers.
- Anyone can enroll. Members collect one point for each dollar of purchases made. The only restriction is that a minimum of $100 of purchases must be made each quarter.
- Each week a half-dozen products are marked as specials and earn double points. In addition, one day a month, double points are awarded for all purchases. The day is unannounced in advance and shoppers will only learn about it if they visit the store.
- Points can be cashed in for store merchandise, local movie theater tickets, or for products and services from a catalog.
- Since its inception, frequent buyers have earned over two million points. They have also cashed in 789,000 points for more than $200,000 in merchandise and services.
- The most points have been collected by Ms. Mary Addis. She has 86,020 points and is saving them till she reaches the 100,000 mark.
- A survey taken by Gretta's indicates that the "Frequent Buyer's Program" has been responsible for attracting over 3000 new customers to the store.
- The oldest participant is Eva Stone, 87, who has collected over 10,000 points. The youngest participant is Arthur Brown, 7, who has 150 points. He has collected them buying gifts for his mother and older sister.
- All participants receive point statements each month.
- It is estimated that 15-20 percent of the points will never be redeemed.
- Minimum redemption at any one time is 1000 points. Largest redemption as of May 15 was 80,000 points by a local resident for a fur coat.
- Several other benefits are available for members of the program. There is a special "Frequent Buyer's" lounge in the store, with

free coffee and tea; a monthly newsletter; and special discounts arranged at ten area restaurants. The discount program is expected to be expanded over the next three months.

Press Release on an Upcoming
Special Event

FOUR NIGHTS OF NEW YEAR'S EVE PARTIES SCHEDULED NEXT WEEK

If you are too tired to go out and celebrate New Year's Eve next Monday evening, don't worry about it. You will have four more chances during the week to get in the mood to ring out the old year, and greet the new one.

Clarkson's Men's Clothing Store is running a New Year's Eve party each evening, Wednesday through Saturday. And to make it even more convenient for those who have to go to work the next day, the clock actually "strikes midnight" at 8 PM.

There will be champagne, music, noisemakers, party hats and all the trimmings including video replays of the Monday evening Times Square celebration. "If you will have already broken the resolutions you made Monday night, you will have a second chance to make a new list at our party," Irving Clarkson, owner of the store, said.

The party is part of Clarkson's annual New Year's sale. An added element to this year's promotion is that a special matinee New Year's party is scheduled for Saturday afternoon at 3 PM for parents who want to share the fun with their children. Milk and soft drinks will be poured.

Clarkson's sales force will be dressed in formal wear during the entire week, and anyone purchasing an overcoat will get a free bottle of champagne.

This is the tenth year Clarkson's has held a New Year's promotion and sale. "It gives everyone a chance to add a few more days of holiday fun, and get to see old friends from our past parties," Clarkson said. "There are people who attend each year just to see people they have met in previous years."

Clarkson's is located at 12345 Standard Avenue.

NOTE: The party is used as the vehicle to get publicity for the store, and attract people to a sale—though the sale is only mentioned once. This is an excellent release to send to disc jockeys.

IF YOU DON'T WEAR RED ON TUESDAY YOU WON'T BE ABLE TO SHOP AT MARVIN'S SPORTSWEAR

Have you ever heard of a retailer who will turn away a customer because he or she is not wearing the color of the day?

Meet Marvin Jones, owner of Marvin's Sportswear. Each year on Valentine's Day, Jones enforces the "red law." No one can enter his 685 Main Street store unless he or she has some red on. Red cheeks, red lipstick, and red nail polish do not count, but red hair does, according to Jones.

"It is Valentine's Day and people have to get into the swing of things," he said. "We are a fashion-oriented store and so are our customers." He did admit that if customers are not wearing red, Marvin's will rent red ties to men, and red scarves to women. "We charge a two-dollar rental fee and give it all to the Thistown Senior Citizens' Center," he said.

In past years, customers have tried to get in with a spool of red tape, red dental floss, and even a can of red beets, but it didn't work. As Jones said, "If you are not wearing it, it just doesn't count."

The one exception Marvin's has ever made to the rule was for a young man who showed up around closing time about five years ago. "He was desperate to get a certain gift for his fiancee and at that time we were not loaning ties or scarves," Jones recalled. "Finally he asked, 'What do you want—a pint of blood?'" Jones cut a deal on the spot: the young man could buy the gift if he promised to donate a pint of blood. A week later he came back with his receipt from the blood bank.

As for Marvin Jones, he will be wearing a red blazer Tuesday and all the sales help at the fashionable women's store will be in red dresses, or suits.

***NOTE**: This type of story can be developed for other days when there is an "in" color, or some other gimmick required to get into the store. It is also a good item to send to disc jockeys.*

Press Release Announcing Special Contest Related to Products Sold by a Store

CUSTOMERS INVITED TO WRITE POEMS ABOUT THEIR JEANS

They have been called dungarees, Levis, denims and jeans and no matter what they have been known as, they have been popular selling products among the customers of Morgan's Army Navy Store at 345 Green Street for over 30 years. According to Joseph Morgan his store has sold over 350,000 pairs during that period.

Now Morgan's is giving its customers a chance to explain their fondness for the blue denim product—in poetry. The store is sponsoring "An Ode To My Jeans," a poetry contest for people of all ages to write poems dedicated to, or about, their jeans.

The rules are simple, according to Morgan. The poem must be between 10 and 25 lines, and must relate to the writer's jeans. "It can be about their durability, their favorite pair, how they decorate them, an experience they shared with their jeans," Morgan said.

The writers of the three best poems will be awarded all-expense-paid weekends for two at the Conninger Resort Hotel.

Judges will be Millicent Jones, head of the English Department at Thistown High School; Professor Arlen Gonder of the English Department of Thistown University; and Harvey Friend, a poet and owner of the Johnson Book Store.

Ten finalists will be selected from among all poems received by the March 15 deadline. The authors will be invited to a final judging read-off at Morgan's on April 10 where the winners will be selected.

Twenty-five of the best poems will be published in a special booklet and distributed to Morgan's customers.

Entry forms and rules can be picked up at the store.

NOTE: This is an excellent item to send to disc jockeys.

Press Release to Announce
Promotional Event

ARMED FORCES SALUTE SCHEDULED FOR MAY 9-15 BY LOCAL RETAILER

Anderson's Sporting Goods Store will honor military units and veterans' groups from the Thistown area during Armed Forces Week, May 9-15, it was announced by Harry Anderson, its owner.

A display of uniforms worn by the military since 1901 will be featured in the store's 123 Main Street windows. Inside will be a display of photographs and memorabilia loaned by local veterans, soldiers from nearby Fort Jones, ROTC cadets from the Thistown University unit, and the 340th Air Force Squadron at Hap Field.

On Saturday, Armed Forces Day, the ROTC precision drill team will perform in the parking lot behind the store at 10 AM and at noon. In addition, there will be special displays of military vehicles, and a 50-foot scale model of the aircraft carrier Kennedy.

As a tribute to the armed forces, Anderson's will feature and hold special sales on all "Made in the USA" products. An additional ten-percent discount will be given to all active military personnel and members of veterans' organizations.

NOTE: *In addition to sending this press release to newspapers, radio and television, you should also send it to military publications in the area, as well as those published by veterans' organizations and patriotic groups.*

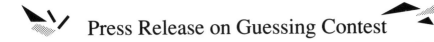

THE WINNER GETS TO KEEP THE BUCKET OF WORMS

Winners of the "Guess The Number In The Bucket" contest held each month at Ralph's Sporting Goods usually look forward to taking home the contents of the ten-gallon container. It may not be the case this month.

Entrants in the June contest must guess the number of worms in the bucket. And who is going to want the hundreds, or thousands of worms, especially if you are not into fishing?

In past months, local residents took home 767 candy Kisses, 1003 pennies, 977 ping pong balls, and 12465 shelled peanuts.

"With the fishing season coming up, we thought we would get into the spirit of things," Ralph Smith, the store's owner, said. "Perhaps we will let the winner sell the worms back to us."

Started three years ago, the monthly guessing game draws as many as 1500 entries a month. "So far with 20 days remaining it looks as though we will get well over 1000 entries," Smith said. "Someone must like worms."

No purchases are required to enter the contest, but all entries must be on official entry forms which are available at the customer service desk at Ralph's, located at 543 Pacific Street.

NOTE: Be sure to send this press release also to the outdoors writers at newspapers, and disc jockeys.

MIDTOWN STORE TO COMMEMORATE "GIVE SOMETHING BACK DAY" SATURDAY BY DONATING PROFITS TO LOCAL SENIOR CITIZEN CENTER

Black's Hardware Store, 263 East Ave., will contribute all profits earned on Saturday, June 14 to the Thistown Senior Citizens Center, it was announced by Thomas Rich, the owner.

"We are firm believers in giving something back to the community which has supported us all these years," Rich said. "This will be the fifth year we are giving one day's profits to a local organization."

According to Rich, the senior citizens center might earn as much as $2400 on June 14. "We have given away over $10,000 during previous 'give something back' days," Rich said, "We think it is good business to share our success with the community."

The Thistown Senior Citizens Center plans to use the money it receives from Black's to improve its recreation and games room, according to Sarah Willis, the center's director. "It will enable us to expand the facility so that we can accommodate another 25 seniors."

In addition to its "give something back day," Black's has donated thousands of dollars worth of tools and hardware supplies to local non-profit and charitable organizations.

NOTE: *In addition to sending this story to conventional media, it should also be sent to senior citizen publications and columnists, as well as disc jockeys.*

SOMEONE'S GOING TO WIN A MILLION DOLLAR STORE IN THIS CONTEST

Someone is going to win a store worth over one-million dollars this Saturday.

Westmates Cosmetics is holding its annual Customer Appreciation Day drawing and the top prize will be all of the store's profits on one day, November 12.

"Whoever is selected as our 'Customer of The Year' will win the store for a day," David West said. "He or she will be the boss on November 12 and at the end of the day can take home all of the profits."

West estimated that the profits could range from $3000-$5000. "We will also give the winner the option of running a sale that day," West said. "While there would be a lower profit margin, the sale might significantly increase the total volume and the winner would end up with more money to take home."

Other prizes to be awarded during Customer Appreciation Day include $100 of free merchandise per month for a 12-month period, a three-minute shopping spree during which the winner can keep as much merchandise as he or she can bring to the checkout counter, and a year's supply of lipstick.

The winner will be selected at a drawing from among the 15,432 entries received by the time the sweepstakes closed last Monday. The public is invited to attend the drawing at 10 AM at Westmates, 3456 Main Street. Mayor John Brown will pick the winning names, and the Thistown Boy's Club Choir and band will entertain. Refreshments will be served.

NOTE: The only way to get publicity for a sweepstakes is by developing a unique or impressive prize like the one in this release. If it is an ordinary prize, it really doesn't pay to send out a release for a sweepstakes.

Press Release on Improved Customer Service Programs

SPECIAL SERVICES FOR THE BLIND AND HEARING-IMPAIRED AVAILABLE AT DOWNTOWN CLOTHING STORE

Special services for the blind and hearing-impaired are now available at Checkster's Clothing on 129 Jupiter Street, it was announced by Arthur Checkster.

The services include price and information tags as well as promotional fliers in Braille, and the addition of a customer service representative who is fluent in sign language and who has previous experience working with the hearing impaired.

"We have always taken pride in our customer service program and have continuously looked for ways to improve it," Checkster said. "We met with various organizations involved with the blind and hearing-impaired, as well as with individual customers to get their input as to which services were needed."

The store's monthly mailing to customers is now available, upon request, in Braille, and all merchandise includes not only Braille on its price tags, but also in its information about the product including color, style, size, design, material, and use and care.

For the hearing-disabled, Checkster's has added Mary Ellen Jones, a former teacher at the Thistown School for The Deaf as a customer service representative. At the school, she taught sign language.

"We will be monitoring these programs to make certain that they are effective in helping our customers," Checkster said. "We will also be looking to see how we might improve them to make them even more effective."

NOTE: *In addition to radio, television and newspapers, send this type of release to the organizations which serve the blind and hearing-disabled.*

Press Release on In-Store Appearance By Celebrity

FORMER MIDDLEWEIGHT CHAMPION JOHN MURPHY TO APPEAR AT EVENS MEN'S SHOP THURSDAY

Former middleweight champion John Murphy will appear at Evens Men's Shop on 141 Broadway Thursday, from noon to 2 p.m.

Murphy, who held the title from 1982 through 1987, will sign autographs and pose for pictures with customers.

While no purchase is required for an autograph, only customers who make a purchase over $25 will have their picture taken with the former champion.

Since retiring from the ring in 1989, Murphy has been the national spokesman for "Dress Up," an organization promoting formal fashions for men. He has traveled over 200,000 miles a year making personal appearances for the group.

NOTE: This should be sent to the sports editors, columnists, broadcasters and boxing writers, as well as to lifestyle editors.

"ODD-SIZE CLUB" STARTED BY MEN'S CLOTHING STORE

For the man who wears different sized gloves on each hand, needs different sized shoes or off-size jackets or suits, there is good news in the offing. Roberts Men's Shop, 9000 Evans Ave, has organized an "odd-sized" club to cater to this growing group.

"We are attempting to create a central registry of all men in the area who require two different sized items," Robert Smith, owner of Roberts, said. "We will then be able to identify men who require different sizes for each hand or foot, and the sizes they need." Smith explained that once they have the sizes, they will be able to match people so that they can coordinate their purchases. "This will save them both time and money."

Smith also noted that many men have difficulty finding properly fitted jackets or suits because they do not wear standard-sized garments. "We are instituting relationships with several clothing factories to accommodate these customers," Smith said. "We expect to be able to search and find the needed sizes within 48 hours after a customer's visit."

Smith is urging all men who require different sizes for each hand or foot, or off-sized clothing to enroll in the registry at Roberts. "It is a long-overdue solution to a lingering problem," Smith said.

NOTE: This press release should be sent to lifestyle editors, disc jockeys, publications of men's organizations, as well as radio and television stations. It is an example of how you can get publicity for a unique service you offer.

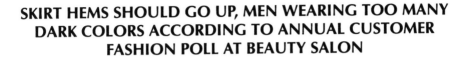

SKIRT HEMS SHOULD GO UP, MEN WEARING TOO MANY DARK COLORS ACCORDING TO ANNUAL CUSTOMER FASHION POLL AT BEAUTY SALON

The third annual fashion poll among customers at Sally's Beauty Salon has come out in favor of shorter skirts, fewer dark color suits for men, and two-piece bathing suits.

Over 1700 customers of the upper Southside salon participated in this year's survey. Seventy-two percent said they preferred that shorter skirts remain in style. As a matter of fact, almost one-third suggested that the skirts be shortened by another inch.

So far as two-piece bathing suits are concerned, it was a runaway vote again. Sixty-eight percent were in favor, with only 20 percent opposed. The other 12 percent had no opinion.

The favorite color among the women was red with 48 percent. Blue at 32 percent was second and brown with 12 percent finished third. When it came to hair coloring, only 20 percent said they would become blondes, and six percent would become red heads.

Forty percent prefer gold necklaces, 39 percent prefer silver, and 20 percent pearls. Diamonds are still a girl's best friend, according to the survey. Ninety percent said it was their favorite ring.

When asked their opinions on men's fashions, the women were very opinionated. Sally's poll showed that 75 percent felt that men wore too many dark-colored suits and sports jackets. Almost 80 percent thought their ties were too conservative, and over 90 percent criticized the dark-blue and black socks most men wear.

The women at Sally's Beauty Salon felt that men were not styling their hair as much as they did five years ago. Fifty-two percent said that there was less styling apparent, and only 17 percent thought there was more. The remaining 31 percent said it was about the same.

Copies of the survey are available from Sally Roberts, Sally's Beauty Salon, 567 Fifth Street North, Thistown 23456.

NOTE: Customer surveys are always of interest to the media, even if they are not scientific. This type of press release should go to newspapers, radio and television, as well as disc jockeys.

RESIDENTS ARE SPENDING TOO MUCH MONEY ON CLEANING BILLS BECAUSE THEY ARE NOT FOLLOWING THE USE AND CARE INSTRUCTIONS

Thistown residents may be spending as much as 20 percent more than they should be on their cleaning bills because they are not following the instructions on their garments, according to a local women's wear store owner.

Alfred Jones, of The Place For Fashion, said that he has based his estimate on comments he has heard from customers in the store. "I always make it a practice to ask them if they follow the instructions on the label and if they do not, what do they do with their garments," Jones said. "You would be surprised by the number of women who dry clean garments which can, and should, be washed."

Jones also said that a smaller number wash garments which should be dry cleaned. "This can ruin some garments, and shrink others," he said. "So can washing or drying garments in cycles other than those recommended by the manufacturer."

He noted that in addition to spending too much on unnecessary cleaning bills, a consumer may not get as much wear out of a garment as she would if she followed the manufacturer's recommendations.

Jones said that The Place For Fashion has prepared an eight-page pamphlet on the use and care of clothing and will give a free copy to anyone who visits the store. He also said that he is planning to run seminars on the subject at the store sometime next winter. "It is important that you take good care of your clothing, but there is a thing called `overkill' and too many people are unnecessarily practicing it," he said. The Place For Fashion is located at 1500 Second Avenue.

NOTE: Statements on consumerism, especially if they show how a customer can save money, are always of interest to media. This can also be sent to the lifestyle editor, as well as to any consumerism writers or broadcasters.

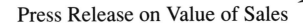

TWO MILLION DOLLARS SAVED BY CUSTOMERS OF LOCAL HOUSEWARES STORE THROUGH TEN SALES LAST YEAR

More than two-million dollars have been saved by customers of Tillie's Housewares through purchases they made at the 10 sales the downtown store held last year.

According to Tillie Caron, its owner, the savings were realized by approximately 12,000 local residents, for an average of $167 each. "While we run these ten sales a year and draw larger crowds to the store during them, we still do a very high volume business when we charge our regular prices," Caron said. "We offer quality and fair prices all year round."

An informal survey taken by Tillie's showed that approximately 20 percent of the savings came right back into the store through increased purchases by customers.

The sales Tillie's Housewares plans to hold during the coming year are on Presidents Day, St. Patrick's Day, Memorial Day Weekend, in mid-July and mid-August, Columbus Day, Veterans Day and the first week of December. Two more sale dates have not yet been selected. Tillie's Housewares is located at 1475 First Ave.

NOTE: This release is for the business pages and also consumer writers and editors.

Press Release to Focus Attention on the Store

MEN ARE BUYING SILVER PINS, GOLD NECKLACES AND PEARL EARRINGS WHILE WOMEN ARE BUYING WATCHES AND GOLD CUFF LINKS IN EARLY VALENTINE'S DAY SHOPPING

With another week left before Valentine's Day, certain purchasing trends have developed, according to Phillip King of King's Jewelry on 444 Pacific Street.

"Men seem to be buying an unusually large number of silver pins this year with the 'X-O-X-O-X' love-and-kisses pin the big seller," King said. "They switch to gold when it comes to necklaces, and to pearl when buying earrings." A previous big selling item, charm bracelets, does not seem to be very popular this year, according to King. Heart-shaped jewelry is not near the top of the list either.

As for women, they seem to be falling back to the old standards: watches and cuff links. "This year, there seems to be a trend toward less expensive watches than last year, with silver being purchased more frequently than gold," King said. "Cuff links are always big sale items for Valentine's Day, with about 60 percent of them gold."

King noticed that men appear to be spending more time shopping this year than in previous years. "They are either having a more difficult time making a selection or are more value-conscious and are looking for the better price," he said. "On the other hand, women still seem to spend about the same amount of time shopping as in previous years."

What about those last-minute shoppers? "Based on the number of shoppers to date, the numbers pattern seems to be about the same this year as in previous years. Women have been shopping in greater numbers early on, while men are continuing to put off their decisions until the last minute," King said.

NOTE: This type of release can be prepared for just about any store during any gift-giving season of the year. It is a good story for all media, including business editors, lifestyle editors, disc jockeys, etc.

Press Release to Announce a
Staff Appointment

LOUIS SMITH APPOINTED CUSTOMER SERVICE MANAGER AT HART'S VARIETY STORE

Louis B. Smith, a veteran retailer, has been appointed customer service manager at Hart's Variety Store, it was announced by William Hart, president.

Smith, a resident of Thistown, had been a men's clothing department manager at the L-Town Department Store for 10 years. He also held managerial positions with Jones Variety Store, and Harry's Clothing.

In his new position, Smith will be responsible for expanding Hart's customer service program. It includes the supervision of the store's frequent buyer program, extended warranty service, and repair department.

"I have known Lou Smith for over 20 years and have always been impressed with his dedication to customer service," Hart said. "I tried to hire him on several occasions because I was convinced that he was the best choice to supervise our program. Now that we are expanding, I am delighted he's coming aboard."

A graduate of Penn State College, Smith and his wife, Mary, have three children, Susan, Sarah, and Sam.

NOTE: *Appointment releases should be sent to business editors and organizations to which the person belongs.*

LOCAL RETAILER LOOKING FOR 100 GOOD MEN AND WOMEN TO SPONSOR IN THISTOWN WALK-A-THON

Jackson's Health Foods Store is looking for 100 local residents to sponsor in next month's Thistown Walk-A-Thon for the Civic Park Fund.

"Civic Park provides unlimited pleasure and recreational facilities for the citizens of this city, and we want to help raise as much money as possible for it," Roberta Barmost, owner of Jackson's, said. "We're willing to pledge five dollars per mile to the 100 competitors we sponsor."

Area residents who want to be sponsored by Jackson's should leave their names in the store at 456 Main Street.

"We are looking for competitors who intend to finish the entire course because we are anxious to make a big donation to the Civic Park Fund," Barmost said.

This will be the third consecutive year Jackson's Health Foods Store will be sponsoring 100 residents in the Walk-A-Thon. In addition to this competition, Jackson's has also sponsored 100 competitors a year in the Civic Park Fund Bike-A-Thon, held each September.

NOTE: This is an example of how a store can get involved in an existing community project in a major way. This type of release should also be sent to the sports pages if they cover such events. Also send to disc jockeys along with a covering letter inviting them to sign up and join the group of 100 competitors.

Letter to Newspapers, Radio and Television Making Them Aware of Your Availability as a Source for Information

Dear :

For the past 25 years I have been involved in retail in Thistown as the owner of Larry's Women's Fashions. I also served for four terms as president of the local merchants' association.

During this quarter century in retail, I have gained considerable expertise in several areas which might be of interest to you.

I would be very pleased to assist you in providing information anytime you need material in the following areas:

- *Women's Fashions.* Our store has an excellent reputation among the fashion-conscious women of the community. We attend both the Paris and New York shows each year, and can provide you with updates after each show. We also have an extensive collection of pictures of fashions from over the past 50 years.

- *The Changing Scene at Retail.* We are active in several national retail organizations (as well as local chapters), attend their conventions, and are up-to-date on what is going on in retail today, and what to expect in the future.

- *Retail in Thistown.* Having been president of the local merchants' association, I am very familiar with the problems local retailers face: taxes, fees, petty crime, zoning regulations, etc. Also the opportunities: good economic environment, loyal local customer base, absence of the big discount chains, good traffic control and parking facilities in the downtown area.

You can call us anytime for information on any of these subjects or in any other areas in which you need input. Along with this letter, I am enclosing cards with both my home and business telephone numbers. Call nights and weekends if necessary.

Hope we can be of help to you in the future.

Sincerely,

You can use two formats in preparing the telephone contact cards you send to media: one with the subject matter at the top of the card, the other with your name at the top. Some people use both formats so that an editor or broadcaster can select the one which fits into his or her file system.

William R. Smith
President, Williams Fashions
123 Main Street
234-5678   (Home) 432-8765

Women's Fashions, Retailing
Local Business Climate

Women's Fashions . . . Retailing
Local Business Climate

William R. Smith
President, Williams Fashions
123 Main Street
234-5678   (Home) 432-8765

Letter to Radio Station and Television Promotion Directors Offering to Provide Prizes for Promotional Contests

Dear :

We have always enjoyed your station's listener ("viewer" for television) promotions, and have even entered a few times ourselves.

While we have never been winners, we were wondering if we could do the next best thing—provide the prizes for the winners of your next contest?

Not only are we willing to provide the prizes, but we will also assist you in promoting the contest in our Main Street windows, on our in-store signage, and in a mailing to our customers.

I will call you in a few days to see if we can get together and discuss this possible participation.

I look forward to talking to you.

Sincerely,

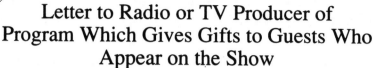

Letter to Radio or TV Producer of Program Which Gives Gifts to Guests Who Appear on the Show

Dear :

Guests are such an important part of your show that we feel that they deserve nothing but the best when it comes to the gifts they get for appearing.

That's why we would very much like to provide the gifts which you give to your guests.

As you may know, we have been in business for over 35 years at the same location and have developed an excellent reputation for the fine quality of merchandise in our store.

We would be willing to provide specific gifts, or even gift certificates. As part of our participation with your program, we will promote the show at our store.

I will call you next week to see if we can arrange this tie-in.

Sincerely,

AND DON'T FORGET YOUR SUPPLIER PRESS RELEASES

As part of their marketing program, manufacturers often prepare press releases about their products and send them to retailers for local use. By filling in a few spaces, you have a good localized press release to send to media.

If your suppliers send such material to you, be sure to use it. If they do not, ask that you be put on the mailing list to receive them. If need be, contact the public relations departments at your supplier companies.

CHAPTER 15

Using Advertising and Other Paid Services to Promote Your Store

Publicity enables you to gain exposure in media without paying for the time and space. It will help you develop a positive image for the store, and will attract people to shop at it. However, you exercise very little control over how, when or where your message appears because it is entirely up to the editors and broadcasters to make that decision. You are at their mercy.

The only guaranteed way of delivering the message you want delivered, when you want it delivered, to your customers and potential customers is through advertising and other paid marketing vehicles.

This chapter is designed to familiarize you with these paid outlets, and suggest the various options you might exercise for organizing your advertising program.

ORGANIZING YOUR ADVERTISING PROGRAM

The amount of money you plan to spend on advertising will generally determine how you should organize your program. If you have a very modest budget and can only afford a minimal effort, you would go in one direction. On the other hand, if you are willing to commit a substantial amount of money to a program, you may not have any alternative but to hire an advertising agency.

Before deciding on how you will organize your effort, it is important that you realize that there are many different components which comprise the planning and execution phases of an ongoing advertising program.

A few of the elements are: planning a strategy that dovetails with your marketing and business plan; evaluating the available media and selecting from among those which will provide the most effective and cost-efficient ways to reach your target audience; writing copy; designing layouts; preparing the artwork; taping and recording; buying time and space; and production.

Your Budget

The first step you should take is to allocate funds for your advertising budget. Only you know your costs of doing business and how much you can afford to spend on advertising. At the end of this chapter on page 285 is a chart which lists the average percent of sales invested in advertising by almost 40 different kinds of stores. It provides you with a good guideline. If your type of store is not listed, use three percent of your gross sales as a starting point for your advertising investment. The figures from the chart will be higher if you are a new store, are in a high-pressure business, have heavy competition, or are in a remote location.

An Advertising Plan

No matter what the size of your budget might be, it is always a good idea to have an advertising plan. It serves as the blueprint for your program. It states your objectives, the budget, your media plan, creative approach, etc. A lot of the research you gathered (see Chapter Two) will be included in the plan, too.

There are several ways to develop the plan. If you use an advertising agency, it will usually develop the plan for you. Or you might contact the closest Small Business Institute of the Small Business Administration (see Chapter Two, page 15). You might be able to get it to develop the plan at no charge. Try checking local universities, especially schools of business, to see if they have internship, or team project programs. If they do, see if you can arrange for your advertising plan to be developed by an intern, or as part of a team project. Other possibilities are for a college marketing professor, a free-lancer, or someone working at an advertising agency who wants to moonlight. Ask friends for recommendations, or place a classified ad in the "Help Wanted" section of the newspaper under "Advertising."

Conducting the Program

Because there are so many different elements to an advertising program, it will be virtually impossible to handle it all by yourself. Perhaps the only exception might be if your entire program consists of Yellow Pages advertising, a few direct mail letters to customers, and/or limited radio spots. In this case, Yellow Pages salespersons will usually help write your ad, some radio stations will do likewise, and you might be able to write your own direct mail letters.

The options for conducting the program include:

- Hiring an advertising agency. It is usually best to use a local agency (one in your city or within a 50-mile radius). Ask for recommendations from friends and other business firms. You can also check the Yellow Pages under the heading of "Advertising Agencies & Counselors." A helpful directory which lists advertising agencies, staffs and clients is the *Standard Directory Of Advertising Agencies.* It can usually be found at public and business libraries.

- Hiring an advertising manager. If you are spending a considerable amount of money, you might hire someone to coordinate and oversee the work of your agency, or set up your own operation. This does not have to be a full-time job for the individual. He or she could be a semi-retired advertising executive who spends a day or two a week working for you, or a person who also has other responsibilities in the store.

- Using free-lance help. These may be individuals who moonlight from their regular advertising jobs, or men and women who free-lance all the time. Call the advertising departments of local business firms for recommendations. Free-lance writers may be found in the Yellow Pages under the heading, "Writers Business," while free-lance artists are usually listed under the heading "Artists." It is important that when you use free-lance artists or writers that their work be supervised and that they be given direction. That's why it would be to your advantage to have some type of advertising manager overseeing the entire program.

• Intern or class team project programs might also be examined. Check with the local universities and see what they might be able to offer. Be sure to examine carefully past campaigns they may have done for local businesses. Remember, chances are a different group of students will be working on your campaign and their work may not be comparable to the work being shown to you. However, the examples of past work should give you a general idea of the pattern of the work and the supervision they received from the faculty. This may be the route to consider carefully if you have a small budget.

Other Support

Look for support for your program from vendors, and the media. Check with your suppliers and determine what, if any, cooperative advertising programs and allowances they have in place. Also check to see if the manufacturers have advertising slicks, or other materials which they will furnish free of charge. Check with local media to see what extras they might offer. Will they offer assistance in preparing ads? Do they offer free or low-cost audio or video taping facilities? Will they provide a free announcer to do audio spots? Do they have special merchandise support programs or allowances? Do they offer research reports on the local population and its purchasing habits?

THE VEHICLES THROUGH WHICH YOU CAN DELIVER YOUR MESSAGE

There are more than 25 different types of paid outlets which you can use to deliver your message. They range from newspapers, radio and television, to bus shelters, bill stuffers, and direct mail; from cable, ethnic and high school publications to outdoor billboards, tourist publications and aerial advertising.

What do they offer you?

Daily Newspapers

On the average, over 60 percent of all adults in the United States read a daily newspaper. To get one, an individual must buy it and is obviously making an investment in something he or she wants to read. Whether or not they see your ad is another question. Dailies normally have an image of credibility among their readers and wide acceptance in the community. They offer a great deal of flexibility to the advertiser. You can pick the day of the week you want to run your ad, its size can vary, and you can target it to the sections of the paper through which you think you can best reach your audience. Moreover, you do not have a long lead deadline. You can quickly schedule an ad if need be. If you see that a competitor has drastically cut prices on a product, you can quickly prepare and run an ad meeting him or her head-on. Another benefit is that since today's newspaper is old tomorrow, readers can cut out and save your ad or coupons. They have a reminder of what to shop for, something they do not get from radio or television. If the newspaper has area sections, you can limit your message to those people you are trying to reach and greatly reduce your cost per thousand circulation. On the other hand, if you are in a very large city and there is only one edition, you may be paying for a lot of wasted circulation. When reading a newspaper, people do not get up to go to the bathroom or refrigerator when they get to an advertisement, something which they may do when a commercial comes on the television set. On the other hand, there is a lot of "clutter" in a newspaper. Since around 57 percent of a newspaper is advertising, readers may flip through pages of ads to get to the stories. There is no guarantee they will read your ad.

Weekly Newspapers

Since weekly newspapers usually cover a specific section of a city, they enable a retailer to target the advertising carefully to the audience he or she wants to reach.

There are several differences between weeklies and daily newspapers. While some weeklies are purchased, others are given away free of charge. The person picking up a paper which is free may not be as committed to it as he or she would be if a purchase was required. On the other hand, if it is the only weekly in that section and it does a good job, it could have as loyal and dedicated a readership as a paid circulation weekly. Unlike daily newspapers, many weeklies may not have their circulations verified by a recognized circulation auditing group. You should ask your local weeklies how you can verify their circulations. Another difference is that, while you can vary the size of your ad, you don't have the flexibility of picking the day you want it to be published, and you have a longer lead deadline. Readers may also have a tendency to keep the paper for a longer period of time and be reluctant to clip out an ad or coupons.

A very positive factor is that many readers look upon their weekly newspaper as their prime source for news about their neighbors and neighborhood. As a result, they probably read it more carefully than they do their daily newspaper. This could mean that they become more aware of the ads and pay closer attention to them. Ask your local weekly newspapers to provide you with any research studies they have done on their readership patterns.

Radio

Radio is the only medium which can be with you all of the time. You can hear it at home, in the car, at work, on the beach, and even when walking down the street. With more than 15 different formats (though all may not be available in your community), it offers you the flexibility to target your audience based on the music (or talk) it prefers. Industry reports indicate that the average American adult tunes into radio almost three hours a day.

Radio can be the least expensive medium when it comes to production time and costs. A simple commercial may be read by an announcer or taped (sometimes at the station). Even a more elaborate radio spot can cost less than that of the production of a print ad or television commercial. Copy changes can be made very quickly, enabling you to react almost instantly to events which might have an impact on your store (snowy weather sale, arrival of a popular product in back order, etc.). A good catchy spot will attract listeners' attention, and through repeated airings will leave an indelible impression in their minds.

A negative is that the listener does not have a permanent record of what is said during a spot and could forget sale items and other important information. Outside the home and office, chances are the listener cannot or will not take notes, and may forget what was said. Another negative is that if you only have a limited schedule with the station, a listener may miss your message because he or she just wasn't tuned in when it ran.

Since radio audiences become attached to on-air personalities, many become highly credible spokespersons for advertisers. If your spots run on a program hosted by such a personality, it would be to your advantage to have him or her read them live.

Television

The medium with which people spend the most time each day is television. It is also the medium which enables you to reach the largest number of people at any one time. A television commercial can be very powerful and convey a strong message about your store, your products and your image.

On the negative side, a good television spot is expensive to produce and may be beyond the reach of the average small retailer. With a limited budget, you would have to decide whether the production costs of a television commercial could be more effectively used to buy time or space in another medium. However, there may be ways to reduce production costs. Your suppliers may have spots about their products which can be localized with your store name. You may be able to get university students studying advertising or television production to shoot spots for you as part of a class project. Your local channels may also have ideas, or offer low-cost production facilities to get your business.

Cable

In deciding whether cable will be an effective medium for you to use, you must determine its penetration in your area. What percentage of television homes in the area from which you draw customers are wired for cable?

You should also determine if there are any statistics available on local cable viewing patterns.

Cable offers relatively low advertising rates. As a result, you can buy a considerable amount of time and achieve high ad repetition. With so much highly specialized programming, you can target specific segments of the population through the channels which appeal to them.

On the negative side, you still have to produce spots and, as explained under "television," it can be expensive. It is a fact that watching broadcast television still dominates the viewing time even in cable homes, and you are also competing against pay cable programming. In addition, there may be so many program options on your cable system that viewership is very segmented.

Magazines

There are three types of magazines you might consider: the locally published general "city" magazines, local business magazines and the local/regional editions of national magazines.

Locally published magazines usually have an upscale readership; if there are any in your area, be sure to get their media kits to determine demographics. The local/regional editions of national magazines enable you to "rub shoulders" with the large national advertisers. It is good image-building for your store to be included in a regional edition. You can then feature the ad on easels with the tag line, "As Seen In XXXXX." Customers will be impressed. Locally published "city" magazines usually project a very high quality image which will rub off on your store if you are an advertiser. Moreover, magazines are usually kept around the home or office for a period of time, and as a result your ad remains alive and visible for a long time. Chances are it will not be clipped.

But there are drawbacks as well. Because of long lead deadlines, your advertising will probably have to be submitted weeks in advance of publication. If you plan to feature products, you will have to be certain that you have them on hand when the advertising breaks. It is going to take a lot of planning and coordination with your suppliers. Costs can also be high if you draw customers from a small concentrated area of the city where the publication has good penetration, but which only represents a small percentage of its circulation. In this case, you will be paying a premium price for the circulation you want. See if you can get from the publications zip code breakdowns of its subscribers. If you have a limited budget, you must determine the value of going into one of these magazines on an infrequent basis. Are you getting maximum value when you combine space costs with ad preparation and production costs? You might be able to reach the same audience more efficiently, for example, with direct mail.

There is an exception. The Christmas gift-giving issues of the local consumer magazines are usually very well read and used as a shopping guide by the readers. It may be worth a "one-shot" effort.

Ethnic Publications

If a large number of your customers belong to an ethnic group and/or you are trying to reach out to the group, you should study its local publication(s) as an advertising medium.

Ask for media kits, and try to determine if the readership is the audience you are trying to attract to the store. As with all media you have under consideration, determine if the publication(s) projects the type of image which you want for your advertising.

A factor to weigh is whether or not you are already reaching your target audience through your general media advertising. If the answer is "yes," you must then determine if this advertising will reinforce your other message with this group, or is of no value. Ask for an audited circulation statement before placing any advertising.

Ethnic publications may fit in the same category as weekly newspapers in that they, too, may be more thoroughly read than dailies. This would have to be determined by reading any research reports they produce.

Foreign Language Publications

If you have large numbers of foreign language-speaking residents in the community who patronize your store or whom you would like to attract, consider advertising in any of the local foreign language newspapers they read. Obtain a media kit and evaluate the publication as an advertising medium. Are its rates in line? Does it have an audited circulation report? Does the publication's image reflect where you want your advertising to appear?

Your advertising should be in the language of the newspaper and you should consider asking the advertising staff at the paper to translate it for you. You should also have the translation checked by at least two other sources to make certain it is correct. Naturally it is important that if you consider advertising in a foreign language publication, you should be prepared to have on the selling floor at least one person who speaks the language.

Tourist Publications

If one of your goals is to attract visitors to the city, you should examine the various tourist publications distributed to visitors at hotels, airports, restaurants and convention centers. You should also consider advertising in the programs of the various trade shows which bring out-of-town visitors to the city. Since these are giveaways, it may be impossible to get an audited circulation report. What you should do is check the various hotel front desks and other places where the magazines are supposed to be distributed in order to make certain that they are actually available. Do this several times over a few months' period. Actually visitors do use these guides for selecting entertainment and dining facilities as well as sightseeing. How often they use these guides for shopping recommendations is something you should check out. Call other advertisers and ask them if they are satisfied with the response to their advertisements. Also ask the publisher for any research he or she might have on the subject.

Advertising in these guides will probably only be successful for you if you are located in the areas where tourists stay or visit, if you are offering a unique product or product line, or exceptionally good pricing on well-known products (watches, etc.). It may be a good idea to offer a discount in your ad if the tourist brings it to the store. This will enable you to pinpoint its effectiveness.

Other Publications

There are probably dozens of other types of publications in your area in which you may consider placing an ad from time to time. They can include high school, college, union and military publications, as well as those published by fraternal, religious, business, civic, veterans, patriotic, senior citizens, and non-profit organizations. There may also be the programs of balls and fundraising banquets, and theater programs. The list can be endless.

You will probably want to consider a regular schedule only if you see a group as a source of important customers. For example, if your product line is aimed at teen-agers, you might advertise in high school and/or college publications. You will probably find that these costs for advertising are quite low. If you offer special pricing for senior citizens, you may want to run ads in their publications, especially around May, which is Senior Citizen Month.

In other publications, you may want to run advertising in conjunction with special promotions aimed at the groups. If you run a Veterans Day promotion, you may want to take out small space ads in the organizations' newsletters "saluting" the veterans on their day, and announcing the promotion. You will probably find that you will get a good response from advertising in these newsletters because the membership appreciates this type of support.

Theater program advertising can be an effective buy for your store if theater patrons are part of your target audience. Ask the publisher to provide you with research about its readers.

Yellow Pages

One of the most important local publications to a retailer may be the Yellow Pages. It is in practically every home in your area, and remains there for an entire year. It is also a well-used reference source. It is estimated that 59 percent of consumers use it weekly.

The Yellow Pages are best used to complement or enhance the effects of advertising placed in other media. Studies have shown that when adding Yellow Pages advertising to newspaper, or television, or radio advertising schedules, the percentage of purchasers influenced by the conventional media increased anywhere from 42 to almost 300 percent. Other studies have shown that 60 percent of consumers who use the Yellow Pages make a purchase, and that 80 percent of consumers turn to the Yellow Pages in urgent situations. Upper-income and college-educated adults are very heavy users of the Yellow Pages. It is a relatively low-cost medium from both a space and production standpoint. The Yellow Pages is also an effective vehicle to use to reach out for new customers in the areas surrounding your city. You can go into as many of the directories as your budget permits, and where you feel you will find potential customers.

Negatives are that your ad can only be changed once a year, and you are lumped together on the same page as your competitors. One way to overcome this latter concern is to consider using more than one listing in the key books. Use as many listings as your budget permits, under various headings which reflect your different product lines.

Shelter Advertising

One of the newer forms of media, and a fast-growing one at that, is bus shelter advertising. While buses stop at these shelters, their passengers are just one group of the audience reached. Motorists and pedestrians are also targets for the advertising. You will probably want any shelter advertising you do to be within a 3-5 mile radius from your store, especially if it is within the area from which you draw most of your customers. You should also consider using the shelters of bus routes which lead to your store. The creative work used on shelters is often coordinated with in-store displays, thus increasing the frequency of exposure to the product near, and at the point-of-purchase.

Telephone Side Panels

Similar in concept to shelter advertising, these back-lit panels are on outdoor telephone kiosks in heavily traveled areas. They are easily visible to both pedestrians and motorists. They offer excellent creative opportunities. You might buy into kiosks on the streets surrounding your store, offering directions on how to reach it: "Turn right on Rush Street and walk 30 feet to our front entrance," "Walk two blocks north, and turn left," etc. As with shelter advertising, the creative work on the telephone panels can be coordinated with in-store displays to increase product frequency of exposure near and at the point-of-purchase.

Transit

Side and rear panels on buses, railroad stations, airport and bus terminals, bus and train interiors, and taxi tops are locations to consider for placing your advertising. Factors to consider include the travel patterns of your customers and potential customers (see Chapter Two), the visibility you can receive in the community, and the cost effectiveness.

Airport advertising would only be effective if you are courting tourists, or your customer base consists of many frequent travelers. Bus terminal and railroad station advertising would also only be effective if your customers use these facilities.

Exterior and interior bus advertising and interior train advertising can be effective if you can target it for those routes and lines which customers would take to reach your store. An advantage of exterior bus advertising is that it is highly visible to both motorists and pedestrians. Motorists stuck in traffic behind or alongside a bus can never forget the advertising on its exterior.

Outdoor

Effective for communicating simple ideas, and reinforcing and reminding consumers of advertising messages communicated through other media, outdoor advertising is a cost-efficient buy and can usually be strategically located on routes leading to stores. It is possible to cover a market completely and achieve high levels of viewing frequency.

There are, however, several negative aspects. You must determine if outdoor advertising will be effective in reaching your audience. It is possible that billboards may never come within view of your customers or target audience, especially if they, and the store, are located within the city's borders. Another negative is public opinion. There are groups of people, and even communities which have been fighting to eliminate billboards. If there is active opposition to billboard advertising in your community, you should carefully study the situation before coming to a decision as to whether or not you will use them. Also, your advertising can be surrounded with other messages. Your outdoor board can provide sports scores, news bulletins, time and temperature. One more point to remember. If your billboard is off a fast-moving highway, motorists will not have much time to read more than one strong message, and it has to be a simple one at that.

Stadium, Aerial and Other Outdoor Advertising

There are so many other ways to advertise your message out-of-doors: at sports stadiums, using outdoor balloons and airplanes, your own trucks and vehicles and even bumper stickers.

Sports stadium and arena advertising can be an exceptionally good buy if your advertising is strategically located so that it will be picked up during television coverage of games. Around the scoreboard is always a good location. Ask the stadium marketing people for game video tapes so that you can study the camera angles.

Aerial advertising always attracts attention, and is effective whether it is in the downtown area of a city, over a park, fairgrounds or stadium, or beach. You can get primarily name identification on such advertising.

Any vehicles you have — especially those of your service force — should carry store signage which projects a positive image of your business. They serve as a moving advertisement for your store as they drive through the streets of the city.

You might also develop a unique and attractive bumper sticker and give it to your customers. If it is unique and non-commercial, many will probably use it.

Circulars and Bulletin Board Posters

Both circulars and bulletin board posters are forms of advertising which might be considered. Each can serve an important function.

Bulletin board posters can be used to support any special sales and promotions you conduct throughout the year for segments of the population. For example, if you run special sales or pricing for senior citizens, send posters to each senior citizen center and organization for their bulletin boards. Same with veterans organizations if you run a Veterans Day promotion. And don't forget business firms if you are running special nights for them. You can also send bulletin board posters to apartment houses, business firms and complexes, fraternal organizations, and military bases when you are running general sales.

Circulars can be used many ways. You could have someone distribute them in the streets around the store (if it is legal in your community, and you do not feel it will reflect negatively on the image of the store). You could also distribute them, in bulk, at apartment complexes, business firms, under doors (again, if it does not compromise your image). Depending upon the type of circulars you use, you may even have them inserted in weekly newspapers or other publications.

Direct Mail

A very effective technique for targeting specific groups by location, interests, product use, and even demographics, direct mail offers you great flexibility in presenting your message, and is an effective way to test market ideas and products.

The disadvantages include relatively high cost per contact, a low response rate, and its image. Direct mail is often called "junk mail" and it is said that almost half of it gets thrown away without being opened. But if your store has a good image and reputation in the community, chances are a higher percentage of people will open the mail it receives from your store.

Any direct mail campaign you conduct will undoubtedly cover three different audiences: your current customers, former ones you are trying to lure back, and new prospects. You undoubtedly have mailing lists for your current customers, as well as former ones. Obtaining updated, accurate mailing lists is a problem since about 18 percent of the public moves each year. But lists of potential customers can be obtained in various ways. Through your research (Chapter Two), you should have a pretty good idea of the demographics of your target audience. You might contact a list broker who compiles and sells mailing lists. You can find them in the Yellow Pages under the heading of "Mailing Lists." Or you could also develop your own list. If you want to reach new mothers, try to get names from local hospitals, or check the birth certificates filed with the city government. Marriage license applications, property transfer records, voting rolls, and tax rolls are all possible sources for mailing list names.

Another source for developing a mailing list is the "address telephone directory," which many telephone companies will sell. Instead of listings by name in alphabetic order, names are grouped by street addresses. This will be a good way for you to develop your list if your research has pinpointed the location of your prospects. You should also try to get mailing lists from various local organizations (they may sell them to you), and local media. The latter may give them to you free if you advertise.

A technique to lower direct mail costs is to go into a group mailing where expenses are shared. Val-Pak, which operates in approximately 250 cities in the United States, breaks its mailings into groupings of approximately 10,000 homes, using carrier routes. By grouping retailers together, it can produce a mailing for a retailer for around $400. This not only includes the mailing but also the design, layout and printing of the mailing insertion.

THERE ARE SO MANY OTHER WAYS . . . .

There are countless other techniques for gaining exposure. They include messages on your postage meter, attractive shopping bags, in-store PA system announcements, a call-in telephone number for recorded messages on specials, advertising messages on the plastic bags newspapers sometimes use for home delivery, and even participation on computer bulletin boards.

Let your imagination run away with itself!

RESOURCES

Many of the resources mentioned in this chapter can be found locally by going to the Yellow Pages. The proper listings for most were given within the chapter. All media you will deal with are located in your community.

Standard Directory of Advertising Agencies

- National Register Publishing, 121 Chanlon Road, New Providence, NJ, 07974

Val-Pak Marketing Systems, Inc.

- Post Office Box 13428, St. Petersburg, FL 33733 (1-800-237-6266).

Aerial Advertising

- For airplane advertising, look in the Yellow Pages under the heading of "Advertising-Aerial." A company with national capabilities is AVIAD (formerly known as National Aerial Advertising), 250 Clark Street, North Andover, MA (1-800-223-7425).

- "Advertising-Aerial" is also the listing for cold-air inflated advertising balloons. A resource with national outlets is ASAP Promotions, 766-A Production Drive, Cincinnati, Ohio 45237 (513-679-6300).

ADVERTISING-TO-SALES RATIOS

The following table lists the average percent of sales invested in advertising by different kinds of stores. This is to be used as a guideline for particular types of stores. Keep in mind that your ad budget will be above the average figures shown here if you are a new store, are in a high-pressure business, have heavy competition, or are in a remote location.

Average figures mean that successful stores are put in with less lucrative operations, and may also include stores which do no advertising at all.

Commodity or Class of Business	Average Ad Dollars as Percent of Sales
Apparel & Accessory Stores (1)	1.9 Percent
Appliance & Electronics (2)	
Appliance & Electronics Sales & Service	2.9
Appliance Sales & Service	2.2
Electronics Sales & Service	4.1
Appliance/Electronics & Furniture Sales	3.6
Auto Dealers (3)	1.2
Auto & Home Supply Stores (1)	1.7
Bakeries (4)	
Full-line	2.9
Limited Line	2.6
Specialty	3.5
Multi-unit	2.9

Commodity or Class of Business	Average Ad Dollars as Percent of Sales
Bicycle Dealers (5)	2.6
Book Stores (6)	2.0
Multiple Independents	1.8
Single Independents	2.0
Building Materials, Hardware, Garden-Retail (1)	3.0
Decorating Retailers (7)	2.9
Department Stores (8)	
All Department Stores	3.9
Under $100-million	4.0
Discount Stores (9)	1.7
Drug & Proprietary Stores (1)	1.4
Dry Cleaning Plants (10)	
$100,000-$200,000	2.5
$200,000-$300,000	2.3
Over $300,000	2.5
Family Clothing Stores (1)	2.3
Florists (11)	2.8
Grocery Stores (1)	1.3
Hardware Stores (12)	
Under $250,000	3.0
$250,000-$749,999	2.6
$750,000-$1,999,999	2.5
$2-million Or More	2.0
Hobby, Toy & Game Shops (1)	1.6
Home Centers (13)	
Under $3-million	1.7
Home Furnishing Stores (14)	6.5
Under $1-million	6.7
$1-million-$3-million	6.8
Jewelry Stores (1)	3.2
Laundromats (15)	2.5
Menswear Stores (16)	3.5
Natural Food Stores (17)	2.5
Office Furniture Retailers (18)	2.5

Commodity or Class of Business	Average Ad Dollars as Percent of Sales
Office Supplies Retailers (18)	
Under $1-million	2.1
$1-million-$2-million	1.6
$2-million-$5-million	1.7
Optical Dispensers (19)	
Optical Chains	10.0
Independents	2.0-3.0
Pet Dealers--Independent (20)	3.8
Photo/Video Stores (21)	
Without On-site Processing	2.5
With On-site, One-hour Processing	2.8
Retail One-hour photo labs	3.5
Radio, TV, Consumer Electronic Stores (1)	4.7
Restaurants (22)	
Full-menu With Table Service	1.9
Limited-menu With Table Service	2.8
Limited-menu With No Table Service	4.2
Cafeteria	2.0
Shoe Stores (1)	4.0
Specialty Stores (8)	
All Specialty Stores	3.3
Under $5-million	4.4
Sporting Good Stores (23)	
General	2.2
Specialty	3.1
Tire Dealers (24)	3.0-5.0
Variety Stores (1)	1.6
Video Specialty Retailers (25)	
Average	2.6
Video Superstores	4.0+
Women's Clothing Stores (1)	3.7

Sources for Chart

(1) Schonfeld & Associates. (708) 948-8080, as reported in *Advertising Age*, 7/13/92

(2) National Association of Retail Dealers of America, 1990

(3) The National Automobile Dealers Association, 1991

(4) "Bakery Production & Marketing Survey Of Retail Bakeries." Retail Bakers of America, 1988

(5) National Bicycle Dealers Association, 1990

(6) *1992 Abacus Expanded: A.B.A's Financial Survey Of Member Book Stores Based on 1990 Operations.* Bookseller's Publishing, Inc., American Booksellers Association

(7) National Decorating Products Association Market Research Bureau, 1991

(8) *Financial & Operating Results Of Department & Specialty Stores in 1990*, National Retail Federation

(9) *Discount Merchandiser*, 1991

(10) *IFI Survey of 1991 Operating Costs*, International Fabricare Institute

(11) *FTD Flower Business Fact Book 1991*, Florists' Transworld Delivery Association

(12) National Retail Hardware Association, 1990

(13) National Retail Hardware Association/Home Center Institute, 1990

(14) *1992 NHFA Annual Operating Experiences Report* (of 1991 results), National Home Furnishings Association

(15) Coin Laundry Association, 1992

(16) *MRA Annual Business Survey*, Menswear Retailers Of America, 1990

(17) "Health Foods Business' Annual Survey of Health Food Stores in America," *Health Foods Business*, 1992

(18) *NOPA Dealer Financial Comparison, 1991*, National Office Products Association

(19) *20/20* Magazine, 1992 estimate

(20) NAA calculation, based on "15th Annual Survey," *The Pet Dealer*, December 1991 (3.0%, per *Pet Supplies Marketing Magazine*)

(21) *1991 Photo Marketing Association Cost Of Doing Business Survey*, Photo Marketing Association International

(22) *The Restaurant Industry Operations Report, 1991*, National Restaurant Association

(23) *Cost Of Doing Business For Retail Sporting Goods Stores 1991-1992*, National Sporting Goods Association

(24) National Tire Dealers and Retreaders Association, Inc., 1992
(25) *1992 Video Store Magazine Retailer Survey*

Chart courtesy of Newspaper Association of America
Newspaper Advertising Planbook For 1993

APPENDIX

Throughout this book are 180 themes for sales which a retailer might conduct. Here in alphabetical order are the themes along with the page on which each is mentioned.

SALES THEMES

- A Green Sale   (70)
- A Lincoln Penny Goes A Long Way   (69)
- A Peek At Winter   (80)
- All A's Sale   (119)
- Anniversary Sale   (88)
- A Torrid Sale   (113)
- April Action Sale   (123)
- April Showers Sale   (71)
- Armed Forces Week Sale   (74)
- August Accessory Sale   (123)
- Back From The Beach Bargains   (77)
- Back To School Savings   (77)
- Bargains From The Old Sod   (70)
- Beach Bargains   (76)

- Best Buys In Town   (123)
- Blackboard Specials   (77)
- Blood Donor Discount   (116)
- Bonus Buys   (121)
- Broomstick Bargains   (80)
- Carnival Of Savings   (123)
- Cast Your Ballot For Savings   (81)
- Celebrate St. Patrick's Day Sale   (70)
- Cheaper By The Dozen (More Or Less) Sale   (120)
- Christmas In August Sale   (115)
- Classroom Classics   (77)
- Clear The Shelves Sale   (123)
- Cold Weather Bargains   (67)
- Come In And Watch Our Prices Melt   (113)
- Cool Prices On A Hot Day   (113)
- Cool Specials   (123)
- Customer Appreciation Day Sale   (116)
- Customer Appreciation Week Sale   (116)
- December Dollar Days   (123)
- Diet Sale   (117)
- Discover A New World Of Values   (78)
- Discover Columbus Day Values   (78)
- Discover (France) Sale   (122)
- Dog Days Of August Sale   (122)
- Dollar And Sense Sale   (123)
- Don't Forget Father On Father's Day   (73)
- Don't Forget Mother On Mother's Day   (73)
- Easter Egg Hunt Sale   (71)
- Easter Savings   (71)
- Election Day Specials   (81)
- End Of Summer Specials   (77)
- Every Day Is A Special Day At (Store Name)   (112)
- Everything Out Of The Store   (123)

- Fabulous Fall Buys   (78)
- Fall Close Outs . . . Winter Previews   (80)
- Fall Preview   (77)
- Fall Values   (78)
- FALLing Prices   (80)
- Farewell Summer of 'XX   (77)
- February Fantasy Sale   (123)
- Fifties Sale   (119)
- Firecracker Of A Sale   (76)
- First Look At Fall   (77)
- First Sale Of The Year   (65)
- Flip Of The Coin Sale   (120)
- 1492 Sale   (78)
- Fourth Of July Specials   (76)
- Gay Nineties Sale   (119)
- Get Acquainted Sale   (117)
- Get To Know Us Sale   (117)
- Give Blood And Save Sale   (116)
- Graduating Seniors Sale   (119)
- Grandparents Day Sale   (121)
- Hail To The Graduate Sale   (75)
- Half Moon Sale . . . Buy One And Half Off The Second   (115)
- Halloween Headliners   (80)
- Hot Prices . . . Hot Values   (123)
- If Your Name Is . . . . . Sale   (114)
- It All Gotta Go Sale   (123)
- It's Snowing Savings   (67)
- January Jamboree   (123)
- July Jumbo Bargains   (123)
- June Jubilee   (123)
- Leap Year Sale   (119)
- Make A Resolution To Shop And Save At (Store Name)   (65)
- Marathon Sale   (122)

- The Carload Sale   (118)
- The Confusion Sale   (120)
- The Daily Knockdown Sale   (121)
- The Good Old Days Sale   (119)
- The Hottest Prices In Town   (113)
- The Lottery Sale   (115)
- The More You Lose, The More You Save   (117)
- The Thermometer And Our Prices Are Down   (67)
- The Truckload Sale   (118)
- Three-Day Sale   (123)
- 3Rs Sale   (77)
- Trade-In Your Old Products   (122)
- Trick Or Treat Sale   (90)
- Turkey Day Clearance   (83)
- Two For The Price Of One Sale   (121)
- Vacation Sale   (123)
- Veterans Day Specials   (82)
- Volumes Of Value Sale   (123)
- Vote For The Best Buys In Town   (81)
- Warehouse Sale   (123)
- Warm Up To Our Cold Day Specials   (113)
- We Hail Those Who Served With This Special Sale   (82)
- Weekly Senior Citizen Sale   (113)
- Welcome Back From The Beach   (77)
- We're Chopping Our Prices   (69)
- We're Cleaning Out The House   (69)
- We're Cutting Our Prices To Help You Through The Tax Season   (117)
- We've Thawed Our Prices   (67)
- Winter Close-outs   (71)
- Winter Wonderland Of Savings   (67)
- X-Percent Off All Made In The USA Products During Armed Forces Week   (74)

Index